T0192015

Communications
in Computer and Information Science 1626

More information about this series at https://link.springer.com/bookseries/7899

Hongxiu Li · Maehed Ghorbanian Zolbin ·
Robert Krimmer · Jukka Kärkkäinen ·
Chenglong Li · Reima Suomi (Eds.)

Well-Being in the Information Society

When the Mind Breaks

9th International Conference, WIS 2022
Turku, Finland, August 25–26, 2022
Proceedings

Springer

Editors
Hongxiu Li (ID)
Tampere University
Tampere, Finland

Robert Krimmer (ID)
University of Tartu
Tartu, Estonia

Chenglong Li (ID)
Tampere University
Tampere, Finland

Maehed Ghorbanian Zolbin (ID)
Åbo Akademi University
Turku, Finland

Jukka Kärkkäinen
Finnish Institute for Health and Welfare
Helsinki, Finland

Reima Suomi (ID)
University of Turku
Turku, Finland

ISSN 1865-0929   ISSN 1865-0937 (electronic)
Communications in Computer and Information Science
ISBN 978-3-031-14831-6   ISBN 978-3-031-14832-3 (eBook)
https://doi.org/10.1007/978-3-031-14832-3

This Springer imprint is published by the registered company Springer Nature Switzerland AG
The registered company address is: Gewerbestrasse 11, 6330 Cham, Switzerland

Preface

"When the Mind Breaks" was the motto of the ninth biannual conference on Well-being in the Information Society (WIS 2022). The conference topic couldn't be timelier than after having endured a pandemic following the COVID-19 virus outbreak. What first seemed like an event that fostered, and even accelerated, the digital transformation in ways almost unimaginable before, also challenged the well-being of those affected by isolation and lack of human contact more than ever. Here, the Russian aggression against Ukraine with all its consequences inside and outside the war-affected territories furthered these tendencies even more.

We felt that the topic was relevant and academic discussion around it was much needed; hence, it was selected as the main theme of this year's conference, which once again was organized by the University of Turku in cooperation with Åbo Akademi University and Tampere University.

The submitted papers consisted of academic contributions on the topics at the intersection of health, ICT, and society as seen from different directions and contexts. Thanks to the international reviewers, we were able to accept 14 papers to be presented at the conference, which was to be held in a hybrid way allowing both remote and in-person presentations. We are grateful for the efforts of the reviewers in identifying relevant and topical research papers for WIS 2022.

This interdisciplinary conference shows nicely how the topic of Well-being in the Information Society requires a thorough understanding of psychology, information systems, medicine, societal development, and systems theory. Dealing with one of these issues alone does not allow one to understand the complexity of the topic as a whole. Only the combination of knowledge, understanding, and contextualization presents the rich details of this topic. If the conference on Well-being in the Information Society didn't exist already, now would certainly be the time when it would be founded again.

The proceedings are structured in four sections: i) Mental Well-being and E-Health, ii) Social Media and Well-being, iii) Innovative Solutions for Well-Being in the Information Society, and iv) Driving Well-being in the Information Society.

The first section includes four papers reflecting the issues of mental health and well-being through the use of information and communication technology (ICT). In the first paper, titled "Well-Being of Hong Kong DSE Students in the Post-COVID-19 age: Opportunities and Challenges for Mental Health Education and Promotion", Wai Sun Derek Chun, Siu Ho Yau, Wai Man Chan, and Ting Ting Fung discuss how the mental health of the student population in Hong Kong, a system which is known for focusing on examinations, was affected by COVID-19. The second paper by Vincent Peter C. Magboo and Sheila A. Magboo focuses on "Important Features Associated with Depression Prediction and Explainable AI", whereby they analyze how artificial intelligence can help to understand and predict being affected by depression. The third paper in this section by Dana Naous and Tobias Mettler discusses the dilemma around "Mental Health Monitoring at Work: IoT Solutions and Privacy Concerns", where employers try to support their staff by monitoring for mental health issues, which raises serious concerns about their privacy. In the final paper of this section, Prima Pangsrisomboon, Aung Pyaea, Noppasorn Thawitsri, and Supasin Liulak present the issues around mental health for Thai students in their study titled "Design and Development of an NLP-Based Mental Health Pre-screening Tool for Undergraduate Students in Thailand: A Usability Study".

The second section collates three papers dealing with how social media is increasingly affecting our society's well-being, not least since the Cambridge Analytica scandal has shown the vulnerability of our political systems, and the fears around the pitfalls of social media become more and more evident. The first of these papers is authored by Linda Achilles, Thomas Mandl, and Christa Womser-Hacker. In their paper focused on "Thinspiration Inspired by K-pop: A Comparison of K-pop Related Thinspiration Imagery and Texts to Regular Thinspiration Content on Tumblr", they explore how social media posts on Tumblr can affect eating disorders and body dissatisfaction. The second contribution titled "Mental Health Communication on Social Media in India: Current Status and Predictors", by Sairaj Patki and Anika Iyer, presents the Indian experience with mental health communication in social media and how COVID-19 supported such communication. Aung Pyae and Shahrokh Nikou, in the concluding paper of this section titled "Understanding University Students' Health Information Seeking Behaviors on Social Media During the COVID-19 Pandemic: A Developing Country Perspective" address how social media affected university students' health (mis-)information during the pandemic, due to lack of alternatives.

The third section provides an overview of three innovative solutions around well-being. The first paper, "Classification of Healthcare Robots" by Rong Huang, deals with how we can differentiate different robots in the area of health. The second contribution reviews how the poor can use information society tools to improve their situation in a paper titled "Digital Solutions for the Marginalised in Society: A Review of Systems to Address Homelessness and Avenues for Further Research" by Michael Oduor. The third paper deals with virtual reality and new ways of working, titled "Investigating Students' Engagement, Enjoyment, and Sociability in Virtual Reality-Based Systems: A Comparative Usability Study of Spatial.io, Gather.town, and Zoom" and authored by Summa Sriworapong, Aung Pyaea, Arin Thirasawasd, and Wasin Keereewan.

The fourth and last section provides an interesting insight into different approaches to providing well-being in the information society. The first paper by Hamed Ahmadinia deals with "A Review of Health Beliefs and Their Influence on Asylum Seekers and Refugees' Health-Seeking Behavior". The second paper, by Eva Collanus, Emilia Kielo-Viljamaa, Janne Lahtiranta, and Antti Tuomisto, is on the important topic of "Measuring the Maturity of Healthcare Testbeds". The third contribution addresses "Study Structures in the Interplay of Stress and Coping in Higher Education" and is authored by Eija-Liisa Heikka, Pia Hurmelinna-Laukkanen, Outi Keränen, and Pia Partanen. The final paper by Tina Long deals with the important issue of "What Drives User Engagement of Theme Park Apps? Utilitarian, Hedonic or Social Gratifications".

We want to express our deepest gratitude to our organizing institutions that have constantly supported us with the conference in several ways. We also want to thank the Finnish Foundation for Economic Education for financial support, all the authors for contributions, and all the reviewers for their hard work to ensure the quality of WIS 2022. Further, we acknowledge the support received through Horizon 2020 funding with grant number 857622 for the work of Robert Krimmer. Our conference management group consisting (in addition to us) of Hongxiu Li, Chenglong Li, Maedeh Ghorbanian Zolbin, Kaisa Mishina, Brita Somerkoski, and Tapio Vepsäläinen also deserves a big thanks. Finally, we are grateful to Springer for again accepting our proceedings for publication.

August 2022
Robert Krimmer
Jukka Kärkkäinen
Reima Suomi

Organization

Organizing Committee

Suomi, Reima (Conference Chair)	University of Turku, Finland
Li, Chenglong (Committee Chair)	Tampere University, Finland
Krimmer, Robert (Program Co-chair)	University of Tartu, Estonia
Kärkkäinen, Jukka (Program Co-chair)	National Institute for Health and Welfare, Finland
Ghorbanian Zolbin, Maedeh	Åbo Akademi University, Finland
Li, Hongxiu	Tampere University, Finland
Somerkoski, Brita	University of Turku, Finland
Widén, Gunilla	Åbo Akademi University, Finland

Program Committee

Ameel, Maria	University of Turku, Finland
Anttila, Maria	Helsinki University Hospital, Finland
Athanasopoulou, Christina	University of West Attica, Greece
Bergum, Svein	Lillehammer University College, Norway
Cacace, Mirella	Katholische Hochschule Freiburg, Germany
Cabral, Regis	FEPRO - Funding for European Projects, Sweden
Halonen, Raija	University of Oulu, Finland
Järveläinen, Jonna	University of Turku, Finland
Krimmer, Robert	University of Tartu, Estonia
Li, Chenglong	Tampere University, Finland
Li, Hongxiu	Tampere University, Finland
Liu, Yong	Aalto University, Finland
Mettler, Tobias	University of Lausanne, Switzerland
Mishina, Kaisa	University of Turku, Finland
Mäntymäki, Matti	University of Turku, Finland
Pakarinen, Anni	University of Turku, Finland
Somerkoski, Brita	University of Turku, Finland
Söderlund, Riitta	University of Turku, Finland
Vold, Tone	Inland Norway University of Applied Sciences, Norway
Widén, Gunilla	Åbo Akademi University, Finland

Contents

Driving Well-being in the Information Society

Mental Well-being and E-Health

Well-Being of Hong Kong DSE Students in the Post-COVID-19 Age: Opportunities and Challenges for Mental Health Education and Promotion

Derek Wai Sun Chun[1]([✉]), Siu Ho Yau[1], Wai Man Chan[2], and Ting Ting Fung[1]

[1] The Education University of Hong Kong, 10 Lo Ping Road, Tai Po, New Territories, Hong Kong
{dwschun,shyau}@eduhk.hk
[2] The Chinese University of Hong Kong, 10 Lo Ping Road, Tai Po, New Territories, Hong Kong
skywmchan@cuhk.edu.hk

Abstract. Hong Kong has been regarded as one of the strong examination-driven systems worldwide. Under the current education system, local secondary school students have to sit for the Hong Kong Diploma of Secondary Education Examination (HKDSE) at the end of Grade 12. Although the continuing assessment reform since 2000 tried to reduce the number of high-stakes examinations for secondary school students (from two to one at the end of the six-year secondary education), it remained a high-stakes public examination because the examination results usually have a significant influence on learners' future pathways, including further education and employment. In respect of the COVID-19 pandemic since 2020, many international public examinations have been tried to be called off, but the Hong Kong government did persist in moving ahead with HKDSE. This aroused criticisms about whether the government has taken students' well-being as a top priority because the annual survey on DSE students' stress recorded the highest levels in 2020, 2021 and 2022. In this paper, the positioning and myth of HKDSE and its tie to Confucian philosophy will be examined. Students' well-being is also discussed regarding rescheduling the examination and the impacts on the mental health of all DSE students, notwithstanding the challenges that can bring to any successful outcomes. It is hoped to urge mental health education and promotion could be carried out systematically to improve its effectiveness.

Keywords: Well-being · HKDSE students · COVID-19 · Hong Kong · Mental health education and promotion

1 Introduction

In light of the 'deep-rooted cultural traditions' of Confucian Heritage Culture (CHC), Hong Kong has been regarded as one of the strong examination-driven systems for a long worldwide. Under the current education system, local secondary school students have to sit for the Hong Kong Diploma of Secondary Education Examination (HKDSE) at the end of Grade 12. Although the continuing assessment reform since 2000 tried

© The Author(s), under exclusive license to Springer Nature Switzerland AG 2022
H. Li et al. (Eds.): WIS 2022, CCIS 1626, pp. 3–22, 2022.
https://doi.org/10.1007/978-3-031-14832-3_1

to reduce the number of high-stakes examinations for secondary school students (from two to one at the end of the six-year secondary education), it remained a high-stakes public examination because the examination results usually have a significant influence on learners' future pathways, including further education and employment.

Humanity has been universally affected by the COVID-19 worldwide pandemic since 2020, and many are experiencing mental health problems stemming from the pandemic. In particular, school closure and lesson time mode re-shifting and re-scheduling have, in turn, influenced students' daily routine and eating, sleeping, and exercising habits, which may harm their learning and psychological health. Besides, many international public examinations have been tried to be called off, but the Hong Kong government did persist in moving ahead with HKDSE. This aroused criticisms about whether the government has taken students' well-being as a top priority because the annual survey on DSE students' stress recorded the highest level respectively in 2020, 2021 and 2022. Since the "No health without mental health" strategy was initiated by World Health Organization (WHO) for more than a decade, Hong Kong DSE students' well-being is surely worth paying much greater attention to [1].

In general, Hong Kong mental health education is embedded in the hidden curriculum, practicing moral and civic education, promoting values education, and some unorganized mental health activities in schools and initiatives in the community. The government will provide relevant learning resources and organize student activities and teacher professional development programmes to support schools in cultivating students' positive thinking and resilience [2]. The Whole School Approach was encouraged to be adopted to promote students' mental health and enhance support for students with mental health needs (including those with suicidal risk). Nevertheless, it appears ineffective during the suspension of face-to-face classes. DSE students' negative emotions had been arising in the past two years from the epidemic and affecting them to maintain a desirable level of well-being. Therefore, the intrinsic case study method will be adopted in this paper to examine how the high-stakes nature of HKDSE has been directly and influentially hazardous to DSE students' psychological health. It also aims to investigate how the COVID-19 pandemic has been intensifying DSE students' negative emotions and stress, given that they have already been tied with poor mental health for a long. It is hoped to urge mental health education and promotion could be carried out systematically to improve its effectiveness.

2   Literature Review

2.1   HKDSE as a High-Stakes System and its Impact on DSE Students' Mental Health

High-stakes assessment and standardized tests are prominent features of globally competitive educational systems. Around the world, examinations are commonly used at the end of secondary schooling to measure academic attainment for certification, achieving subject scores, or establishing rankings for university entrance. According to UNESCO [3], high-stake assessment is understood as assessments with important consequences for test-takers based on their performance. Success in the examination would benefit students by progressing to a higher grade, a high school diploma, a scholarship, entering the labor market, or getting a license to practice a profession. On the other hand, failing may result in negative consequences, such as being forced to take remedial classes or not being able to practice a profession. As such, the high-stake examination is inevitably associated with the problems of equity and meritocracy and normalized an essential consequence of pressure on teachers and students to "teach to the test" [4]. UNESCO Bangkok [5] raised their concerns about a growing culture of testing in the Asia–Pacific region and continuous disproportionate attention placed on tests and exams because this will oversimplify the essentials of teaching and learning and the notorious impact on the functions of education.

HKDSE is a new public exam under the New Academic Structure (NAS) in Hong Kong since 2012. Every senior secondary student takes the exam at the end of their third year of Senior Secondary education. The new system is 'standards-referenced,' indicating students' performance will be assessed based on a pre-defined standard. There are five levels, and each level is accompanied by descriptors that clarify what a typical student at a given level can do [6]. The NAS consists of 6-year secondary education proposes to offer students a longer period of secondary schooling, with the chance to explore their abilities and interests more thoroughly than their counterparts in the old academic structure. In the past, the Hong Kong Certificate of Education Examination (HKCEE) served as the exit exam for secondary education within five years of schooling; approximately 10,000 candidates obtained zero points every year [7]. The reality is that low achievers intend to feel disillusioned in the face of a more difficult examination at The Hong Kong Advanced Level Examination, which was formally the major university entrance examination until the academic year 2011/2012. Under this new system, HKDSE becomes the single examination among the whole secondary schooling with the aims of basic competency benchmarking and university entrance screening; academic stress for our youths has been structurally increased. Moreover, the desire for university admission has aroused more stress. Hong Kong has been criticized for having a low tertiary enrollment ratio, with the rate at around 18% over the last two decades [8]. In fact, the rate has increased in recent years, but the stress on the students remained high because the competition is still extremely keen on public-funded tertiary education. Although government officials have initiated multiple pathways for our youths, students within the NAS are endlessly overwhelmed by uncertainty and enormous stress.

Provided that CHC is placing great importance on the exam-driven education system, there is a consequence that Hong Kong students are spending the most prolonged learning hours on an international study. In addition, they could not perceive a high level of life satisfaction, sense of belonging, and motivation in their learning and reading. They also reported a higher than average level of experiencing bullying, a higher level of loneliness, and a higher occurrence of being unable to find a way out when facing difficulties with a lower resilience level [9, 10]. Bhugra et al. [11] point out that the continuous passive attitudes toward mental health are a significant barrier to connecting those in need. Hong Kong adolescents still view mental health with the least understanding compared to other age groups. This insufficient awareness and acceptance of mental health among peers make young people reluctant to seek help at the earliest possible and affects their life outcomes and conditions. According to Save the Children [12], the drivers of mental health hardships contain school performance, HKDSE, uncertainty about the future, and family relationships. The social and political turmoil and the pandemic have compounded the mental health burdens of Hong Kong children and youth when almost 40% of primary and secondary students might have developed mental health disorders in these past years. In a survey sampled more than 2,600 secondary school students before the pandemic in 2019, more than 50% of respondents reported symptoms of depression, 34% were unable to stay focused, and 30% were feeling anxiety [13]. Another study reflects that pandemic has also further led to "alarming" levels of fear, anger, self-doubt, and thoughts of death in the Hong Kong population, with young people the worst affected, apart from social turmoil and academic stress effects [14]. The discovery echoes Save the Children's [12] study that more than 60% of sample respondents indicated increased negative feelings during school suspension. Summing up, the existing alienation of the high-stake natures remained unchanged, which aligns with Ho's [15] observation a long time ago that high-stakes exams had adverse outcomes for Hong Kong students academically, emotionally, and socially. With the increasingly detrimental effects and epidemic impacts, students' learning performance, environment, daily life, and physical and psychological health have also been drastically influenced. This paper hence will tend to focus on examining the academic stress and pandemic effects rather than the longitudinal effects of the social turmoil in 2019.

2.2 Mental Health Promotion in an Educational and Communal Settings

Mental health education was not officially stated as a formal curriculum in Hong Kong, but some initiatives had been long in progress. Starting from the 2004/05 school year, "Understanding Adolescent Project (Primary)" was launched, aiming at helping students acquire the necessary knowledge, skills, and attitudes for facing adversities. However, it is not directly related to mental health matters. A few years later, Healthy School Policy (HSP) was carried out in the 2010/11 school year to encourage more schools to design a school-based HSP by reintegrating their existing resources to develop a holistically enjoyable and healthy school environment. It is anticipated that students could develop healthy lifestyles, positive values, and proactive attitudes at a young age, enhancing their resilience and immunization against adversity. Although the supportive measures seem sufficient, all-rounded planning remains inexistent until the turning point occurs. The Education Bureau (EDB) and the University of Hong Kong have been jointly holding the Mindshift Educational Programme to promote the culture of positive mental health among secondary schools. Later, during the school years of 2016/2017 to 2018/2019, EDB cooperated with the Department of Health in holding the Joyful@School Campaign. It consists of the elements of "Sharing," "Positive Thinking" and "Enjoyment of Life", and the objectives were incorporated into the plan of the school curriculum, guidance, and discipline work to increase students' understanding and awareness of mental health and significantly strengthen their coping ability for environmental changes [16]. In respect of its fruitfulness, this campaign has transferred to a stable policy initiative called Health Promoting School (HPS) Programme starting in the 2019/20 school year, which fosters a self-sustaining and health-enhancing learning environment for students [17]. Participating schools will be assisted in identifying specific health priorities and developing school-based health promotion action plans by referring to the health needs of their students and working towards the goal of building a healthy campus. It echoes the World Health Organization's agenda to strengthen the school's capacity as a healthy setting for living, learning and working through a concerted effort of all its members and the community [18].

At the same time, EDB has continuously provided schools with additional professional support to cater to the learning, social, emotional, and behavioral needs of students, such as implementing "School-based Educational Psychology Service (SBEPS)," "two school social workers for each school" and "Student Mental Health Support Scheme" in primary and secondary schools. Besides, the category of mental illness was also officially included in the Learning Support Grant to support students with special education needs since the 2017/18 school year. To support teachers in providing mental health guidance with professional skills and knowledge in schools, EDB has been organizing several programmes, workshops, seminars, and experience-sharing sessions for primary and secondary teachers every school year. In particular, at least one teacher and one designated teacher from every public sector-funded mainstream school had to complete the Elementary Course and the in-depth course of "the Professional Development Programme for Mental Health" within the three years from the school year of 2017/18.

During the epidemic, the "Mental Health@School" website (mentalhealth.edb.gov.hk) was created to provide appropriate resources and strategies for the whole community to support students' mental health in different ways to sustain their resistance to the threat of disease (HKSAR Government, 2021). Generally, the Whole School Approach to mental health operates in a three-tier support model, including the Universal, Selective, and Indicated levels. Every school is continuously encouraged to provide mental health support for needy students. Regarding the Universal level, diversified adventure-based, team-building, problem-solving development programmes were widely promoted among primary and secondary schools to raise the students' awareness of mental health and strengthen their resilience in facing challenges. At the Selective level, it mainly provided teachers with structured mental-health-related educational training programs to enhance early identification and support for at-risk students. Regarding the Indicated level, all-rounded mental health grants, schemes, and support were specially provided for students with mental health needs to support them through a school-based platform [19].

Apart from the school perspective, the government has also paid great attention to public education on mental health promotion. The "Joyful@HK" Campaign was regarded as territory-wide mental health promotion and publicity campaign launched by the Department of Health in 2016. This new campaign aims to reduce the stigma toward persons with mental health needs, making Hong Kong a mental-health-friendly society and facilitating their reintegration into the community. The campaign seeks to promote higher acceptance of people with mental health needs, enhance their employment opportunities, and generate economic, social, and health benefits in the longer term. With the recurrent funding supports by the government for the ongoing mental health promotion and public education initiative, "Shall We Talk" was the newest initiative for mental health promotion and public education since July 2020. It aims to increase public engagement in promoting mental well-being and reduce the stigma toward people with mental illness [20].

2.3 Class Suspensions and Resumptions Since Early 2020 and HKDSE Arrangements in 2020, 2021 and 2022

After the first outbreak of COVID-19 in January 2020, the government quickly decided to have class suspension at all levels of educational institutions till March 2020. The Secretary for Education, Mr. Kevin Yeung Yun-hung, announced the two different plans that the EDB and the Hong Kong Examinations and Assessment Authority (HKEAA) considered arranging the 2020 HKDSE examination [21]. For instance, if those candidates cannot take the exam, their final grade in the subject would only be determined based on their school performance, and the maximum grade that they would obtain was only Level 5.[1] With a sharp increase in the number of confirmed cases in mid-March, arrangement on class suspension has been prolonged on the one hand, but on the other hand, the dates of those written examinations were postponed again from 24 April to 25 May [22]. Lots of candidates expressed dissatisfaction with the latest arrangement of the HKDSE examination as the risk of virus transmission would be high as candidates had to stay in indoor examination areas for long periods. Some of them reflected that cancellation of the HKDSE examination could be a better option for the candidates, given that the examination preparation has been heavily influenced by the outbreak of this pandemic [23]. Fortunately, there was no report on any confirmed case related to the HKDSE examination, and the results for the 2020 HKDSE examination were released on 22 July 2020. With this success, the HKDSE examination was a regular practice without any interruptions, even under the territory-wide outbreak of COVID-19.

In early August 2020, the EDB announced that all schools should suspend face-to-face teaching upon the commencement of the new academic year 2020–21, having regard to the epidemic situation of the COVID-19 at the time. With the subsided COVID-19 cases, schools in Hong Kong have gradually resumed face-to-face classes in two phases on a half-day basis to minimize the risk of infection. However, class resumption did not last long in light of another worsening outbreak of COVID-19, and suspension of face-to-face classes and school activities started again in late November 2020 until the beginning of schools' Chinese New Year holidays 2021 in mid-February [24]. Remarkably, schools were given more flexibility on face-to-face classes arrangement from mid-January. Secondary schools could arrange for students of any individual level to return to school (either in the morning or in the afternoon) to attend face-to-face classes or take examinations. Thus, the number of students who could return to schools kept increasing after the Chinese New Year holidays because EDB announced that all kindergartens, primary and secondary schools (including special schools and schools offering non-local curriculum) as well as 'tutorial schools' would be allowed to arrange more students to return to campuses on a half-day basis, with the number of students capped at one-third of the total number of students [25]. After the completion of the HKDSE 2021 in May, all kindergartens, primary and secondary schools (including special schools and schools offering a non-local curriculum) as well as "tutorial schools" were allowed to fully resume face-to-face classes on a half-day basis [26]. From the academic year 2021/22, all teachers and school staff who provide on-campus services will be required to have received at least

---

[1] Grade point conversion for Category A subjects (Elective subjects): Level 5** as 7 points, level 5* as 6 points, level 5 as 5 points, level 4 as 4 points, level 3 as 3 points, level 2 as 2 points, and level 1 as 1 point.

two doses of the COVID-19 vaccine to normalize the operation of half-day face-to-face classes in the 2021/22 school year. Once schools have achieved a high vaccination rate (70% or more), meaning teachers and school staff, and students have received two doses of COVID-19 vaccine for more than 14 days), may arrange for whole-day face-to-face classes [27].

Considering the 2021 and 2022 HKDSE, as the epidemic continues and keeps fluctuating, on-campus teaching and activities were suspended again in early 2021. The HKEAA and EDB made one-off contingency measures for the 2021 HKDSE to provide more flexibility for this specific cohort of students. The 2021 revised examination timetable had been slightly compressed and shortened to 20 examination days. The start of the written examinations of the 2021 HKDSE Category A subjects,[2] were postponed until 23 April to 18 May. Moreover, the speaking examinations in both the Chinese Language and English languages were canceled. Due to the rescheduling of the examination, the examination results were released on 21 July 2021 [28]. While the fifth outbreak wave occurred in January 2022, the EDB announced that in light of the changing COVID-19 situation, the detailed exam arrangement would be confirmed by early April, but with the exam duration to be shortened from one month to three weeks. Every candidate must undergo Covid-19 self-testing before their examinations; those who test positive will not be allowed to sit the exam. Absentees may get an assessed mark from their internal test result, but the highest score would be level 5 rather than 5**. Fortunately, the exam commenced smoothly in mid-April, and the date of release of the examination results remains to be July 20 [29]. The extended class suspension has severely disrupted normal school operation in these years, adversely affecting the learning and teaching cohort of students sitting the 2021 and 2022 HKDSE. Based on the arrangements in the past few years, the students' endeavors might be tantamount to getting neglected if they are unexpectedly and unfortunately infected. The high-stakes essence of HKDSE in the post-pandemic even further sharpens the devastating impacts on students' prospects.

3 Existing and Potential Challenges to DSE Student's Well-Being and Mental Health Education and Promotion in Hong Kong

Given the great efforts paid for the last two decades in mental health education and promotion, why does the well-being of the whole population keeps declining? In particular, why does the number of suicides of the youngsters in Hong Kong keeps at a worrying level? In addition to the COVID-19 epidemic, what are the factors causing the deterioration of the well-being of the HKDSE students? What should be done for future mental health education and promotion? The responses to these queries will be illustrated in the following sections.

3.1 Realization of Cultural Heritage Culture: East Asian Educational Model

Hong Kong has been named one of the high-performance education systems for a long [30, 31]. As a CHC, Hong Kong has long been dominated by test scores, textual transmission, and drills [32]. Instead of tests and exams that have become "the baton directing

---

[2] Twenty-four secondary subjects and four compulsory core subjects.

learning and teaching," the education reform in the early twenty-first century had tried to incept the "new assessment culture" to advance student learning and progress for the twenty-first century. However, the dominant powerfulness of CHC in its key features, such as the importance of education; the high expectation for students to achieve; an exam culture; an emphasis on personal effort; the use of repeated practice and memorization, and the virtue of modesty have undermined the effects of the reform [33]. As a result, Hong Kong has contended as one of the regions exemplified by the East Asian Educational Model (EAEM). It is a model that [34]:

- rooted in and shaped by *Confucian habitus*: unconscious and ingrained worldviews, dispositions, and habits that reflect the standards of appropriateness in a Confucian Heritage Culture;
- aspiring *high performance*: a balance between academic excellence and holistic development; and
- utilized *educational harmonization*: the art of bringing together different and contradictory means and ends to achieve desired educational outcomes.

Confucian habitus is defined as unconscious and ingrained worldviews, dispositions, and habits that reflect the standards of appropriateness in a CHC [34]. It can appear from different angles in Hong Kong, focusing a socio-cultural emphasis on diligence in studying, parental dependence on private tutoring, and public support for terminal exams. In the local context, the impact of Confucian habitus and practices can be generally displayed through the value of education, the prominence of high-stakes exams (i.e., Territory-wide System Assessment, Pre-Secondary One Hong Kong Attainment Test), substantial homework, and the ubiquity of private tutoring. There is no doubt that in CHC, the legacy of the exam system signifies the opportunity to become government officials, so learning tends to be instrumental. Students are also more likely to acquire the necessary skills and qualifications to conform to today's knowledge-based economy [35]. The high-stakes assessment reinforces the ideology that examination scores are highly valued, and self-cultivation is suppressed. This situation can be conceptualized as a modern form of oppression since a narrow sense of success oppresses students: to secure a university degree, get a well-paid job and eventually reach top positions in their careers. Private tutoring has been deemed a commodity that students can purchase to increase their chance of "success" [31]. Within this localized high-stakes environment, Yung [36] problematized this particular oppressive education context as a source of oppression in the education system, along with the demand for performativity in mainstream schooling and the commodification of education in private tutoring.

In addition, the parents' mindset is still heavily influenced by CHC, which emphasizes order, stability, hierarchy, self-discipline, and obedience [37]. With this deeply rooted culture, the success in examinations, which are considered the fairest approach for assessing the learning progress and the academic achievement of the students in order to respond to the value placed by Confucian societies, is commonly considered one of the significant ways to attain social mobility [38]. The Chinese parents always place high expectations on their children's academic success, so the HKDSE becomes the unique "battlefield" that the parents are willing to pay any effort to ensure their children could "win the battle" [39]. According to Hong Kong Research Association's survey [40], the respondents' children and youth daily spent 5 h for school, 2.2 h for homework, 1.7 h for private tutoring, and 1.4 h for extra-curricular activities on average, resulting in 62.2 h per week for study. Although the government estimated that the time spent on studying among the primary and secondary school students was a bit less than 55 h [41], it was still higher than those studying in the UK. This scenario not just greatly reduced the sleeping time of the students, which might cause an adverse effect on their physical and mental health; insufficient leisure time could further negatively influence the development of creativity.

Against this oppressive climate, Hong Kong students tended to adopt a surface learning approach to tackle the summative assessment mode, emphasizing memorizing the critical learning points and mastering skills for tackling the questions to achieve good grades in the assessment. Echoed this phenomenon, major respondents from another study commented that they had private tutoring "to improve academic performance as they are not good now" (37.8%), "to achieve best possible improvement on a current good level" (25.1%), or "to take examination" (18.8%). As reported, 72% of Secondary Six students in Hong Kong were receiving private tutoring as a better way of preparation for the HKDSE in 2012, which was observed to be higher than the average level (63.3%) at that time [42]. Without notable factors, this percentage was believed to be further increased after introducing the HKDSE as some examination papers were commented to be too difficult for Secondary Six Students. For example, the Chinese language paper has been dubbed the "paper of death" as a significant portion of students could not get the passing mark in the paper, which will further influence their admission to the bachelor's degree programme [43]. In a nutshell, CHC unwittingly becomes an enabling factor by oppressing our DSE students to suffer a higher pressure resulting from their well-being at an alarming level.

3.2 HKDSE Must go on in the Pandemic: Well-Being or Personal Prospects Matter?

According to the survey conducted by a local student counseling group between 2020 to 2022, DSE students are sustainably anxious mainly due to the COVID-19 pandemic. In 2021, more than 1,700 Form Six students rated their stress levels toward the HKDSE reached the second-highest since it was first introduced in 2012, with an average score of 7.6 out of 10 [44]. It was understandable that the high-stress level among Form Six students was due to the insufficient time for preparation caused by the prolonged outbreak of this pandemic. From the annual records prepared by Hok Yau Club, the average stress scores ranged from 6.75 in 2018 to 8.10 in 2020, indicating the stress level of Form Six students was relatively high, which deviated from the expectation. In 2022, more than 2,100 DSE students rated their stress score 7.87 out of 10, the second-highest score. Not only around 40% of students reported perceiving "Very stressful" before a month of the commencement of HKDSE, but 90% of students had also experienced burnout, 87% expressed difficult concentration, and 78% said they were prone to mood swings. When this year's candidates have been affected by the epidemic since they were in Grade 10, they need to face the significant uncertainties without guidance from teachers and the support of their friends and classmates [45].

When HKDSE became the only university entrance examination, the General Entrance Requirements (GER) of undergraduate programmes under the NAS were set as "3322", which refers to a minimum level of Level 3 for Chinese Language and English Language, and Level 2 for Mathematics and Liberal Studies. To better secure the admission to a bachelor's degree programme funded by the University Grants Committee, a more conservative estimation based on the past admission records was that students should have Level 4 or better results for all four core subjects, together with Level 4 or better result for the elective subjects. In addition, the Secondary Six Students' Pathway Survey revealed that 93.9% of the respondents would like to further pursue full-time study after completion of the secondary school study and the percentage was similar to the observation from the same study in 2019 (92.0%) [46]. Unfortunately, only 48.7% of the respondents could continue their bachelor's degree programme studies. The respondents who took post-secondary programmes and other full-time courses were 30.1% and 20.6%, respectively. The deviation between GER and the estimated requirements and the keen competition for university admission have driven the senior secondary students to work hard on preparing for the HKDSE since their Grade 10 study, and their study stress remains unchanged.

Given that aspiring to the bachelor's degree programme is still set as the top priority among the Secondary Six students and the GER focuses on the four core subjects, even though some students might get excellent performance in the chosen elective subjects, some would fail to admit to the bachelor's degree programme as they could not fulfill the GER on the four core subjects. Hence, this group of disadvantaged students could only apply for the subjects under Vocational and Professional Education and Training (VPET), for example, the higher diploma (HD) programmes offered by the Vocational Training Council (VTC). This mindset encourages the VPET programmes' inferior position and treats it as one of the transitional steps on their academic career paths. The graduates of the VPET programmes still set their ultimate goals of obtaining degree qualifications, but also monotonies the concept of multiple pathways [47]. In the same vein, the results of Applied Learning (APL) subjects, which is one of the elective subjects offered in HKDSE, are only set in three levels – "Attained," "Attained with Distinction (I)," and "Attained with Distinction (II)," which is comparable to Level 4 or above of the Category A subjects of the HKDSE examination. This setting might underscore the advantages for students to admit to the bachelor's degree programme they want. According to the latest registration statistics, the number of candidates registered for examination on APL subjects (i.e., Category B subjects.[3]) were 3,430, accounting only for 6.58% of the total number of candidates [48]. In sum, there are still significant gaps between the outstanding achievements of multiple pathways; HKDSE maintained its high-stakes nature under such a cultural context.

In contrast, while Territory-wide System Assessment.[4] has been suspended in these two years because of the volatility of the epidemic, the decision to move towards HKDSE can further exaggerate its high-stakes natures, and the government is seen as unwilling to shoulder the responsibility for prioritizing candidates' well-being. As HKDSE has

---

[3] Applied Learning (APL) subjects (about 40 subjects are offered).

[4] It is an annual territory-level assessment to objectively assess the basic learning competencies and learning progress of the students at different stages of learning.

become the sole qualification examination for local university admissions, its stakes level keeps rising as candidates view it as an examination that "determines whether they live or die" [49]. Moreover, the consequences of canceling HKDSE may result in the only determinants for matriculation that would rely on the performance in internal examinations and the candidate's secondary school academic record. This would give candidates from resource-rich and prestigious secondary schools an advantage while dealing a devastating blow to underprivileged students and those resitting the exam. Since HKDSE as standardized testing can ensure ostensible fair environments and rules, it is noted that the government officials are afraid to face the music. Undoubtedly, DSE students' well-being is sacrificed by bureaucracy and so-called students' prospects, proved by the annual survey that HKDSE creates a medium level of test anxiety and negatively affects their well-being and personal development [44, 45]. The intensification of alienation and the myth of public exams in Hong Kong persisted.

3.3 Unsystematic and Fragmented Mental Health Education Implementation in the Formal Curriculum

Mental health education is not on the pivotal policy agenda in the current local educational setting. As aforementioned, mental health education is incorporated mainly into different parts of the informal curriculum to infuse the understanding and knowledge of mental health. Little emphasis is placed on the formal curriculum in a school setting. According to the secondary education curriculum guide, helping students develop a healthy lifestyle is instigated as one of the seven learning goals of the school curriculum so that they can lead a healthy lifestyle with active participation in physical and aesthetic activities and appreciate sports and the arts [50]. In this respect, schools must offer students learning opportunities for quality physical and aesthetic education beyond the classroom to nurture their confidence, perseverance, and aesthetic appreciation in becoming lifelong learners and facing personal and social challenges. Besides, moral and civic education (MCE) has been promoted as one of the Four Key Tasks for school curriculum reform. Given the school-based flexibility and arrangements echoing with schools' vision and students' individual needs, every school should carry out MCE through school assemblies, life education periods, class teacher periods, or life-wide learning activities to foster students' positive values and attitudes [2]. Apart from MCE, elements of psychological health are covered in various subjects. For instance, Health Management and Social Care curriculum implemented at the senior secondary level, including "Mental disorders" and "Services for mental patients" as part of the study units; the meaning of "life and death" is reflected in Ethics and Religious Studies subject [51]. Even though the elements related to mental health or psychological health are embedded in such study areas, the coverage of mental health education in formal education is still inadequate. With its unsystematic and fragmented curriculum design, related elective subjects are not popularly offered by mainstream secondary schools.

With the newest curriculum review in 2020 initiated by the government, the notion of "learning time" is delineated to provide more flexibility for schools in planning curriculum-related activities. It is designated for schools to review, reflect on and fine-tune their whole-school curriculum plans for student learning to plan the "learning time" of students and foster their whole-person development [52]. Furthermore, schools are advised to carry out appropriate measures to broaden students' exposure and cater to their balanced development, with due consideration given to their physical and social developmental needs and the promotion of a healthy lifestyle. However, the mental health or psychological health issues have not been addressed concretely. Actually, with the ongoing school curriculum renewal since 2014, each school is requested to set aside 8% and 10–15% of its junior and senior secondary school hours, respectively (i.e., 220 h over three years in junior form and a minimum of 250 h in senior form) for cross-curricular teaching and learning, including values education which has to contain the cultivation of right attitudes in personal growth, family, school, and social interaction with life exemplars. Notwithstanding, the government has indeed infiltrated preventive and developmental educational contents like value education into different subjects to help students develop basic psychological literacy. Nevertheless, it helps less for mental health education development. The core problem is not precisely about textbook teaching instead of preventive and developmental element for mental health education, which has never been considered included in the class time and teaching materials allocated by the government.

In reality, many schools rely heavily on outsourced services to provide mental health education and support activities based on individual school needs. The effectiveness may vary subject to the school commitment and teachers' intention because they need to prepare additional materials and organize activities to meet their school needs. Early intervention and identification will be difficult if social workers and teachers cannot spend extra time understanding students and their family problems in a more profound sense in the post-COVID-19 context. Although the government has adopted preventive mental health strategies in recent years, "school-based" flexibility causes a lack of comprehensive policy coordination for a better outcome. The top priority for schools is to make more efforts to remove the stigma of emotional health and mental health issues on campus. At the same time, emotions can be divided into positive and negative types. Understanding each emotional state and need can accurately create a peer and mutual support environment and increase the trust among teachers, students, social workers, counselors, and parents. If the status quo remains, the effectiveness will depend on the school's willingness and goodwill toward mental health issues.

4   Implication and Recommendation

Under the existing CHC context, DSE students are forced to face extreme pressure from schools and parents, and it raises the question if they have sufficient awareness to cope with the ensuring mental health issues. The stigmatization of mental disorders is a social barrier that stops young people who have suicidal thoughts from seeking help. Therefore, the community should perform the gatekeeper role in raising community awareness and breaking down taboos to make more considerable progress in helping our youth with mental health problems. When they can foster self-awareness and self-care from various channels, they can learn how to accept their limitation and appreciate themselves. Hence, it is suggested that Hong Kong should have new policy initiatives on mental health education curriculum and tackle children and youth mental health by a whole-of-society approach.

4.1 New Policy Initiative in Education: Mental Health Education Curriculum

In view of the school's weakness in over-focusing on developing positive emotions, reacting and tackling negative emotions are also crucial to our DSE students to enhance their resilience in overcoming challenges and stresses. In light of the general lack of awareness of mental health among students, a "Mental Health Ambassador Scheme" should be launched to instill relevant knowledge and a more positive attitude towards mental health. The scheme can target primary and secondary students by planning activities related to mental health, such as visiting people who have recovered from mental illness and holding awareness-building activities in schools [53]. The aims are to raise awareness of mental health among primary and secondary students, thus dispelling myths and lowering the stigmatization of people with mental illness among the student body. Activities can be counted as extra-curricular hours to motivate DSE students to participate.

If we start treating mental and physical health equally, it will become the norm to have everyday conversations about feelings and emotions. Against this backdrop, Cairns [54] argues that overly rigid alignment of high-stakes assessment with curriculum engenders curricula and curricular practices in COVID-19. It leads to a complete reconsideration of the future function of standardized assessment; at least, we should try to design a robust mental health education curriculum as a little move. It is believed that mental health education can provide an opportunity for youth to acquire the knowledge, understanding, language, and confidence about their own positive or negative emotions and help develop proper processing strategies for themselves and others. Students should be able to seek consultation with school counselors or other clinical professionals with the assurance of anonymity so that they can speak freely and without judgment. It is worth providing the necessary support and training to enable teachers to teach and communicate about mental health knowledge and handling skills effectively. Alongside teaching mental health and well-being in the curriculum, the curriculum objective of mental health education is to lead students to explore the understanding of mental health, such as what stress is and its causes, knowledge of mental health and mental disorder, and respect for the value of life [55]. It could become a means that mental health should play an essential role in the syllabus to enhance students' self-awareness. The guidelines are further suggested not to restrict the teaching methods for the curriculum and encourage the adoption of communicative methods (e.g., communication with professionals, teachers, and students) and experience-sharing methods hosted by experienced patients [56]. Schools may choose what best suits their students so they can assimilate basic information about mental health and establish a positive sense of life value. They should also be taught the correct attitude when handling mental illness to reduce stigmatization and discrimination. Because of the importance of educational function, schools should incorporate student suicide prevention strategies into their school development plan with guidance on when and how to intervene. They are also required to help promote a common language and understanding of mental health in their community by sharing vital tools, resources, and information with parents because parental support is empirically proved as the most effective channel to prevent mental health.

4.2 New Policy Initiative in Community: Localized Whole-of-Society Approach to Manage Children and Youth Mental Health

According to The State of the World's Children 2021, urgent investment is called in child and adolescent mental health across governments, public and private sector partners to commit, communicate and act to promote mental health for all children, adolescents, and caregivers. It can protect those in need of help and care for the most vulnerable so that the *whole-of-society approach* can be effectively implemented in the post-COVID-19 era [57]. OECD [58] states that an integrated whole-of-society response means that access to existing mental health services should be assured either in-person, via telemedicine, or both. Increasing access to evidence-based services should be a priority. Mental health promotion programmes in schools should be included for children and adolescents, which have been particularly disrupted. Policymakers should look further at the implications of long-term teleservice provision on mental health. Every country should consider scaling-up mental health support services through public medical and social services.

In this connection, a *localized whole-of-society approach* to manage Hong Kong children and youth mental health initiatives is recommended. It is a comprehensive approach to ensuring how different stakeholders and social systems can cope with children and youth mental health issues in a more effective and organized manner to maximize the outcomes adapted from Hochlaf and Thomas [59] and Bronfbrenner [60]. In this model, five system levels are identified below:

Individual-level (Sex, Age and Health etc.): Children and youth have a role in raising their awareness of mental health and nurturing positive well-being. They are strongly encouraged to be more involved in the personalized mental health management process so that a whole-of-society approach can be started from each individual.

Microsystem (Interpersonal, school, family, and peers): Schools should proactively become the gatekeeper of children and youth's mental health because they are a site for mental health education and prevention. Family and peers are the critical determinants in protecting their mental health when the family has supposed to have a vital role in children's well-being. The microsystem should enhance children and adolescents' awareness of their stress status and well-being, nudge and influence their lifestyle choices and career and life development. It is also vital to help children and adolescents foster positive well-being from family, schools, and peers.

Mesosystem (Community and mass media): Communities will provide different mental health support programmes and services and become the transited destination if children and youth have unique mental health conditions that are hard to manage by families and schools. Media should have regular information exchange about children and youth mental health as parts of public education and socialization. The mesosystem should enable to co-create a facilitating environment for stress management and suicide prevention to empower children and adolescents to engage in social inclusion. It can prevent their social withdrawal and provide mental health assessment programmes, follow-ups, and monitoring support services closely and effectively.

Exosystem (Organizational structure, public services, neighborhoods, and professional expertise): Organizational support should be executed through accessible public services because it could encourage different stakeholders to increase social connectedness to include children and adolescents with mental disorders. Different professionals should educate the expert insights and knowledge to deepen public understanding of children and youth mental health and improve their support for children and youth's good well-being. They should proactively manage children's and adolescents' mental health conditions and bring up synergy through direct communication and intervention (i.e., public promotion and activities). Non-government organizations can become the bridge and platform for all related stakeholders to engage in children and youth mental health issues more keenly and fruitfully with their mediate support role. It can assist children and adolescents in managing their stress well and providing better well-being. Within the exosystem, it is expected that a synergic effect can be realized.

Macrosystem (Policy, attitudes, and ideologies of social culture): The government should fund and empower various stakeholders to work on their behalf. She could also consider revamping or setting up a young health policy framework to meet the varied needs of children and adolescents, particularly mental health and well-being supports. Improving the social-ecological support system for children and youth mental health requires a comprehensive reform in different social settings (i.e., preventing destigmatization and undermining CHC impacts) should be attempted to prevent their well-being from further deterioration [61]. The macrosystem is ultimately aimed at undermining the structural suppression of CHC in children and adolescents and destigmatizing help-seeking action to encourage children and adolescents to manage their mental health conditions in the soonest occasions (Diagram 1).

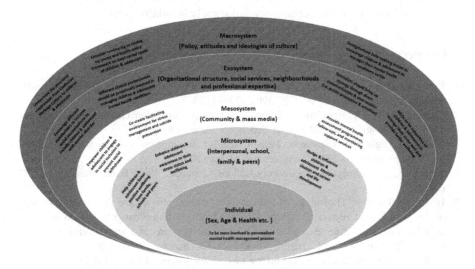

Diagram 1. Socio-ecological model depicting the whole-of-society approach to manage children and youth mental health in Hong Kong (Adapted from Hochlaf and Thomas [60])

5   Concluding Remarks

Hong Kong children and youth's mental health are deteriorating caused by different factors, especially among senior secondary students. The COVID-19 effects are still not yet fully emerged, and the gatekeeper role of the schools should remain but not be overemphasized because it should work out altogether from the society and community by a whole-of-society approach instead. It could provide more holistic and coordinated support to children and youth's mental health and good well-being. The success of a mental health support initiative can only be actualized if all sectors can hold mental health, healthcare, social care and welfare programmes, educational settings, and local governmental and non-governmental organizations accountable [62].

DSE, three letters that strike fear into every Hong Kong senior secondary student and result in debilitating anxiety, have already drawn special attention from the community to raise awareness of the tremendous pressure and be mindful of its dangers. Under the long-term effect of CHC and the pandemic, the stress level of DSE students was inevitably recorded at the highest level in the post-pandemic age. While DSE students of the 2022 cohort are the most affected group, it is hoped that future research could investigate how prolonged school closures, social distancing measures, and pandemics affect their psychological health and attempt to enhance their mental health literacy [63]. Understandably, teacher' supports and care for students' well-being might not be as similar as before the pandemic. Therefore, the suggested mental health education curriculum and whole-of-society approach initiative should be significantly considered to address the increasing needs of Hong Kong senior school students' mental well-being, so every child and youth can become psychologically healthily literate.

References

1. Prince, M., Patel, V., Saxena, S., Maj, M., Maselko, J., Phillips, M.R., Rahman, A.: No health without mental health. Lancet. **370**(9590), 859–77 (2007)
2. Curriculum Development Council: Secondary Education Curriculum Guide, Booklet 6: Moral and Civic Education: Towards Values Education. Hong Kong (2017)
3. UNESCO: High-stake assessment. Paris: UNESCO. http://uis.unesco.org/en/glossary-term/highstake-assessment (2020). Last accessed 11 June 2022
4. Kellaghan, T., Greaney, V.: Public examinations examined. World Bank, Washington, DC (2020)
5. UNESCO Bangkok: The culture of testing: Socio-cultural drivers and the effects on youth in the Asia-Pacific region. Bangkok: UNESCO (2015) https://bangkok.unesco.org/sites/default/files/assets/themes/education/quality_education/culture_of_testing/UNESCO_Bangkok_Culture_of_Testing_Literature_Review.pdf. Last accessed 11 June 2022
6. Chan, W.: A review of educational reform-new senior secondary (NSS) Education in Hong Kong. International Education Studies **3**(4), 26–35 (2010)
7. Yau, S.Y., Tsui, Y.C.: Options and pathways for students under the new academic structure. Journal of Youth Studies **15**(1), 105–115 (2012)
8. UNESCO: Statistical annual report. Paris, France: Author (2010)
9. Organisation for Economic Co-operation and Development Programme for International Student Assessment (PISA) (2015) https://www.oecd.org/pisa/pisa-2015-results-in-focus.pdf Last accessed 11 June 2022

10. Organisation for Economic Co-operation and Development Programme for International Student Assessment (PISA) (2018) https://www.oecd.org/pisa/pisa-2018-results-in-focus.pdf Last accessed 11 June 2022

11. Bhugra, D., Tse, S., Ng, R.M.K., Takei, N.: Routledge handbook of psychiatry in Asia. Handbook of Psychiatry in Asia, Routledge (2015)

12. Save the Children: Protect Children's Wellbeing in Hong Kong (2020). https://resourcec entre.savethechildren.net/pdf/mental_health_matters_-_save_the_children_hong_kong_-_2020.pdf Last accessed 11 June 2022

13. The Hong Kong Federation of Youth Groups: Survey results 'Emotional Stress Situation of Secondary School Students' (2019). https://hkfyg.org.hk/wp-content/uploads/2019/11/% E6%96%B0%E8%81%9E%E7%A8%BF_%E9%9D%92%E5%8D%94%E5%85%AC% E5%B8%83%E3%80%8C%E4%B8%AD%E5%AD%B8%E7%94%9F%E6%83%85% E7%B7%92%E5%A3%93%E5%8A%9B%E7%8B%80%E6%B3%81%E3%80%8D% E8%AA%BF%E6%9F%A5%E7%B5%90%E6%9E%9C.pdf Last accessed 11 June 2022

14. Choy, G.: One-two punch of protests, coronavirus playing havoc with mental health in Hong Kong, study finds. South China Morning Post (2020). https://www.scmp.com/news/ hong-kong/healthenvironment/article/3096326/one-two-punch-protests-coronavirus-pla ying-havoc Last accessed 11 June 2022

15. Ho, E.: High-stakes testing and its impact on student and schools in Hong Kong: What we have learned from the PISA studies. KEDI journal of educational policy 3(1) (2006)

16. Advisory Committee on Mental Health.: Work report of the advisory committee on mental health (1 December 2017 – 30 November 2019) (2020). https://www.fhb.gov.hk/download/ committees/acmh/work_report_of_ACMH_201_2019_e.pdf Last accessed 11 June 2022

17. Department of Health: The Briefing on the Health Promoting School (HPS) Programme (in Chinese) (2019). https://www.studenthealth.gov.hk/english/hps/hps_snapshots/snapsh ots_hps_briefing.html Last accessed 11 June 2022

18. World Health Organization: Health promoting school (n.d.) https://www.who.int/health-top ics/health-promoting-schools#tab=tab_1 Last accessed 11 June 2022

19. Education Bureau: Whole school approach (2021). https://mentalhealth.edb.gov.hk/en/whole-school-approach/policy-highlights.html Last accessed 11 June 2022

20. Hong Kong SAR Government: "Shall We Talk" initiative launches to promote mental health (2020). https://www.info.gov.hk/gia/general/202007/11/P2020071100548.htm Last accessed 11 June 2022

21. News.gov.hk.: New HKDSE plan to be announced (2020) https://www.news.gov.hk/eng/ 2020/02/20200206/20200206_150218_291.html Last accessed 11 June 2022

22. The Hong Kong Examinations and Assessment Authority: Press release: 2020 HKDSE written examinations postponed to late April (2020). https://www.hkeaa.edu.hk/DocLibrary/Mai nNews/PR_contingency_HKDSE_0321_ENG.pdf Last accessed 11 June 2022

23. Hong Kong Free Press: Coronavirus: Possible delay in critical exams causing anguish among Hong Kong secondary students (22 Feb 2020). https://hongkongfp.com/2020/02/22/corona virus-possible-delay-critical-examscauses-anguish-among-hong-kong-secondary-students/ Last accessed 11 June 2022

24. The Government of the HKSAR: Primary school classes suspended (2020). https://www. news.gov.hk/eng/2020/11/20201120/20201120_143157_604.ht Last accessed 11 June 2022

25. Education Bureau: Class Arrangements for Schools after Chinese New Year Holidays (2021). https://www.edb.gov.hk/attachment/en/sch-admin/admin/about-sch/diseases-preven tion/edb_20210205_eng.pdf Last accessed 11 June 2022

26. The Government of the HKSAR: Press releases: First phase of face-to-face class resumption for all schools in Hong Kong runs smoothly (2020). https://www.info.gov.hk/gia/gen eral/202009/23/P2020092300629.htm Last accessed 11 June 2022

27. Education Bureau: Face-to-Face Class Arrangements for Schools in Hong Kong in the 2021/22 School Year (2021). https://www.edb.gov.hk/attachment/en/sch-admin/admin/about-sch/diseases-prevention/edb_20210802_eng.pdf Last accessed 11 June 2022

28. The Hong Kong Examinations and Assessment Authority: Press release: 2021 Hong Kong Diploma of Secondary Education examination arrangements for release of results (2021) https://www.hkeaa.edu.hk/DocLibrary/Media/PR/PR_Arrangements_for_Release_of_2021HKDSE_Results_E.pdf Last accessed 11 June 2022

29. The Government of the HKSAR: HKDSE Examination commences smoothly (2022) https://www.info.gov.hk/gia/general/202204/22/P2022042200552.htm Last accessed 11 June 2022

30. Waldow, F.: Projecting images of the 'good' and the 'bad school': Top scorers in educational large-scale assessments as reference societies. A J. Comparat. Int. Edu. **47**(5), 647–664 (2017)

31. Zhang, H. A.: Vision for one's own life: Lessons from Hu Shi and Liang Shuming on education in China. In: Zhao, G., Deng, Z. (eds.) Re-envisioning Chinese education: The meaning of person-making in a new age, pp. 74–90. Routledge, New York, NY (2016)

32. Lee, I., Coniam, D.: Introducing assessment for learning for EFL writing in an assessment of learning examination-driven system in Hong Kong. J. Second Lang. Writ. **22**(1), 34–50 (2013)

33. Tan, C.: Parental responses to education reform in Singapore, Shanghai and Hong Kong. Asia Pacific Education Review **20**, 91–99 (2019)

34. Tan, C.: Comparing high-performing education systems: Understanding Singapore, Shanghai, and Hong Kong. Routledge, Oxon (2018)

35. Carless, D.: From testing to productive student learning: Implementing formative assessment in Confucian-heritage settings. Routledge, New York, NY (2011)

36. Yung, K.W.H.: Shadow education as a form of oppression: conceptualizing experiences and reflections of secondary students in Hong Kong. Asia Pacific Journal of Education **41**(1), 115–129 (2021)

37. Salili, F., Chiu, C. Y., Lai, S.: Goals and motivation of Chinese students – Testing the adaptive learning model. In: Salili, F., Chiu, C.Y., Hong, Y.Y. (eds.) Student motivation: The culture and context of learning, pp. 340–386. Plenum, New York (2001)

38. Li, J.: Learning to self-perfect: Chinese beliefs about learning. In: Chan, C.K.K., Rao, N. (eds.) Revisiting the Chinese learner: Changing contexts, changing education, pp. 35–70. Comparative Education Research Centre, Hong Kong (2009)

39. Kennedy, P.: Learning cultures and learning styles: Myth-understandings about adult (Hong Kong) Chinese learners. Int. J. lifelong Edu. **21**(5), 430-445 (2002)

40. Hong Kong Research Association: The average weekly study hours of Hong Kong students are higher than the working hours of "wage earners". (in Chinese) (2014). http://www.rahk.org/research/1162/1162newsX.pdf Last accessed 11 June 2022

41. Legislative Council Secretariat: Information note: Overall study hours and student well-being in Hong Kong (IN05/17 – 18) (2018). https://www.legco.gov.hk/research-publications/english/1718in05-overall-study-hours-and-student-well-being-in-hong-kong-20180130-e.pdf Last accessed 11 June 2022

42. South China Morning Post: Hong Kong schools still emphasise exam scores rather than learning (11 May 2015) https://www.scmp.com/lifestyle/families/article/1789423/hong-kong-schools-still-emphasise-exam-scores-rather-learning Last accessed 11 June 2022

43. South China Morning Post: This year's HKDSE Chinese exam was a lively "paper of death" (5 April 2017). https://www.scmp.com/yp/discover/news/hong-kong/article/3073804/years-hkdse-chinese-exam-was-lively-paper-death. Last accessed 11 June 2022

44. Hok Yau Club: Stress level of DSE candidates remained high. Pandemic influence on learning progress was even larger than last year (in Chinese) (18 April 2021). http://hyc.org.hk/files/press/20210418_PR.PDF. Last accessed 11 June 2022

45. Hok Yau Club: Pandemic and school closure cause DSE candidates experiencing very high levels of stress (in Chinese) (10 April 2022). https://hyc.org.hk/files/press/20220410_001.pdf Last accessed 11 June 2022
46. Education Bureau: 2020 Secondary 6 Students' Pathway Survey (2021). https://www.edb.gov.hk/attachment/en/about-edb/publicationsstat/figures/S6_20.pdf Last accessed 11 June 2022
47. Yau, T.S.H, Chung, M.L., Li, H.C., Chun, D.W.S: Myth of the Inferior Status of Vocational Education: The Case of Hong Kong. Chinese Education & Society **51**(6), 476–490 (2019)
48. The Hong Kong Examinations and Assessment Authority: Category B: Applied learning subjects (2021). https://www.hkeaa.edu.hk/en/HKDSE/assessment/subject_information/category_b_subjects/faq_index/faq_03.html Last accessed 11 June 2022
49. Legislative Council: Council meeting of 21 May 2014: Amendments to Hon Michael Tien's motion on "Returning a happy childhood to students" [Memorandum] (2014). https://www.legco.gov.hk/yr13-14/english/counmtg/motion/m_papers/cm0521cb3-663-e.pdf Last accessed 11 June 2022
50. Curriculum Development Council: Secondary Education Curriculum Guide, Booklet 2: Learning Goals. School Curriculum Framework and Planning, Hong Kong (2017)
51. Legislative Council Panel on Health Services: Mental Health of Adolescents. LC Paper No. CB(2)512/17–18(01) (2017). https://www.legco.gov.hk/yr17-18/english/panels/ed/papers/edhsws20171220cb2-512-1-e.pdf Last accessed 11 June 2022
52. Task Force on Review of School Curriculum Final report: Optimise the curriculum for the future, Foster whole-person development and diverse talents (2020). https://www.edb.gov.hk/attachment/en/curriculum-development/renewal/taskforce_cur/TF_CurriculumReview_FinalReport_e.pdf Last accessed 11 June 2022
53. Education Council: Australian student wellbeing framework. Education Services Australia (2018). https://studentwellbeinghub.edu.au/media/9310/aswf_booklet.pdf Last accessed 11 June 2022
54. Cairns, R.: Exams tested by Covid-19: An opportunity to rethink standardized senior secondary examinations. Prospects (2020)
55. Pubic Health England: Promoting children and young people's mental health and wellbeing: A whole school or college approach (2021). https://assets.publishing.service.gov.uk/government/uploads/system/uploads/attachment_data/file/1020249/Promoting_children_and_young_people_s_mental_health_and_wellbeing.pdf Last accessed 11 June 2022
56. Department of Education and Skills: Wellbeing Policy Statement and Framework for Practice. Government of Ireland (2018)
57. UNICEF: Impact of COVID-19 on poor mental health in children and young people 'tip of the iceberg' (5 Oct 2021). https://www.unicef.org/press-releases/impact-covid-19-poor-mental-health-children-and-young-people-tip-iceberg Last accessed 11 June 2022
58. OECD: Tackling the mental health impact of the COVID-19 crisis: An integrated, whole-of-society response (2021). https://www.theconsumergoodsforum.com/wp-content/uploads/2021/06/OECD-Tackling-Coronavirus.pdf Last accessed 11 June 2022
59. Hochlaf, D., Thomas, C.: The whole society approach: Making a giant leap on childhood health. IPPR (2020). http://www.ippr.org/research/publications/the-whole-society-approach Last accessed 11 June 2022
60. Bronfenbrenner, U.: The ecology of human development: Experiments by nature and design. Harvard University Press, Cambridge, Massachusetts (1979)
61. Cho, E.Y.N., Chan, T.M.S.: Children's wellbeing in a high-stakes testing environment: The case of Hong Kong. Children and Youth Services Review. Elsevier **109**(C). 2020

62. AGE Platform Europe: Mental health in the eye of the COVID-19 hurricane. (8 May 2020). https://www.age-platform.eu/sites/default/files/JointPR_MentalHealth%26COVID19-Joint_recommendations_May2020.pdf Last accessed 11 June 2022
63. Lee, J.: Mental health effects of school closures during COVID-19. Lancet Child Adolesc Health. 4(6), 421 (2020)

Important Features Associated with Depression Prediction and Explainable AI

Vincent Peter C. Magboo$^{(\boxtimes)}$ (ID) and Ma. Sheila A. Magboo (ID)

Department of Physical Sciences and Mathematics, University of the Philippines Manila, Manila, Philippines
{vcmagboo,mamagboo}@up.edu.ph

Abstract. Depression is a debilitating disease that leaves individuals persistently feeling sad or hopeless for more than two weeks affecting more than 300 million people globally. We applied several machine learning models with model explainability to a publicly available depression dataset. Several experiments were performed to assess the use of feature selection methods and technique to address dataset imbalance on diagnostic accuracy. The top performing model was obtained by logistic regression with excellent performance metrics (91% accuracy, 93% sensitivity, 85% specificity, 93% precision, 93% F1-score and 0.78 Matthews correlation coefficient). Feature importance was also generated for the best model. Explainable artificial intelligence method using LIME was applied to help understand the reasoning behind the model's classification of depression leading to better understanding of physicians, thus demonstrating its use in clinical practice.

Keywords: Depression prediction · Machine learning · Feature selection · Feature importance · LIME

1 Introduction

Depression, characterized by persistent sadness and a loss of interest in activities a person normally enjoys or accompanied by the inability to do usual daily activities for at least two weeks, is very common nowadays affecting more than 300 million people globally [1]. It significantly affects the over-all well-being and functioning at school, family, and workplace often leading to self-harm or even suicide. With COVID-19 pandemic, depression has become even more pronounced as shown in the study by Rossi et al., indicating COVID-related stressful events to be associated with depression and anxiety symptoms in the Italian general population [2]. Depression has also been shown to be highly associated with numerous chronic diseases such as diabetes, heart disease caner, stroke, and chronic obstructive pulmonary disease [3]. Prompt recognition of the disease coupled with early professional intervention can significantly improve mental symptoms, resolve somatic problems such as gastrointestinal problems and sleeping disorders, thereby mitigating the negative implications for over-all well-being [4]. To assess depression, it is crucial to determine important contributing factors to plan the appropriate intervention. It is in this area of early diagnosis where machine learning

H. Li et al. (Eds.): WIS 2022, CCIS 1626, pp. 23–36, 2022.
https://doi.org/10.1007/978-3-031-14832-3_2

(ML) can be utilized, thus enhancing the whole diagnostic process leading to institution of the much-needed early intervention efforts and medical therapy.

Our objective is to predict depression using a variety of ML classification algorithms namely: Logistic Regression (LR), Naive Bayes (NB), k-Nearest Neighbor (kNN), Support Vector Machine (SVM), Decision Tree (DT), Random Forest (RF), Adaptive Boosting (AdaBoost), and Extreme Gradient Boosting (XGBoost) evaluated on publicly available dataset. It is also our aim to determine the important features relevant to depression prediction and the logic employed by the classifiers to explain their prediction.

2 Literature Review

In the study by Grzenda et al. involving depressed 60 years and above, authors compared ML classifiers - SVM, RF, and LR on sociodemographic characteristics, baseline clinical self-reports, cognitive tests, and structural magnetic resonance imaging features to predict treatment outcomes in late-life depression [5]. RF obtained an area under receiver operating characteristic curve (AUROC) of 0.83 while SVM and LR recorded AUROC of 0.80 and 0.79, respectively. They also reported anterior and posterior cingulate volumes, depression characteristics, and self-reported health-related quality scores as the most important predictors of treatment response. Lin et al. [6], compared regression-based models (LR, lasso, ridge) and RF in depression forecasting among home-based elderly Chinese. Authors concluded that these models have good diagnostic performance in differentiating depression versus no depression. They reported life satisfaction, self-reported memory, cognitive ability, activities of daily living impairment to be the major determinants. In [7], authors applied XGBoost model to classify current depression versus no lifetime depression with a 0.86 AUROC. They further concluded that XGBoost and network analysis were useful to discover depression-related factors and their relationships and can be applied to epidemiological studies.

Sabab Zulfiker et al., applied six ML classifiers coupled with three feature selection methods and synthetic minority oversampling technique (SMOTE) to assess for presence of depression [8]. Their results showed AdaBoost with SelectKBest feature selection technique to be the best performing model with a 92.56% accuracy rate. Nemesure et al. [9], applied a novel ensemble of ML models (SVM, kNN, LR, RF, XGBoost, and neural network (NN)) to predict depression and Generalized Anxiety Disorder (GAD) with moderate predictive performance (AUROC of 0.73 for GAD and 0.60 for depression). Shapley Additive Explanations (SHAP) was used to generate feature importance.

Sousa et al. [10], determine predictors of depression and reported that sex, living status, mobility, and nutritional status appear to be the important factors to be associated with depression. They concluded that these important predictors would be crucial for prevention and for customization of interventions. In the study by Richter et al., evaluated several ML-based approaches that use behavioral data in the classification of depression and other psychiatric disorders. Authors classified these studies into laboratory-based assessments and data mining which was further divided into (a) social media usage and movement sensors data and (b) demographic and clinical information. Authors summarized the benefits and constraints and suggested future research directions to develop interventions and individually tailored treatments in the future [11].

In the study by Vincent et al. [12], they used a multilayered neural perceptron (MLP) and experimented with the backpropagation technique to assess for depression involving data collected from IT professionals. Authors reported that deep-MLP with backpropagation outperforms other machine learning-based models for effective classification of depression with a 98.8% accuracy. Jan et al., reviewed several ML algorithms for diagnosis of bipolar disorders [13]. Their survey identified 18 classification models, five regression models, two model-based clustering methods, one natural language processing, one clustering algorithms and three deep learning -based models. Magnetic resonance imaging data were mostly used for classifying bipolar patients whereas microarray expression data sets and genomic data were the least commonly used.

3 Methodology

In our research, the first step is the loading of the dataset. This is to be followed by pre-processing steps which include data cleaning, dataset normalization, feature selection techniques to select important predictors, and addressing data imbalance. We then applied various ML algorithms followed by assessment of their performance using accuracy, precision, sensitivity/recall, specificity, F1-scores, and Matthews correlation coefficient. Feature importance and AI explainability assessment were also done. The pipeline for this study is seen in Fig. 1.

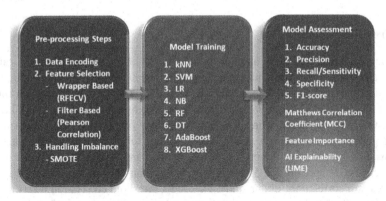

Fig. 1. Machine learning pipeline for depression prediction

3.1 Dataset Description

We used a publicly available depression dataset from github [14]. The dataset contains 604 instances involving 455:149 male–female sex ratio, with 30 predictor variables and 1 target variable (depressed or not) based on Burns Depression Checklist. The description of these attributes is shown in Table 1.

Table 1. Description of attributes of depression

Attribute	Attribute	
Age in years (AGERNG)	Physical Exercise (PHYEX)	Felt Cheated (CHEAT)
Gender	Smoker (SMOKE)	Faced threat (THREAT)
Educational Attainment (EDU)	Alcohol Drinker (DRINK)	Felt Abused (ABUSED)
Profession (PROF)	With Illness (ILLNESS)	Lost someone (LOST)
Marital Status (MARSTS)	Has Insomnia (INSOM)	Has Work/Study Pressure (WRKPRE)
Type of Residence (RESDPL)	Has Eating disorder (EATDIS)	Inferiority Complex (INFER)
Lives with Family or not (LIVWTH)	Average sleep hours (AVGSLP)	Suicidal thoughts (SUICIDE)
Satisfied with Environment or not (ENVSAT)	Taking Prescribed Med (PREMED)	In Conflict with Family or Friends (CONFLICT)
Satisfied with current position or achievements or not (POSSAT)	Ave hours in social network (TSSN)	Depressed
Financial stress (FINSTR)	Feels anxiety (ANXI)	
Had Debt (DEBT)	Feels deprived (DEPRI)	

3.2 Pre-processing Steps

Pre-processing methods were applied to the dataset in preparation for ML training. There were no missing values but there were 10 duplicate records which were promptly removed. It also shows mild data imbalance with 391 (65.82%) with depression and 203 (34.18%) without depression. We performed data encoding for the attributes and feature scaling with normalization using the StandardScaler function of scikit-learn library. All categorical predictors were dummified resulting to an increase in the number of columns. For feature selection procedure, we applied and compared a wrapper method using recursive feature elimination with cross validation (RFE-CV) and a filter method using Pearson correlation. In our study, we used a threshold correlation with the target variable of > 0.20 and a correlation between predictors of less than 0.80. As the dataset is imbalanced, we applied Synthetic Minority Over-sampling TEchnique (SMOTE). The correlation heatmap is seen in Fig. 2.

3.3 Machine Learning Models

The dummified dataset was divided into 30% testing involving 179 records and 70% training involving 415 records with tenfold cross validation. We utilized python 3.8 and its various machine learning libraries (scikit-learn, keras, tensorflow, pandas, Matplotlib, seaborn, NumPy, and LIME) in our experiment. The models tested were LR, NB, kNN, SVM, DT, RF, AdaBoost, and XGBoost. Hyperparameter tuning was performed on each

ML model. To determine the best performing model, Matthews correlation coefficient (MCC) was used.

3.4   Feature Importance and Model Explainability

For the best performing models, we generated the feature importance scores to determine the most important attributes relevant to depression prediction. To understand the local behavior of the model for a single instance of a patient with or without depresssion, we applied Local Interpretable Model-agnostic Explanations (LIME). LIME is used to explain individual prediction of a black-box machine learning model.

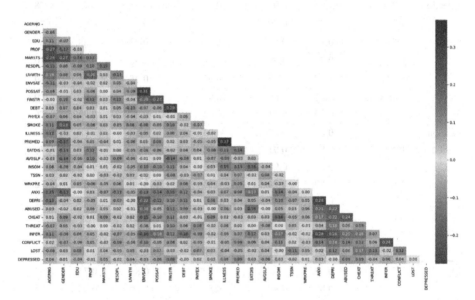

Fig. 2. Correlation heatmap of predictor variables for depression

4   Results and Analysis

The performance metrics of the 8 ML models for our dataset are shown in Table 2 where the effects of feature selection method are assessed. LR is the best performing model when there is no feature selection technique used as well as when Pearson correlation is used as a feature selection with accuracy rates of 91% and 89%, respectively. For Pearson correlation, a mild increase in the accuracy rate ranging from 1- 4% is seen for DT, RF, NB, kNN and SVM while a slight decrease of 2–5% is noted for LR, AdaBoost and XGBoost. Nonetheless, LR still remains to be the top model when Pearson correlation method is used as a feature selection. On the other hand, the top model for the RFE-CV feature selection is XGBoost with 85% accuracy. When RFE-CV is applied, generally there is a decrease in accuracy ranging from 3%-7% for most of the models while the rest of the models (DT, NB, kNN) did not show any significant changes. Overall, after considering the effects of feature selection, LR with no feature selection is the best performing model as it obtained the highest MCC score at 0.78, and 91% accuracy. Hence in this dataset, it appears that all attributes seem to be important in depression prediction and no attributes need to be eliminated.

Table 2. Performance metrics for predicting depression – assessment of feature selection

	ML Model	Accuracy	Precision	Sensitivity	Specificity	F-score	MCC
No Feature	DT	0.82	0.91	0.81	0.83	0.85	0.61
Selection	LR	0.91	0.93	0.93	0.85	0.93	0.78
	RF	0.87	0.89	0.92	0.78	0.91	0.71
	NB	0.84	0.95	0.82	0.92	0.88	0.69
	kNN	0.83	0.99	0.76	0.98	0.86	0.70
	SVM	0.87	0.88	0.93	0.75	0.91	0.70
	AdaBoost	0.87	0.89	0.91	0.78	0.90	0.69
	XGBoost	0.89	0.91	0.93	0.81	0.92	0.76
Pearson	DT	0.83	0.82	0.95	0.58	0.88	0.59
Correlation	LR	0.89	0.91	0.93	0.81	0.92	0.76
	RF	0.85	0.91	0.86	0.83	0.88	0.67
	NB	0.87	0.94	0.85	0.90	0.89	0.72
	kNN	0.87	0.93	0.87	0.86	0.90	0.71
	SVM	0.88	0.90	0.93	0.80	0.91	0.73
	AdaBoost	0.83	0.89	0.85	0.80	0.87	0.63
	XGBoost	0.84	0.87	0.90	0.73	0.89	0.64
RFE-CV	DT	0.83	0.91	0.82	0.83	0.76	0.63
	LR	0.84	0.90	0.87	0.80	0.88	0.65
	RF	0.84	0.90	0.87	0.80	0.88	0.65
	NB	0.84	0.90	0.86	0.80	0.88	0.64
	kNN	0.83	0.89	0.85	0.80	0.87	0.63
	SVM	0.83	0.91	0.82	0.83	0.86	0.63
	AdaBoost	0.80	0.86	0.84	0.71	0.85	0.55
	XGBoost	0.85	0.89	0.90	0.76	0.89	0.67

To address the issue of imbalance, SMOTE was applied to the dataset. Assessment of SMOTE for the feature selection methods is seen in Table 3. The application of SMOTE to the dataset when there is no feature selection resulted to a decrease in the accuracy rate with a range of 3%-18% for most models. The only model which posted a slight increase (2%) in the accuracy is NB while there was no change for RF and AdaBoost. Nevertheless, LR obtained the highest accuracy and MCC at 84% and 0.74 respectively. The application of SMOTE to the dataset when Pearson correlation was used as a feature selection generally resulted to a very small decrease in the accuracy (1%-4%) for most

Table 3. Comparative Performance Metrics of ML Models with and without SMOTE

	ML Model	Accuracy	Precision	Sensitivity	Specificity	F-score	MCC
No Feature Selection plus SMOTE	DT	0.64	0.97	0.47	0.97	0.64	0.44
	LR	0.88	0.92	0.91	0.83	0.91	0.74
	RF	0.87	0.90	0.91	0.80	0.90	0.71
	NB	0.86	0.93	0.86	0.86	0.89	0.70
	kNN	0.74	0.91	0.68	0.86	0.78	0.51
	SVM	0.83	0.91	0.83	0.83	0.87	0.64
	AdaBoost	0.87	0.89	0.74	0.81	0.81	0.53
	XGBoost	0.85	0.89	0.89	0.78	0.89	0.67
Pearson Correlation plus SMOTE	DT	0.83	0.89	0.85	0.78	0.87	0.62
	LR	0.89	0.94	0.90	0.88	0.92	0.77
	RF	0.86	0.92	0.87	0.85	0.89	0.70
	NB	0.85	0.94	0.83	0.90	0.88	0.70
	kNN	0.86	0.95	0.83	0.92	0.89	0.71
	SVM	0.85	0.91	0.86	0.83	0.88	0.70
	AdaBoost	0.83	0.89	0.85	0.80	0.87	0.67
	XGBoost	0.88	0.92	0.90	0.83	0.91	0.72
RFE-CV plus SMOTE	DT	0.83	0.91	0.82	0.83	0.86	0.63
	LR	0.84	0.90	0.86	0.80	0.88	0.64
	RF	0.84	0.90	0.87	0.80	0.88	0.65
	NB	0.80	0.91	0.78	0.85	0.84	0.60
	kNN	0.83	0.91	0.82	0.83	0.86	0.63
	SVM	0.84	0.90	0.86	0.80	0.88	0.64
	AdaBoost	0.83	0.91	0.82	0.83	0.86	0.63
	XGBoost	0.84	0.90	0.87	0.80	0.88	0.65

models while a small increase of 1% is seen for RF. No change in the accuracy was noted for DT, LR and AdaBoost. For the case when SMOTE was applied for RFE-CV, there were no significant changes in the accuracy rates across all models – a very slight increase of 1%-3% for SVM and AdaBoost, a decrease of 1%-4% for NB and XGBoost, while the rest of the models had no changes. Overall, LR posted the highest accuracy and MCC at 89% and 0.76, respectively for this experiment assessing the effects of SMOTE.

Table 4 highlights the confusion matrix of the best performing models for the six experiments (no feature selection (FS), with Pearson correlation, with RFE-CV, without SMOTE and with SMOTE). Comparative performance of the best models is also shown in Fig. 3. It can be deduced that the performance of the six models in the experiments seem to be similar or comparable to each other across all metrics. This suggests that for this particular dataset, we may or may not do feature selection method nor may or may not apply SMOTE to address imbalance. Nonetheless, the overall best performing model is LR without any feature selection method and with no SMOTE.

Table 4. Confusion Matrix of the best Performing ML Models in various Experiments

Actual	LR (No FS, No SMOTE) Predicted		LR (With Pearson Correlation, No SMOTE) Predicted		XGBoost (RFE-CV, No SMOTE) Predicted		LR (No FS, With SMOTE) Predicted		LR (With Pearson Correlation, with SMOTE) Predicted		RF/XGBoost (RFE-CV, with With SMOTE) Predicted	
	+	-	+	-	+	-	+	-	+	-	+	-
With depression	[[50	9]	[[48	11]	[[45	14]	[[49	10]	[[52	7]	[[47	12]
No depression	[8	112]]	[8	112]]	[12	108]]	[11	109]]	[12	108]]	[16	104]]

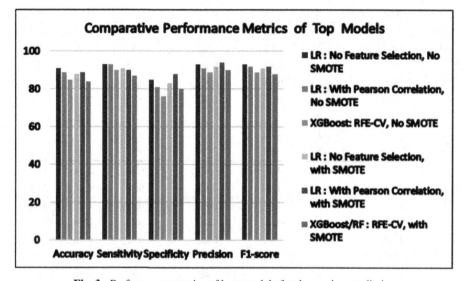

Fig. 3. Performance metrics of best models for depression prediction

The feature importance of the attributes of LR is seen in Fig. 4. The most important features relevant to depression prediction are ANXI (feels anxiety), DEPRI (feels deprived), POSSAT (satisfied or not with current position/achievement), INFER (inferiority complex) and ENVSAT (satisfied or not with environment). These features are also in consonance with clinical assessment of depression.

For the explainable AI part of this research, we used LIME which is a technique that approximates any black box machine learning model with a local, interpretable model to explain each individual prediction. LIME is model agnostic hence can give explanations for any supervised machine learning model. To illustrate how LIME works, we randomly selected two patients the first one without depression while the second one has depression. Let us take the case of our first patient diagnosed as having no depression and was correctly classified by LR to be 0 or "not depressed" as illustrated in Fig. 5. The LIME output in Fig. 5 consists of 3 parts: left, center, and right. The left shows the classification predicted by LR which in this case is 0 or "not depressed" and with a confidence of 90%. The center shows the features that influenced the classification. For this patient, LIME was able to generate the important features for LR to arrive at the classification "no depression" and these are: patient has no anxiety (ANXI_Yes = 0), has no inferiority complex (INFER_Yes = 0), has no suicidal thoughts (SUICIDE_Yes = 0), has not recently lost someone close to him (LOST_YES = 0), was not in conflict with family or friends (CONFLICT_Yes = 0), was not physically, sexually, or emotionally abused (ABUSED_YES = 0), never felt cheated by someone recently (CHEAT_YES = 0), and average sleep of was not 8 h (AVGSLP_8 = 0). Note that there are also feature values that are leaning towards "depression" for this particular case which are: not satisfied with his current position or achievements (POSSAT_YES = 0) and felt deprived of something he deserves (DEPRI_YES = 1). However, the effects of these two features are not enough to oppose the effects of the other features contributing to a "no depression" classification. The rightmost part of the LIME output shows the actual values of the first 10 most important features for this patient. LIME can be an effective tool to explain the logic by the model to arrive at the prediction.

For the second patient who was diagnosed as "depressed", the LIME output in Fig. 6 shows the classification predicted by LR which in this case was 1 or "depressed" and with a confidence of 100%. The center shows the features that influenced the "depressed" classification which are: patient is not satisfied with current position or achievements (POSSAT_True = 0), has anxiety (ANXI_Yes = 1), felt deprived of something he deserves (DEPRI_YES = 1), has inferiority complex (INFER_Yes = 1), and is undergoing financial stress (FINSTR_True = 1). Note that there are also values contributing to "no depression" for this particular case which are: did not lost someone (LOST_Yes = 0), nor felt abused (ABUSED_Yes = 0), nor cheated (CHEAT_Yes = 0), is not in conflict with family or friends (CONFLICT_Yes = 0) nor threatened (THREAT_Yes = 0). However, the effects of these features are not enough to oppose the effects of the features contributing to a "depression" classification. The top features that influenced the "depression" classification for this patient is in agreement with the top features selected by LR as most influential to a "depression" classification as seen in Fig. 3. The explainability feature of LIME can help health professionals understand and interpret classifier's prediction leading to increased trust in the use of these methods.

In our study, we applied a filter method using Pearson correlation with the target variable (presence of depression) and among predictor variables. Feature selection aims to remove redundant features which can be expressed by other attributes and irrelevant features which do not contribute to the performance of the model in predicting depression [15]. RFECV reduces model complexity by removing attributes one at a time until it automatically finds an optimal number of features based on the cross-validation score of the model [16, 17]. It is a commonly used due to its ease of use. Using the associated feature weights, those attributes with small feature weights close to zero contribute very little to predicting depression. But we must take note that removing a single attribute would also lead to a change in the feature weights, which suggest that elimination of the features should be done in a stepwise fashion. On the other hand, pairwise correlation identifies highly correlated features and keeps only one of them to achieve predictive power using few features as possible since highly correlated features bring no new information to the dataset. These highly correlated features only increase model complexity, increase the chance of overfitting, and require more computations [18, 19].

SMOTE is an oversampling method that creates artificial minority data points within the cluster of minority class samples in a balanced way which render it to be an effective method in reducing negative effects of imbalance leading to increased performance [8, 20–24]. It works by utilizing a kNN algorithm to create synthetic data by first selecting a random data from the minority (no depression) class and then kNN from the data are set. That is, synthetic data is created between the random data and the randomly selected kNN. As such, there is not only an increase in the number of datapoints but an increase in its variety. However, SMOTE has its disadvantages such as sample overlapping, noise interference and blindness of neighbor selection as well as their suitability for clinical datasets [22, 25, 26].

Feature importance allows us to detect which features in our depression dataset have predictive power by assigning a score to each feature based on its ability to improve predictions and allow us to rank these features. The increase in the model prediction error after permuting the values of that feature determines its feature importance. An increase in the model error also increases the importance of that feature for predicting depression, while if the accuracy of the model remains the same or slightly decreases, then the feature is deemed unimportant for depression prediction [27–29]. However, this method has also some disadvantages such as prohibitive computational cost and cannot be used as a substitute for statistical inference [30].

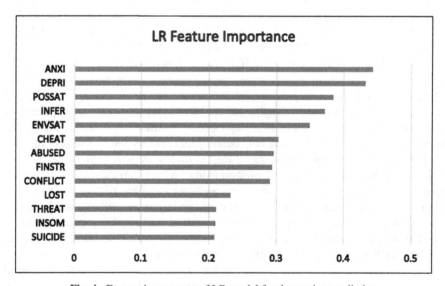

Fig. 4. Feature importance of LR model for depression prediction

Our results are comparable with the other studies [5, 6, 9, 13] in the literature with respect to depression prediction. Our top performing models have very good sensitivity and specificity rates allowing the mental health professionals to use these models as a screening tool for depression in their clinical practice. Additionally, we highlighted the importance of utilizing LIME as an XAI tool in depression prediction. In [31], authors have validated the use of their XAI-ASD in improving diagnostic performance

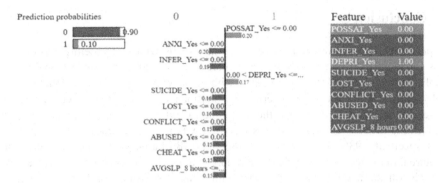

Fig. 5. A sample of feature explainability for a correctly classified patient without depression by logistic regression

Fig. 6. A sample of model explainability for a correctly classified patient with depression by logistic regression

in predicting presence of depression and reported that explainability allows humans to appropriately understand and trust the emerging AI phenomenon. It has brought the machines closer to humans because of its capability to explain the logic behind the diagnosis. It needs to be emphasized that insufficient explainability and transparency in most existing AI systems seem to be a major reason for unsuccessful implementation and integration of AI tools in the routine clinical practice. Our findings suggest the utility of XAI models to make a diagnosis of depression with acceptable results. The clinical relevance of our experiment is even more highlighted with XAI models that can provide faster and with high reliability to help physicians in the screening of patients for depression. An early accurate diagnosis leading to prompt intervention efforts is very crucial to improve patient's quality of life, diminished risk for developing chronic diseases, improve productivity and prevention of suicide cases [5, 8, 24, 32]. This research, thus, provided useful insights in the development of an automated models that can assist healthcare workers in the assessment of depressive disorders.

5   Conclusion

Depression is debilitating disease that leaves individuals persistently feeling sad or hopeless for more than two weeks affecting more than 300 million people globally. We
applied several machine learning models with model explainability to a publicly available depression dataset. After a series of experiments to assess the effects of the use
of feature selection methods and the technique to address dataset imbalance, the best
performing model was logistic regression (LR) with a 91% accuracy, 93% sensitivity,
85% specificity, 93% recall, 93% F1-score and 0.78 Matthews correlation coefficient.
Feature importance identified the most important attributes necessary to make a depression classification are also in consonance with clinical assessment of depression. LIME
method provided tools to visualize the reasoning behind the classification of depression
by the machine learning model for better understanding of physicians. Incorporation
of XAI tools in clinical practice can further enhance the diagnostic acumen of health
professionals. The primary limitation of our research is the use of small datasets due
unavailability of large and open-source depression datasets.

Future enhancement of this study should focus on inclusion of other tools for feature
importance as well as techniques in XAI such as SHAP for better understanding of the
models by healthcare providers. Moreover, mixed type of datasets combining symptoms
with neuroimaging features seen in functional magnetic resonance imaging can also be
explored to generate more superior diagnostic accuracy. Our findings are promising and
have generated useful insights in the development of automated models that are faster
and with high reliability which can be of use to physicians in predicting depression.
Nonetheless, early intervention efforts and treatment for depression ensure the best
quality of care for our patients.

References

1. World Health Organization: Mental Health and Substance Abuse (2021). http://www.emro.
   who.int/mnh/what-you-can-do/index.html#accordionpan4 Last accessed 10 Jan 2022
2. Rossi, R., Jannini, T.B., Socci, V., Pacitti, F., Lorenzo, G.D.: Stressful life events and resilience
   during the COVID-19 lockdown measures in italy: association with mental health outcomes and age. Frontiers in Psychiatry **12**, 635832 (2021). https://doi.org/10.3389/fpsyt.2021.
   635832
3. Li, H., Ge, S., Greene, B., Dunbar-Jacob, J.: Depression in the Context of Chronic Disease in
   the United States and China. Int. J. Nurs. Sci. **6**(1), 117–122 (2019). https://doi.org/10.1016/
   j.ijnss.2018.11.007
4. Uddin, M.Z., Dysthe, K.K., Følstad, A., Brandtzaeg, P.B.: Deep learning for prediction of
   depressive symptoms in a large textual dataset. Neural Comp. Appl. **34**, 721–744 (2022).
   https://doi.org/10.1007/s00521-021-06426-4
5. Grzenda, A., Speier, W., Siddarth, P., Pant, A., Krause-Sorio, B., Narr, K., Lavretsky,
   H.: Machine learning prediction of treatment outcome in late-life depression. Frontiers in
   Psychiatry **12** (2021). https://doi.org/10.3389/fpsyt.2021.738494
6. Lin, S., Wu, Y., Fang, Y.: Comparison of regression and machine learning methods in depression forecasting among home-based elderly chinese: a community based study. Frontiers in
   psychiatry **12**, 764806 (2022). https://doi.org/10.3389/fpsyt.2021.764806

7. Nam, S.M., Peterson, T.A., Seo, K.Y., Han, H.W., Kang, J.I.: Discovery of depression-associated factors from a nationwide population-based survey: epidemiological study using machine learning and network analysis. J. Medi. Intern. Res. **23**(6), e27344 (2021). https://doi.org/10.2196/27344

8. Sabab Zulfiker, M., Kabir, N., Biswas, A.A., Nazneen, T., Shorif Uddin, M.: An in-depth analysis of machine learning approaches to predict depression. Curr. Res. Behavi. Sci. **2**, 100044 (2021). https://doi.org/10.1016/j.crbeha.2021.100044

9. Nemesure, M.D., Heinz, M.V., Huang, R., Jacobson, N.: Predictive modeling of depression and anxiety using electronic health records and a novel machine learning approach with artificial intelligence. Scientific Reports **11**, 1980 (2021). https://doi.org/10.1038/s41598-021-81368-4

10. Sousa, S., Paúl, C., Teixeira, L.: Predictors of major depressive disorder in older people. Int. J. Environm. Res. Pub. Health **18**, 11894 (2021). https://doi.org/10.3390/ijerph182211894

11. Richter, T., Fishbain, B., Richter-Levin, G., Okon-Singer, H.: Machine Learning-Based Behavioral Diagnostic Tools for Depression: Advances, Challenges, and Future Directions. J. Personal. Medi. **11**, 957 (2021). https://doi.org/10.3390/jpm11100957

12. Vincent, P., Mahendran, N., Nebhen, J., Deepa, N., Srinivasan, K., Hu, Y.C.: Performance assessment of certain machine learning models for predicting the major depressive disorder among IT professionals during pandemic times. Computational intelligence and neuroscience **2021**, 9950332 (2021). https://doi.org/10.1155/2021/9950332

13. Jan, Z., et al.: The role of machine learning in diagnosing bipolar disorder: scoping review. J. Medi. Intern. Res. **23**(11), e29749 (2021). https://doi.org/10.2196/29749

14. Sabab31/Depression-Repository: https://github.com/Sabab31/Depression-Repository.git last accessed 10 Nov 2021

15. Demircioğlu, A.: Measuring the bias of incorrect application of feature selection when using cross-validation in radiomics. Insights Imaging **12**, 172 (2021). https://doi.org/10.1186/s13244-021-01115-1

16. Chang, W., Ji, X., Wang, L., Liu, H., Zhang, Y., Chen, B., Zhou, S.: A machine-learning method of predicting vital capacity plateau value for ventilatory Pump failure based on data mining. Healthcare **9**, 1306 (2021). https://doi.org/10.3390/healthcare9101306

17. Li, D., et al.: Application of machine learning classifier to candida auris drug resistance analysis. Frontiers in Cellular and Infection Microbiology **11** (2021). https://doi.org/10.3389/fcimb.2021.742062

18. Rieta, J.J., Senan, E.M., Abunadi, I., Jadhav, M., Fati, S.M.: Score and correlation coefficient-based feature selection for predicting heart failure diagnosis by using machine learning algorithms. Computational and Mathematical Methods in Medicine **2021**, article 8500314 (2021). https://doi.org/10.1155/2021/8500314

19. Magboo, V.P.C., Magboo, M.S.A.: Machine learning classifiers on breast cancer recurrences. Procedia Computer Science **192**, 2742–2752 (2021). https://doi.org/10.1016/j.procs.2021.09.044

20. Çakır, H., İncereis, N., Akgün, B.T., Taştemir, A.S.Y.: Comparison of sampling methods using machine learning and deep learning algorithms with an imbalanced data set for the prevention of violence against physicians. In: 2021 15th Turkish National Software Engineering Symposium (UYMS), pp. 1–7 (2021). https://doi.org/10.1109/UYMS54260.2021.9659758

21. Huang, C.Y., Dai, H.L.: Learning from class-imbalanced data: review of data driven methods and algorithm driven methods. Data Sci. Fina. Econo. **1**(1), 21–36 (2021). https://doi.org/10.3934/DSFE.2021002

22. Wang, S., Dai, Y., Shen, J., Xuan, J.: Research on expansion and classification of imbalanced data based on SMOTE algorithm. Scientific Reports **11**, 24039 (2021). https://doi.org/10.1038/s41598-021-03430-5

23. Risi, M., Wang, J.B., Zou, C.A., Fu, G.H.: AWSMOTE: An SVM-based adaptive weighted SMOTE for class-imbalance learning. scientific programming **2021**, article 9947621 (2021). https://doi.org/10.1155/2021/9947621

24. Magboo, V.P.C., Magboo, M.S.A.: Imputation techniques and recursive feature elimination in machine learning applied to type II diabetes classification. In: 2021 4th Artificial Intelligence and Cloud Computing Conference (AICCC '21), pp. 201-207. Association for Computing Machinery, New York, NY, USA (2021). https://doi.org/10.1145/3508259.3508288

25. Jiang, Z., Pan, T., Zhang, C., Yang, J.: A new oversampling method based on the classification contribution degree. Symmetry **13**, 194 (2021). https://doi.org/10.3390/sym13020194

26. Beinecke, J., Heider, D.: Gaussian noise up-sampling is better suited than SMOTE and ADASYN for clinical decision making. BioData Mining **14**, 49 (2021). https://doi.org/10.1186/s13040-021-00283-6

27. Ljubobratovic, D., Vukovic, M., Brkic Bakaric, M., Jemric, T., Matetic, M.: Utilization of explainable machine learning algorithms for determination of important features in 'Suncrest' peach maturity prediction. Electronics **10**, 3115 (2021). https://doi.org/10.3390/electronics10243115

28. Mi, X., Zou, B., Zou, F., Hu, J.: Permutation-based identification of important biomarkers for complex diseases via machine learning models. Nature Communications **12**, 3008 (2021). https://doi.org/10.1038/s41467-021-22756-2

29. Inglis, A., Parnell, A., Hurley, C.: Visualizing variable importance and variable interaction effects in machine learning models. J. Compu. Graphi. Statis. https://doi.org/10.1080/10618600.2021.2007935

30. Oh, S.: Predictive case-based feature importance and interaction. Information Sciences **593**, 155–176 (2022). https://doi.org/10.1016/j.ins.2022.02.003

31. Uddin, M.Z., et al.: Deep Learning for prediction of depressive symptoms in a large textual dataset. Neural Comp. Appl. **34**, 721–744 (2022). https://doi.org/10.1007/s00521-021-06426-4

32. Magboo, V.P.C., Abu, P.A.R.: Deep neural network for diagnosis of bone metastasis. In: 2022 The 5th International Conference on Software Engineering and Information Management (ICSIM) (ICSIM 2022), pp. 144–151. Association for Computing Machinery, New York, NY, USA (2022). https://doi.org/10.1145/3520084.3520107

Mental Health Monitoring at Work: IoT Solutions and Privacy Concerns

Dana Naous[(⊠)] and Tobias Mettler

IDHEAP, University of Lausanne, Lausanne, Switzerland
{dana.naous,tobias.mettler}@unil.ch

Abstract. The fast-paced business environment and new work arrangements have elevated mental health risks, especially occupational stress and burnouts. Mental health becomes a critical aspect for occupational safety and health in office settings. Therefore, employers aim to improve employees' well-being and safety at the workplace through dedicated health initiatives. Internet-of-things (IoT) technology is increasingly being used for such purposes. However, its implementation in the workplace is accompanied by privacy concerns. In this study, we aim to provide a meta-synthesis of existing IoT solutions for supporting employees' mental health in office settings. We classify existing studies into use cases with possible implementation options. We discuss main challenges emerging from privacy concerns along the IoT data lifecycle. We contribute to the design of the future workplace through emphasizing the opportunity for the connected workplace in improving occupational health.

Keywords: IoT · Mental health · Connected workplace · Meta-synthesis

1 Introduction

For companies to be successful in the digital era, adapting to the ever-changing business environment and worldwide trends is essential. This creates a fast-paced working environment in companies undergoing digital transformation. Companies strive to provide the optimal working conditions for their employees to be more efficient and productive. The current COVID-19 pandemic brought additional challenges and change to the workplace. With the increased numbers of cases worldwide, companies were obliged to shift to remote working and home-office mode. In today's workplace, flexibility is key. Flexible work arrangements, with respect to work schedule and location (such as remote working or working from home), are essential today to help employees concurrently manage work and personal life with the increased digitalization. However, this flexibility comes with a price: the normalized extended availability.

Tamers et al. [1] illustrated that the blurred boundaries between work and personal life can result with constant pre-occupation with work and work-family conflicts which increases stress. In fact, work stress and mental health are important topics when it comes to occupational health. Not only because of the work arrangements, but also with the increased pressure given the fast-paced business environment [2]. Schneider and

H. Li et al. (Eds.): WIS 2022, CCIS 1626, pp. 37–45, 2022.
https://doi.org/10.1007/978-3-031-14832-3_3

Kokshagina [3] explained that the digital workplace creates a pressure of constant connectivity and availability, which can result in technostress. Han et al. [4] explained that work-related stress can occur when there is a poor match between people's working ability and assigned tasks. They emphasized that heavy stress might lead to depression and other health problems, such as cardiovascular diseases and musculoskeletal disorders, which can affect productivity and performance.

Excessive stress has been proven to lower work efficiency and also lead to negative emotions and illnesses [4]. People working under stress or with precarious employment conditions are likely to smoke more, exercise less and have an unhealthy diet. Moreover, in the specific case of office workers, previous research has highlighted several risks associated with the working behavior and environmental conditions for facility management that can affect the employees' mental health. While employees spend 90% of their time indoors, the environmental conditions in the workplace critically affect the employees' well-being and productivity [5]. Sun et al. [6] explained that indoor air quality has a significant impact on the person's health, comfort, and performance. Also, environmental conditions such as thermal comfort and noise can impact the individual's blood pressure and stress levels, which affects concentration and productivity [5, 7].

The World Health Organization (WHO) emphasized that the health of employees is an essential prerequisite for economic development [8]. To address the different possible health risks in today's workplace, WHO urged companies to develop workplace health initiatives that allow them to monitor employees' health and provide the necessary services [8]. Accordingly, employers have been continuously investing in digital solutions and interventions to measure physical or physiological parameters such as movement, body temperature, and heart rate, and sensor networks that enable measuring quality parameters for ensuring the well-being of their employees and avoiding health and safety risks [9–11].

Yassaee et al. [12] explained that the Internet-of-things (IoT) initiatives can help in detecting and preventing root causes for certain health issues, and in mitigating health risks. They also mentioned that introducing IoT into the workplace can help employees be more conscious about their health and proactive in terms of actions. However, the implementation of such initiatives for mental health monitoring in the workplace remains challenging. The use of IoT technology is always accompanied by privacy concerns as it often trespasses the boundary between monitoring online and offline behavior during work time but also outside working hours (e.g., while commuting or at home). The use of wearable devices and sensor networks for continuously tracking and monitoring employees is considered to be a major privacy concern [13, 14]. Due to the sensitive nature of health data, many employees have serious doubts about participating in company-sponsored (or mandated) health and well-being initiatives. Employees fear that personal data is processed by the employer for other purposes, such as, performance appraisals or lay-off decisions [15].

In this paper, we investigate the following question: What are existing solutions for mental health monitoring at work and what are associated implementation challenges? In answering this question, we aim to provide an overview of IoT implementation options for monitoring and improving the mental health of employees in office settings. We highlight privacy concerns associated to the collection of sensitive data and discuss future research avenues. Through reviewing IoT initiatives aiming at improving office workplaces, we contribute to research in the information systems (IS) field through theoretical knowledge on the meta-requirements for privacy-preserving IoT design in occupational settings. For practice, we assist employers by providing an account of existing technologies and realization options as well as outline privacy considerations for successful implementations.

2 Research Approach

We opted for a review of existing literature to better understand the state-of-the-art concerning IoT solutions for mental health monitoring in office environments. The IS discipline continues to grow various applications of information technology for individuals, organizations, and societies, which results in an increased need for synthesizing this type of research to pave the path for future research and to build cumulative knowledge [16]. "Meta-synthesis" is a novel method that is becoming more popular in IS research [17]. It allows the combination of results from qualitative studies to synthesize theoretical knowledge on a specific domain of research. Based on Siau and Long [18], the general procedure of the meta-synthesis involves: First, selecting a group of studies related to a defined research problem. This includes the definition of the research question(s) and the relevant literature to be synthesized. Second, synthesizing translations of the studies. This includes reviewing the literature, identifying relationships and patterns within the collection of studies. Finally, expressing the overarching synthesis through classifications or categorization to postulate or advance theoretical knowledge for further development in a research domain. Accordingly, we perform a meta-synthesis of the existing studies on IoT initiatives for mental health monitoring in office settings. This approach allows us to have an overview of the domain to understand the existing implementation scenarios and associated challenges.

3 IoT Solutions for Mental Health Monitoring

Based on our review, we were able to identify use cases with alternative implementation options to provide an overview and support the derivation of implementation guidelines. Table 1 presents the different studies with indications on the study purpose, devices used, and data collected for each use case.

Emotional health monitoring is crucial for detecting occupational stress or burnouts that can affect the health of employees and compromise the quality of work in the long run. For that purpose, wearable devices are distributed among employees that enable the measurement of biomedical data including heart rate and body temperature for estimation of emotional levels. Han et al. [4], Zenonos et al. [19] and Stepanovic et al. [20] illustrate how wearable wrist bands can help in supporting emotional health by measuring physiological indicators for detecting stress.

Another specific use case is the monitoring of the emotional and psychological state of employees through behavioral indicators. Fugini et al. [21] illustrate a scenario of a sensor network linked with a video camera for capturing facial expressions and processing posture and hand gestures as well as audio sensors for speech recognition to assess the employee's state and provide suggestions for healthier habits based on the analyzed data.

Another use case of IoT technology in the workplace for supporting mental health monitoring is related to thermal comfort. This is necessary to have a well-suited ambient environment that allows focusing and productive work. Rabbani and Keshav [22], van der Valk et al. [23], and Nižetić et al. [24] all focus on measuring ambient conditions including temperature and humidity sensors for detecting abnormalities and optimal settings. There is also a possibility in such implementations to use wearables [23, 24] to obtain a metabolic reaction to detected discomfort and provide insights on corrective measures as a supporting evidence.

Finally, the "connected workplace" is a combination of the different use cases that enable health monitoring at work. It relies on a combination of technology options including wearables and sensor networks. Bhatia and Sood [25] and Benhamida et al. [26] envision the connected workplace as a smart office with hybrid technology involving wearables and an inclusive sensor network to combine multiple information on the physical, emotional and environmental conditions to promote a holistic approach to well-being and safety at work. Thus, allowing stress detection and environmental comfort based on the type of data to be processed.

Table 1. Overview of studies on IoT solutions in the workplace.

Purpose	Study	Device	Data collected
Stress detection	[19]	Wearables	Heart rat, skin temperature, acceleration
	[4]	Wearables	ECG sensor: impedance pneumography, accelerometer, body temperature sensor, photoplethysmography sensor
	[20]	Wearables	Heart rate, blood oxygenation, skin temperature, skin blood perfusion, respiration rate, heart rate variability, blood pulse wave
Emotional and psychological state	[21]	Sensor network	Frontal face camera, profile face camera, speech and voice body pose (images), hand gestures (images)
Thermal comfort	[22]	Sensor network	Temperature, occupancy
	[24]	Sensor network + Wearables	Metabolic rate, air temperature, relative humidity, level of carbon dioxide

(*continued*)

Table 1. (*continued*)

Purpose	Study	Device	Data collected
	[23]	Sensor network + Wearables	Metabolic rate, air temperature, mean radiant temperature air speed, humidity
Connected workplace	[26]	Sensor network + Wearables	Ambient light intensity, background noise, amount of phone calls, computer built-in camera (e.g., eye gaze), smart devices
	[25]	Sensor network + Wearables	Data about health (temperature, blood pressure, heart rate, vital signs), data about environment (cleanliness, room temperature, noise, oxygen level, toxic waste), data about meals (nutritional value, quantity), data about movement (pedometer, accelerometer)

4 Employees' Privacy Concerns

Through our analysis of the different IoT solutions in office settings for supporting mental health at work, we were able to determine a set of challenges that employers face in their implementation. These challenges stem from the employees' privacy concerns related to "big brother" work surveillance practices that aim to collect, store and process their data [27]. This data-based management ideology can result in excessive data collection and an illusionary sense of control [28], which ultimately leads to a climate of distrust, fear, and cynical employee attitudes [29].

Sensitive data collection is of major concern when implementing IoT initiatives at work. In fact, IoT generates a large volume of data and allows collecting personal data, which is frequently not work-related. Solutions for mental health monitoring involving data collection from wearable devices, where the individual can be identified, are considered the most critical. Data collected indicate health information that might be problematic in certain situations and are considered private. Emotional health data on stress levels and mood are strictly sensitive information. Therefore, employers should pay attention to the privacy management of all the data collected from sensors used for emotional health purposes [4, 20]. On the other hand, data about environmental conditions collected from temperature or thermal sensors could be considered less problematic [22, 23].

In addition, with the blurred lines between the use of wearable devices in private and professional lives, the ownership of data collected remains a dilemma. Stepanovic et al. [20] raise an important issue with the use of wearable devices, where there exist measurements done outside of working days. In their study on work-related stress, the elimination of these data points sounds logical. While the type of data collected from wearables (including activity data, physiolytics and location) can be considered sensitive, entities in possession of this data have an advantage and can eventually process it in combination with other personal data to create user profiles for different purposes – whether occupational or commercial.

While the main purpose of IoT initiatives is supposed to improve the health and well-being of employees, the possibility of the data misuse or being used for other purposes than initially agreed upon is a matter of concern for both, employees (e.g., worried by possible measures their employer can introduce against them) and employers (e.g., fearing improper re-use and data breaches of device manufacturers). Fugini et al. [21] explain that the use of IoT technology in the workplace has the potential to capture the employee's behavior. As mentioned earlier, activity tracking data could infer certain work behavior not only for health purposes, including absence/presence and working time at desk. Sensor networks can additionally be used for facial expression detection, voice recognition, and vital signals, which can be indicators of actual and mental workloads.

Finally, these initiatives can be seen as a pathway to behavioral control through nudging and interventions imposed on the employees who somehow lose their freedom and do not have the choice anymore to decide on their reactions to certain events. All these considerations become more and more critical with the discussion of the connected workplace where data is collected in an integrated manner and for the different purposes [25, 26], as discussed previously.

5 Conclusion

Our meta-synthesis provides an overview of the currently discussed implementation options as use cases. IoT initiatives rely on wearable devices that gather data on the employee's physical and emotional health status with the aim to trigger corrective behavioral interventions for preventing harm and improving outcomes. Other studies rely on sensor networks that measure ambient environmental parameters for the purpose of increasing an employee's comfort and well-being in the workplace. The combination of these use cases results in a fully integrated workplace design fueled by different technological components. We discuss concerns related to employee health data privacy along the different phases of the data lifecycle. We emphasize that companies need to take a responsible and active role in reflecting about what is reasonable and ethical when implementing IoT-enabled occupational health initiatives for mental health monitoring. While we highlight different implementation options for the same purpose, we conclude that there exist alternative designs that minimize the collection of individual data for each use case. These options should be considered and further tested to assess their reliability.

Our synthesis highlights the concept of the connected workplace. This concept is worth consideration by researchers in the field of IoT technology as it embeds a true vision of the future work environment in our ever-changing world. The changing work practices and arrangements, as well as the new health and safety regulations accelerated by the COVID-19 pandemic require further studies on the optimal future work environment design. Based on the list of studies and the identified concerns, we suggest solutions that minimize individual data collection. Certain studies promote alternative design options for specific design objectives that require less interactions and collection of sensitive data. These studies suggest using IoT solutions that can be considered less intrusive and are specific to the workplace context only. Once data is collected by the IoT device, the employer should plan for an appropriate technical architecture that is trustworthy and that guarantees the safety and integrity of data.

A promising technology choice was suggested by Bhatia and Sood [25] and Benhamida et al. [26] for the connected workplace, the Fog-Cloud. It is described as a "highly virtualized platform that provides compute, storage, and networking services between end devices and traditional Cloud" [25]. It is specifically relevant to the IoT scenario as it relies on edge decision mechanism, that is, the data is processed at the edge of the network where it is collected. Thus, the user has the option to filter and transform the data before sending it to the Cloud, which ensures privacy of user data and eliminates ownership concerns. Our analysis of the studies also suggests minimizing work interruptions as much as possible. Benhamida et al. [26] promote the use of non-intrusive designs that do not affect the employee's routine. These designs combine passive data collection through the use of technologies surrounding the employee such as sensor networks or connected digital devices. This is an important point in determining how users interact with the system and how their concerns are formed based on this interaction.

We contribute to both research and practice. For the research community, we illustrate the use of a novel method in the IS discipline corresponding to meta-synthesis. The knowledge synthesis we performed adds to the academic debate on the "future workplace" through discussing the potential of IoT technology for improving employee mental health. Researchers in the domain can benefit from this overview to build a cumulative research tradition on the applications of IoT in organizational environments. While IoT technology has a great potential in ameliorating the work environment in the future workplace and can play an effective role in increasing productivity, we also highlight existing downsides to this digital trend. Our synthesis also accounts for data-related challenges in the implementation of IoT initiatives in office settings.

For practitioners, we provide implementation options, through the presented use cases, that can guide their implementation decisions and choices when engaging in IoT initiatives for occupational health. We present "sensitive issues" related to employees' privacy risks which they need to have in mind when implementing IoT, and we recommend actions against malicious practices as a way forward for protecting employees' privacy and establishing further engagement in health initiatives at the workplace.

Acknowledgements. This research has been conducted within the Swiss National Research Programme (NRP77) on "Digital Transformation" and received funding from the Swiss National Science Foundation (grant no. 187429).

References

1. Tamers, S.L., et al.: Envisioning the future of work to safeguard the safety, health, and well-being of the workforce: a perspective from the CDC's national institute for occupational safety and health. Am. J. Ind. Med. **63**, 1065–1084 (2020)

2. Giorgi, G., Arcangeli, G., Ariza-Montes, A., Rapisarda, V., Mucci, N.: Work-related stress in the Italian banking population and its association with recovery experience. Int. J. Occup. Med. Environ. Health **32**, 255–265 (2019)
3. Schneider, S., Kokshagina, O.: Digital technologies in the workplace: a Ne(s)t of paradoxes. In: Proceedings of the 41st International Conference on Information Systems, India (2020)
4. Han, L., Zhang, Q., Chen, X., Zhan, Q., Yang, T., Zhao, Z.: Detecting work-related stress with a wearable device. Comput. Ind. **90**, 42–49 (2017)
5. Marques, G., Pitarma, R.: A real-time noise monitoring system based on internet of things for enhanced acoustic comfort and occupational health. IEEE Access **8**, 139741–139755 (2020)
6. Sun, S., Zheng, X., Villalba-Díez, J., Ordieres-Meré, J.: Indoor air-quality data-monitoring system: long-term monitoring benefits. Sensors **19**, 4157 (2019)
7. Saini, J., Dutta, M., Marques, G.: A Comprehensive review on indoor air quality monitoring systems for enhanced public health. Sustainable Environment Research **30**, 6 (2020)
8. World Health Organization. https://www.who.int/news-room/fact-sheets/detail/protecting-workers'-health
9. Lewis-Wilson, C.: Strategies to reduce employee turnover to increase profitability in a college workplace. scholarworks.waldenu.edu (2019)
10. Bernal, G., Colombo, S., Al Ai Baky, M., Casalegno, F.: Safety++ Designing IoT and wearable systems for industrial safety through a user centered design approach. In: Proceedings of the 10th International Conference on Pervasive Technologies Related to Assistive Environments, pp. 163–170. Island of Rhodes, Greece (2017)
11. Asadzadeh, A., Arashpour, M., Li, H., Ngo, T., Bab-Hadiashar, A., Rashidi, A.: Sensor-based safety management. Autom. Constr. **113**, 103128 (2020)
12. Yassaee, M., Mettler, T., Winter, R.: Principles for the Design of Digital Occupational Health Systems. Elsevier (2019)
13. Kao, Y.-S., Nawata, K., Huang, C.-Y.: An exploration and confirmation of the factors influencing adoption of IoT-based wearable fitness trackers. Int. J. Environ. Res. Public Health **16**, 3227 (2019)
14. Oesterle, S., Trübenbach, B., Buck, C.: Intent and the use of wearables in the workplace – a model development. In: Proceedings of the 14th International Conference on Wirtschaftsinformatik, pp. 972–986. Siegen, Germany (2019)
15. Ajunwa, I.: Algorithms at work: productivity monitoring applications and wearable technology as the new data-centric research agenda for employment and labor law. St. Louis University Law Journal **63**, 21 (2018)
16. Jeyaraj, A., Dwivedi, Y.K.: Meta-analysis in information systems research: review and recommendations. Int. J. Inf. Manage. **55**, 102226 (2020)
17. Stafford, T.F., Farshadkah, S.: A method for interpretively synthesizing qualitative research findings. Commun. Assoc. Inf. Syst. **46**, 6 (2020)
18. Siau, K., Long, Y.: Synthesizing e-Government stage models – a meta-synthesis based on meta-ethnography approach. Ind. Manag. Data Syst. **105**, 443–458 (2005)
19. Zenonos, A., Khan, A., Kalogridis, G., Vatsikas, S., Lewis, T., Sooriyabandara, M.: Healthy-Office: mood recognition at work using smartphones and wearable sensors. In: Proceedings of the IEEE International Conference on Pervasive Computing and Communication Workshops (PerCom Workshops), pp. 1–6. IEEE (2016)
20. Stepanovic, S., Mozgovoy, V., Mettler, T.: Designing visualizations for workplace stress management: results of a pilot study at a swiss municipality. In: Lindgren, I., et al. (eds.) EGOV 2019. LNCS, vol. 11685, pp. 94–104. Springer, Cham (2019). https://doi.org/10.1007/978-3-030-27325-5_8
21. Fugini, M., et al.: WorkingAge: providing occupational safety through pervasive sensing and data driven behavior modeling. In: Proceedings of the 30th European Safety and Reliability Conference, pp. 1–8. Venice, Italy (2020)

22. Rabbani, A., Keshav, S.: The spot* personal thermal comfort system. In: Proceedings of the 3rd ACM International Conference on Systems for Energy-Efficient Built Environments, pp. 75–84. Palo Alto, CA, USA (2016)

23. van der Valk, S., Myers, T., Atkinson, I., Mohring, K.: Sensor networks in workplaces: correlating comfort and productivity. In: Proceedings of the 10th International Conference on Intelligent Sensors, Sensor Networks and Information Processing (ISSNIP), pp. 1–6. IEEE (2015)

24. Nižetić, S., Pivac, N., Zanki, V., Papadopoulos, A.M.: Application of smart wearable sensors in office buildings for modelling of occupants' metabolic responses. Energy and Buildings **226**, 110399 (2020)

25. Bhatia, M., Sood, S.K.: Exploring temporal analytics in fog-cloud architecture for smart office healthcare. Mob. Netw. Appl. **24**, 1392–1410 (2019)

26. Benhamida, F.-Z., Navarro, J., Gómez-Carmona, O., Casado-Mansilla, D., López-de-Ipiña, D., Zaballos, A.: SmartWorkplace: a privacy-based fog computing approach to boost energy efficiency and wellness in digital workspaces. In: Proceedings of the 1st Workshop on Cyber-Physical Social Systems (CPSS2019), pp. 9–15. Bilbao, Spain (2019)

27. Richter, A.: Do Privacy Concerns Prevent Employees' Acceptance of Smart Wearables and Collaborative Robots? SICHERHEIT (2020)

28. Lyytinen, K.: MIS: the urge to control and the control of illusions – towards a dialectic. J. Inf. Technol. **26**, 268–270 (2011)

29. Mettler, T., Wulf, J.: Physiolytics at the workplace: affordances and constraints of wearables use from an employee's perspective. Inf. Syst. J. **29**, 245–273 (2019)

Design and Development of an NLP-Based Mental Health Pre-screening Tool for Undergraduate Students in Thailand: A Usability Study

Prima Pangsrisomboon, Aung Pyae[✉] ⓘ, Noppasorn Thawitsri, and Supasin Liulak

International School of Engineering, Faculty of Engineering, Chulalongkorn University, Bangkok, Thailand
aung.p@chula.ac.th

Abstract. Fear of stigmatization has been a barrier for Thai undergraduate students to actively reach out to health practitioners for support when they experience a mental health problem. Commercially available mental health systems struggle to find a balance between effective clinical diagnostic capability and engaging user experience. In natural ambience, it is proven that users could better articulate their thoughts, which results in a higher efficacy of prescreening results in mental health assessment. Natural language processing (NLP) techniques are promising to enable this by developing a human-like digital assistant for mental health. The usability and user interface design of such mental health assessment tool should support the frictionless interaction while being compatible with the Thai context (e.g., language). To fill these gaps, in this study, we developed an NLP-based digital healthcare assistant as a pre-screening tool that can be used to detect undergraduate students' anxiety levels and identify their needs for psychological support. We conducted a pilot usability evaluation of the system focusing on the system's usability effectiveness, efficiency, and reliability. The findings can be concluded that creating a natural and user-friendly experience for users, with flexibility that allowed for individual preferences through a chat-based NLP system, results in an engaging user experience and less friction towards the adoption of the tool. These findings can be used to support the future development of an effective and user-friendly pre-screening tool for this particular user group.

Keywords: Mental health · Natural language processing · Usability · User experience

1 Introduction

Mental illness is one of the most prevalent public health challenges in the 21st century [1], yet it is also one of the most neglected areas [2]. According to the World Health Organization (WHO), nearly 1 billion people worldwide experience mental disorders. Although mental health issues are common across all age groups, they are exceptionally high among university students [3]. Also, Jurewicz [4] states that 75% of people who have

H. Li et al. (Eds.): WIS 2022, CCIS 1626, pp. 46–60, 2022.
https://doi.org/10.1007/978-3-031-14832-3_4

a mental health disorder have had the first onset during young adulthood. The situation has worsened as the COVID-19 emerges. A survey conducted by [5] showed that 56% of undergraduate students claim that the COVID-19 pandemic has affected their mental health. Son et al. [6] also confirm that the pandemic has accentuated new sources of stressors, such as excessive stress due to distance learning and fear of future uncertainty [7]. Most students are unaware of the consequences and risks of changes in emotional health, whereas, for those who are aware, the fear of stigmatization impedes them from reaching out for immediate support [8]. Moreover, some users especially undergraduates find it frustrating to overcome the self-stigma barrier or perform a solid pre-screening standardized questionnaire when approaching the therapists. Thus, mental illness could significantly hinder undergraduate students from proper and early intervention.

In the clinical setting, several standardized questionnaires have been developed to detect early signs of mental illness such as the WHO self-reporting questionnaire, and the Depression, Anxiety, and Stress Scale (DASS-21). The existing literature shows that the DASS-21 is an effective and reliable tool for mental health assessment, as well as it is a psychometrically adequate and valuable instrument for measuring depression, anxiety, and stress among university students [9]. However, these tools are not currently used widely among the target group particularly in the university student population in Thailand, who are reluctant to seek medical advice due to several constraints including fear of stigmatization or limited medical access. The existing research has suggested the potential of using up-to-date technologies for mental health solutions with promising results and efficiency (e.g., telemedicine for mental health) [10]. Wearable passive sensing is another promising technology that concedes to the well-rounded and bias-less monitoring system, including sleeping duration, heart rate, skin temperature, and more. Of these up-to-date technologies, NLP and machine learning algorithms are regarded due to the comparable level of effectiveness of such tools. Also, it provides the ability in speech analysis to identify the correlation with the psychological disorder [11]. Furthermore, they are affordable and easily accessible when compared to traditional mental health treatment. Using up-to-date technologies (e.g., IT security), most of them satisfy the requirement of data control regulation regarding user privacy and transparent policy, which are among the top users' concerns.

Despite the promises of digital mental health tools, most of them are not carefully designed for undergraduate students [12]. More importantly, these tools are still not applicable to most Thais. The existing literature has shown the critical dispute on the ineffectiveness of the existing digital tools in terms of usability and user experience. Those perspectives result in limited use for a mass community and ineffectiveness in the actual practice [13]. Furthermore, when users use such mental health assessment tools, they prefer to naturally express feelings in a user-friendly way without external pressure (e.g., talking to a friend or family member) [14]. On the other hand, the existing applications of NLP for mental health are still limited to the language variety that does not align with the local norms and cannot produce effective results when the local language (e.g., Thai) is not supported. Thus, this factor impedes an engaging user experience for Thai undergraduate students to use such existing mental health assessment tools. Considering the limitations mentioned above, in this study, we designed and developed an NLP-based mental health pre-screening tool for undergraduate students in Thailand. The main objective of this system is to provide a user-friendly and easily accessible system that undergraduate students can use as a pre-screening tool when they immediately need to access mental health advice and support before reaching out to a health professional.

2 An NLP-Based Mental Health Screening Tool

2.1 Overview

Our solution is designed using an NLP model that can predict the mental health status through idiomatic inputs from the target users (e.g., an undergraduate student in Thailand), which is aimed to assist the pre-screening process [15]. Referring to the real-world situation when a psychiatrist pre-screened a patient's mental health status, they would ask him/her some questions. That set of questions lets the patient express their thoughts, perceptions, emotions, and moods that reflect their mental health status. Similarly, our NLP-based system will ask users queries, process the text inputs into risk indications, and result in the mental health status along with the treatment suggestions to users. Our system was developed through an NLP model training with the use of cloud architecture for storing the dataset. A set of raw inputs would consist of the word of choices mapped with the risk indications on mental illness status. Afterward, the trained model would be stored in the database for later prediction. The presentation layer for this system is a web interface interacting with users by asking them a set of questions using a chat feature of the system. Users will answer those questions in the form of text phrases or sentences, which are then processed and responded to with their personalized mental health condition along with treatment suggestions suited for them. Hence, our system consists of an NLP model as the main processor of the system, features and functionalities of the system, and the web-based user interface. The NLP is trained to have a pre-screening ability based on the DASS-21, which is a standard self-reporting questionnaire designed to assess the emotional states of depression, anxiety, and stress [16].

2.2 Implementation of an NLP Model

Preparing the Dataset. First, dataset preparation is the first and foremost activity for developing any machine learning model since the intelligence of the machine depends highly on the data. In this study, users will be answering the questions in the text-based format with varying lengths while our system will produce the processed mental health status back to the users. Thus, the dataset required for this system is the idiomatic text mapped with the mental health status referred from the DASS-21 scores. Our dataset was collected from Thai undergraduate students from diverse backgrounds by using a questionnaire. After that, the dataset was cleaned up to yield higher accuracy in the model. A bunch of words or phrases were then labeled with negative, neutral, and positive signs of mental health status. For example, the word "*happy*" was labeled with a positive, "*I*" or "*do*" were labeled with a neutral sign, while "*bored*" was labeled to indicate a negative sign of a mental disorder. Next, a bunch of words was then labeled with the mental health status with severity level calculated from DASS-21; in this case, our model covers three labels including '*normal*', '*moderate*', and '*severe*' groups. The normal label represents a DASS-21 score from 0 to 3, the moderate label represents a score from 4 to 7, and the extreme label represents a score greater than 8.

Selecting and Training the Model. The second main task for NLP development is the selection of a model that is most suited to the characteristics of the dataset to yield the highest accuracy of prediction. From a total of 483 respondents to the questionnaire, all of them were classified regarding the disorders and the severity of each symptom. To maintain acceptable accuracy in results, the development proceeded with the most equally distributed dataset which is the classifications of '*anxiety*'. An early prototype integrated with the NLP would be launched with anxiety pre-screening, followed by depression and stress in the forthcoming phases. In this study, PyCaret, an open-source machine learning library, is one of the tools used for enhancing the analysis of model selection. With PyCaret, the experiments of model selection are fast and efficient since it will go through several machine learning models such as Naïve Bayes, SVM, and Decision Trees and will give an analysis of each model's performance [17]. We would randomly split the dataset into '*train*' and '*test*' sets. As shown in Fig. 1, the model would be trained with a training set and would be evaluated using a testing set. The main criteria are model accuracy, which is the error the model has made with the testing set [18]. After obtaining the analysis, the classification model was chosen since it is compatible with assigning a class label to the input [19]. Moreover, each label will have its dedicated model since it has better performance than using one model with multi-class output. For example, the predicted output will be 0 or 1 from each model. In the end, it can be aggregated into {0, 1, 0} which indicates that the user has a moderate anxiety level in this case. The following Table 1 shows the selected model which will be used in the system.

Table 1. Selected model and accuracy of each class.

Description	Model	Accuracy
Normal	Logistic regression	0.6854
Moderate	Logistic regression	0.6780
Extreme	SVM – radial kernal	0.6195

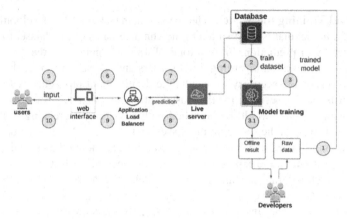

Fig. 1. Overview of the system architecture.

3 Features of '*WELLO*'

Through the chat feature (see Fig. 2), which is presented in the form of a short con-
versational chat, users can express their moods, thoughts, and perceptions. This feature
was developed under the concept of the system is a '*listener*' to the users that can
respond to each answer naturally. The chat feature also supports interactive two-way
communication. To fulfill this, the chat feature of '*WELLO*' allows users to perform
self-pre-screening questionnaires via text-based communication and terminate the system at their convenience. The system processes and analyzes the dataset after receivin
five inputs from the user.

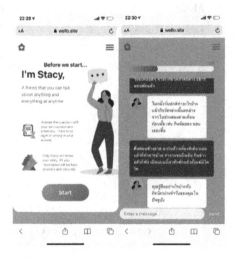

Fig. 2. The interface of the chat feature.

The other feature includes the processed output from the chat feature. It was developed with the primary initiative to notify users of their mental health status to have the illness detected at an early stage. The mental health status will be visualized in the scale, along with the historical graph showing their changes relative to the previous results (Fig. 3).

Fig. 3. The interface of the results & analytics features with the link to suggestions.

As there is a need to track and monitor one's mental health over some time, the dashboard shows all the historical results oneself. It records the pre-screening result and visualizes it in the form of continual line charts showing the emotional levels on a particular day. With this feature, users will be aware of the changes in emotional levels over a particular timeframe for them to maintain their mental healthiness over time.

4 Method: Experimental Set-Up and Procedures

We conducted a pilot usability evaluation of '*WELLO*'. Firstly, we aimed to understand the usability, users' acceptance, and their satisfaction with the system. Secondly, we aimed to evaluate the reliability of system results from the user perspective. Lastly, we aimed to identify problems in the current design and uncover opportunities for further improvement. This pilot study included three main usability testing tools: interviews, questionnaires, and observations. For the usability aspect of the system, we used the *System Usability Scale* (SUS), which is a reliable and widely accepted usability assessment tool [20]. For user satisfaction, we used the Customer Satisfaction Score (CSAT), which is used to measure users' overall satisfaction [21]. In addition to these questionnaires, we also used the DASS-21 questionnaire [22, 23], which was used to validate the results of our system with the self-reported results of the participants' DASS-21. We conducted a short interview with all participants, as well as observation techniques to understand usability problems encountered by the participants during the test. The team would observe the participants' behavior in a controlled environment with a limited set of tasks assigned for participants to minimize external factors that could affect the result of the study.

Due to the restriction of the COVID-19 pandemic, the evaluation was performed remotely via ZOOM software and in a controlled environment where participants were requested to stay in a silent room with a stable Wi-Fi connection and power plug-in. There are four main tools and equipment involved in the data collection process: The system's final prototype is accessible through 'www.wello.site', ZOOM software as the primary communication channel to interact with the test participants, and recordings of keystrokes and expressions. In this study, we used the *Google Form*, containing the DASS-21, SUS, and CSAT questionnaires. During the test, each session took approximately an hour per participant. We recruited a total of 9 participants based on the target user profile, and most of them are undergraduate students in Thailand. The age of participants must be between 18 and 22 years old to meet the inclusion criteria. We recruited the participants through a social media platform (e.g., Facebook) and an instant messaging app (e.g., LINE). During each usability session, there were 2 researchers; the moderator and the observer; each with different roles and responsibilities. The detailed descriptions of the test session are provided in Table 2. There was a total of 4 tasks to be assessed, containing user's profile management, chat, information hub, and navigation. Each task will take about 3–5 min to complete. The data collected from this section was used to evaluate the effectiveness and efficiency of the interface design. In the post-test session, participants were asked follow-up interview questions to understand their overall experience using our system. The detailed design and procedure of the system are provided in Table 2.

Table 2. Details of the test procedure and description.

Activity	Duration	Task description	Responsibility
Pre-test questionnaire	–	Completing DASS-21 questionnaire	Participants shall complete the standard self-assessment test before joining the session to have an experience with the standard tool in mind
Introduction to usability testing	10 min	- Icebreaking - Explanation of testing procedures	Mainly an interaction between the moderator and the user
Pre-testing consent taking	5 min	- Consent for recording agreement	Moderator and participant orally agree on the consent in participating in the studies and allowing information recording during the session

(*continued*)

Table 2. (*continued*)

Activity	Duration	Task description	Responsibility
Usability testing	20 min (5 × 4 tasks)	- Evaluation of usability, efficiency, effectiveness, and learnability	The moderator asks the user to perform 4 tasks while the observer takes note of user interaction and errors
Post-test questionnaires	3 min	- Evaluation of usability: SUS, CSAT, and Trustworthiness	The moderator hands on the questionnaire form for the user to sign and answer
Post-test interview	7 min	- General questions about the user's experiences using the system	The moderator asks the user open-ended probing questions regarding user experience focusing on the rationale of the answers

5   Results

In this pilot study, we used descriptive analysis for the quantitative data and thematic analysis for the qualitative data [24]. Based on the findings from the demographic data analysis, we found that all participants in this study are Thai, and it was aligned with our research's objective to develop a pre-screening tool for the mental health assessment that applies to the context of Thailand. Five of them are male while the other four participants are female. The average age among this sample was 22.3 years old, with a range of 20–25 years old.

5.1   Questionnaires

According to [20], SUS contains ten items that could be classified into a group of positive and negative items. The positive opinions are assigned to the odd items, while the even items contain a negative perspective toward the system's usability. When considering the group of odd items, the overall mean score lies between 3.4 and 4.8, indicating that most participants found it easy to use, usable, and learnable according to the SUS interpretation [25]. On the other hand, the overall mean score of even items lies between 1.4 and 1.6, indicating that the negative aspect of the system's usability was low. When considering the overall result (see Table 3), our system gained an average SUS final score of 82.5, referring to the acceptable range of the system's usability and learnability.

Table 4 summarizes the SUS score with interpretation on the acceptability scale and adjective rating from each participant. The SUS scores majorly fall into an acceptable range in the acceptability scale. When complimenting the interpretation with an adjective scale, it shows that most participants perceived our system as the best imaginable tool.

Table 3. Summary of SUS scores with an adjective rating and acceptability interpretation.

Item's description	M	SD
1. I think that I would like to use this system frequently	3.4	0.7
2. I found the system unnecessarily complex	1.6	0.5
3. I thought the system was easy to use	4.3	0.7
4. I think that I would need the support of a technical person to be able to use this system	1.4	0.5
5. I found the various functions in this system were well integrated	4.3	0.7
6. I thought there was too much inconsistency in this system	1.6	0.5
7. I would imagine that most people would learn to use this system very quickly	4.8	0.4
8. I found the system very cumbersome to use	1.6	0.7
9. I felt very confident using the system	3.8	0.8
10. I needed to learn a lot of things before I could get going with this system	1.6	1.0
SUS raw score = **33.0**; Calculated SUS overall score = **82.5**		

Table 4. SUS adjective rating and acceptability.

Participant no.	SUS scores	Adjective rating	Acceptability
P1	90	Best imaginable	Acceptable
P2	85	Best imaginable	Acceptable
P3	60	OK	Marginal
P4	87.5	Best imaginable	Acceptable
P5	90	Best imaginable	Acceptable
P6	97.5	Best imaginable	Acceptable
P7	77.5	Good	Acceptable
P8	82.5	Excellent	Acceptable
P9	72.5	Good	Acceptable

The *Customer Satisfaction Scale* is a single-item question used to ask about users' satisfaction with the overall system (see Table 5). The rating ranges from *1* to *5*, referring from '*strongly dissatisfied*' to '*strongly satisfied*'. Nine participants rated the mean score of user satisfaction as 3.8 (SD = 0.83), which implies somewhat positive satisfaction. However, after participants were asked an additional question to explain their score. Most feedback mentioned satisfaction with the system's functionality, which is designed to assist an intensive pre-screening methodology with agreeable learnability and suggestions for improvements. For example, it included the more advanced chat feature, personalization, smoother conversation, etc.

Table 5. Customer satisfaction scale (CSAT scores)

	P1	P2	P3	P4	P5	P6	P7	P8	P9	M	SD
Mean score	5	3	3	5	4	4	3	4	3	3.78	0.83

The system results' reliability was assessed by comparing the results processed by the system and the scores calculated from the DASS-21 questionnaire. The mental health status processed by two tools (our system and DASS-21) was aligned with 8 out of 9 records of nine participants (see Table 6). On one record, our system labeled this user as being in a normal condition; however, the result from DASS-21 reported this user to have mild symptoms. It indicates that the results of the system were mostly reliable while suggesting improving the accuracy of the results in the enhanced version in the future.

Table 6. Adjustment between DASS-21 results and the system's results

Participant no.	Anxiety scores	DASS-21 results	System's results	Reliability
P1	2	Normal	Normal	Aligned
P2	1	Normal	Normal	Aligned
P3	3	Normal	Normal	Aligned
P4	5	Mild	Mild	Aligned
P5	4	Mild	Normal	Not aligned
P6	3	Normal	Normal	Aligned
P7	3	Normal	Normal	Aligned
P8	4	Mild	Mild	Aligned
P9	2	Normal	Normal	Aligned

5.2 Interview

Most users agreed that "*WELLO*" is a potential intervention for mental health pre-screening in terms of its functionalities and interface design. It satisfied them with the all-in-one features that provide an end-to-end assistant for them, starting from figuring out the issues to assisting them in resolving anxiety accordingly. Moreover, with the concept of "*a friend who can listen to the users whenever they are not in a good emotion*", this feature suits the needs of people, particularly undergraduates who are seeking help for mental health. Based on the interview results, we found that this group of users need to call for some help from their friends or families when they felt down. They would prefer to talk to close friends or family members before reaching out to health practitioners. To fulfill this, the participants mentioned that this is an effective tool with easy accessibility. For instance, P1 stated, "*I think it is better not to interrupt my friends all the time, and having this tool makes me even feel comfortable in expressing thoughts out of my mind because I do not have to be considerate like I am, with people".*

All users agreed that this intervention created a genuine feeling while using the chat. For instance, each time, the chat gradually asked a question that guided them to think about the circumstances in exemplary steps so the users could understand themselves better. For example, P7 mentioned, *"I understand myself better when I am asked with the step-by-step question guiding me to think about what is going on rather than asking me to consider whether I am feeling down without any context which I do not know how to describe my feeling at that time".* Furthermore, the participants praised that although there was room for improvements, the chat performed a human-like behavior (e.g., a conversation between two friends) to enhance the user engagement and effectiveness of the tool. Thus, most of the users were interested and would like this intervention to become more advanced for a more engaging experience, leading to the second interest, personalization of the system. P4 said, *"It would be more fun if I could continue chatting with the system after the deep conversation. Like when I talked with my friend, we would end up with simple conversation and jokes to relax".* P1 suggested, *"It is excellent to have a new counseling experience with the chat and it could understand me".* Most participants also suggested compliance in offering more input as they would like to receive the complete results personally. The system could ask for more information such as health condition, age, gender, occupation, or non-identifiable information since they believed that the more the system perceived them, the more profoundly processed results from the system. By interpreting all results, it could be summarized that their opinion towards those dimensions affected perceptions of the system's reliability. Their agreement on the results was 4 out of 5, indicating some room for improvements. P7 suggested, *"The system is reliable in my opinion. However, if the chat could perform a human-like conversation with me, I would entirely trust him. It is the same dilemma as when we want to consult with a professional physician."* Overall, based on the interview results, the feedback on the system's usability, its features, and reliability of the results was positive, considering insights by the participants into future enhancements.

5.3 Observation

The observation was conducted simultaneously with the interview process to validate the participants' experiences with the system's effectiveness, efficiency, and reliability. Each time the users were asked to complete a task, a researcher would observe their keystrokes and movements to justify task completion, measure the time spent on each task, and monitor their user experiences during the interview process. The keystrokes and movements would help in reflecting the effectiveness of the system since they revealed their genuine actions whether they were understanding, confused, or randomly accomplished the task. Moreover, justifying the termination action for each task reduced bias on data in the collection of time spent on each task. The time would be calculated into a mean time spent and standard deviation for analyzing the overall efficiency of the system. The results indicated that the usability of the system was acceptable in all aspects. For the system's effectiveness, no one failed in completing the assigned tasks. However, we noted that there was a common confusion on the dashboard on the home page which took some users longer to learn the function. However, the average time spent on the registration, chat feature, information hub, and navigation were 0.7, 3.7, 1.6, and 0.6 min, respectively, which yielded a standard deviation lower than one except for the chat feature. The time spent on this feature deviated in 2–9 min, reflecting the dynamic due to individual preferences. Additionally, applying three-click rules on each task aligned with the user's behavior and helped to optimize the time spent [26]. Regarding the system's reliability, regarding the participant's feedback, most of them were positive with noteworthy insights for future enhancements.

6   Discussion

From conducting the usability test, the study was fulfilled with the validation of its importance and effects on users' acceptance of the system. In the user's perception, the term 'Usability' does not mean whether the tool is usable or not, but the test has proven that it is a cornerstone of the overall user experience on the system, which involves the system's effectiveness, efficiency, reliability, learnability, and satisfaction. When users perceived that a product could support the achievement of their goals, they are motivated to accept that product [27]. For instance, it makes users feel safe, competent, and confident. Following that statement, it occurred in the real scenario as proven by our findings from the usability testing. As discussed in the results, the users tend to adopt this tool according to its usability and positive and engaging user experiences. They also showed a great interest in the intelligence of the chat feature as it complemented their experience with effective and efficient interaction. Thus, it highlights the consideration of the balance in all usability components.

From the usability test, the study was fulfilled with the validation of the research that the effectiveness of the tool is related to the level of user engagement, which can be maintained through the appropriate user interface design, user experience, and the system's usability [28]. By analyzing the task success rate and the error rate, the effectiveness of the current prototype is considered acceptable. All elements exist with their main essential and they are placed in a position relative to their importance which helps facilitate the users to complete the task. Also, designing an input touchpoint to be a chat-based questionnaire has led to more effectiveness in the data collecting process, because most participants were more engaging to continue describing their stories. They stated that higher engagement naturalized their emotion which indicates the positive sign or feasibility of further improvements.

Also, the efficiency of the tool conforms to the incremental of the system's effectiveness, either the technology behind or the apparent presentation. Through the analysis of the system's efficiency, the averages of time the users spent on the system could indicate the moderately high-efficiency rate of the system's usability due to low deviation among the results. However, there is a notice on the time spent with chat that is significantly higher than the average time on the others. This occurrence might be due to the more complicated and intensive interactions of this function. All the same, the long period spent on this feature is not a factor causing dissatisfaction according to the feedback since the journey on chat introduces a friendly and easy-to-use property on this touchpoint. Users mentioned their satisfaction and low pressure in the test session, which means the collected data was considered accurate and reliable.

The reliability gap was analyzed through the cross-validation manifested the alignment between the results processed by the system and the score calculated from the prerequisite DASS-21, which refers to the acceptable reliability of the NLP on its clinical diagnosing ability [29]. From our study, most participants accepted our system according to their higher engagement and natural feeling toward the system. With those feelings, they could provide more comprehensive input to the system which they considered genuine insights. As a result, they believed that the system produced increased efficacy of the clinical interpretation. However, there was a user who did not completely agree with the result processed by the system even though the result was an accurate one. This denial might occur due to the lack of insight or lack of awareness of their mental health [30], which could be one of our future works in increasing mental health literacy and self-awareness for our target users. Good usability and user satisfaction over the current prototype demonstrated the right direction in developing this intervention with moderate to high user acceptance and feasible improvements. The components causing satisfaction for this tool over other conventional tools are the new dimension of the pre-screening process and the interface design that creates an enjoyable journey. Most users were impressed with the mental health elicitation process that eliminates the self-stigma resulting in low to zero friction during the pre-screening process. Moreover, the interface design with increased friendliness leads to higher accessibility and a safe feeling for the users.

Considering all points that we discuss in this section; we fulfilled the research objectives as follows. First, the study has proven that creating a more natural experience for the users could result in an engaging user experience through the complimentary of user experience and user interface design. Moreover, to eliminate the self-stigma towards a mental health assistant, increasing flexibility according to individual preferences might address the barrier of each user. Second, the findings from the study showed that with the application of chat as a touchpoint for users, this approach satisfies the users for those who seek help or would like to maintain healthier mental health. It can be concluded that the users do not give priority only to the competency of the tool like most existing tools are. Yet, either the user interface or user experience shall comply with the user's behavior and its purpose of usage. Thus, this chat-based anxiety pre-screening assistant has uncovered a significant need for a more intensive tool among this group of users, which should be further addressed by the health practitioners in this field. It has introduced a new experience for Thai undergraduate students in approaching mental healthcare services with a more accessible, engaging, human-like, affordable, yet still acceptable clinical intelligence.

To successfully develop this intervention to its full potential and make it widely adopted by Thai undergraduate students, it would be fulfilled by enhancing NLP's intelligence, parallelly with the continuous development of user experience and user interface of the system. Additionally, by collaborating with a mental health wellness center, it would be beneficial in terms of clinical intelligence to be able to cover other common mental disorders in the field. In the end, the promising implementation could highlight the opportunities of integrating such a frontage for early detection to support the mainstream clinical care in communities, such as schools, universities, or any organizations.

The limitations of the study include a small sample size in user testing, the functionalities of the current system, and limited dataset to feed ML algorithm in this study. In the future study, we will address the limitations of the current system.

7 Conclusion

Our study aims to design and develop a user-friendly NLP-based digital mental health pre-screening tool particularly for anxiety to fulfill the needs of Thai undergraduates seeking mental health advice and support. Our prototype design consists of four primary features: a chat feature & NLP-based questionnaire, results & analytics, suggestions, and a dashboard feature. The prototype was then developed and evaluated amongst users to generate results to support the study's objective. The results have uncovered a positive sign of user acceptance and adoption as most participants showed satisfaction with the usability and usefulness of this pre-screening intervention. With the design of a human-like interaction that enhances naturalism and flexibility to users, they experienced a low to frictionless journey with engaging emotions. Additionally, our system has gained user credibility with the integration of NLP for mental health assessment. Moreover, the compliment interface design is user-friendly, it enhances the overall experience to be more accessible, free of stigma, and compatible with the Thai users. This study suggests the potential for using digital mental health assessment tools for student populations in Thailand, as well as in other countries with proper research and system development.

References

1. Iorfino, F., et al.: A digital platform designed for youth mental health services to deliver personalized and measurement-based care. Front. Psych. **240**, 112552 (2019)
2. International Science Council: Mental health is one of the most neglected areas of public health. https://council.science/current/blog/mental-health-is-one-of-the-most-neglected-areas-of-public-health/. Last Accessed 30 Apr 2022
3. Pedrelli, P., Nyer, M., Yeung, A., Zulauf, C., Wilens, T.: College students: mental health problems and treatment considerations. Acad. Psychiatry **39**(5), 503–511 (2015)
4. Jurewicz, I.: Mental health in young adults and adolescents – supporting general physicians to provide holistic care. Clin. Med. J. **15**(2), 151–154 (2015)
5. State of the Student. https://www.chegg.org/state-of-the-student-reports. Last Accessed 02 May 2022
6. Son, C., Hegde, S., Smith, A., Wang, X., Sasangohar, F.: Effects of COVID-19 on college students mental health in the US: interview-survey study. J. Med. Internet Res. **22**(9), e21279 (2020)
7. Jiang, N., Yan-Li, S., Pamanee, K., Sriyanto, J.: Depression, anxiety, and stress during the COVID-19 pandemic: Comparison among higher education students in four countries in the Asia-Pacific region. J. Popul. Soc. Stud. **29** (2021)
8. Henderson, C., Evans-Lacko, S., Thornicroft, G.: Mental illness stigma, help seeking, and public health programs. Am. J. Public Health **103**(5), 777–780 (2013)
9. Jiang, L.-C. et al.: The depression anxiety stress scale-21 in Chinese hospital workers: reliability, latent structure, and measurement invariance across genders. Front. Psychol. **11**, 247 (2020)

10. Kazdin, A., Blasé, S.L.: Rebooting psychotherapy research and practice to reduce the burden of mental illness. Perspect. Psychol. Sci. **6**(1), 21–37 (2011)
11. Rebhan, A.: Natural language processing: how this emerging tool can improve mental health treatment. https://www.advisory.com/blog/2019/05/nlp-mental. Last Accessed 02 May 2022
12. Mental Health Commission of Canada: Discover mental health. https://mentalhealthcommis sion.ca/. Last Accessed 02 May 2022
13. Inchaithep, S., Puasiri, S., Punsawat, M., Thungmepon, P., Robkob, W.: Development of mental health literacy indicators for the public. Boromarajonani College of Nursing, Uttaradit Journal **10**(2), 97–109 (2018)
14. Alqahtani, F., Orji, R.: Insights from user reviews to improve mental health apps. Health Informatics J. 2042–2066 (2020)
15. Glaz, A.L., et al.: Machine learning and natural language processing in mental health: A systematic review. J. Med. Internet Res. **23**(5), e15708 (2021)
16. Bayram, N., Bilgel, N.: The prevalence and socio-demographic correlations of depression, anxiety and stress among a group of university students. Soc. Psychiatry Psychiatr. Epidemiol. **43**(8), 667–672 (2008)
17. PyCaret. https://pycaret.gitbook.io/docs/. Last Accessed 02 May 2022
18. Brownlee, J.: A gentle introduction to model selection for machine learning. Machine Learning Mastery. https://machinelearningmastery.com/a-gentle-introduction-to-model-selection-for-machine-learning/. Last Accessed 03 May 2022
19. Brownlee, J.: 4 types of classification tasks in machine learning. Machine Learning Mastery. https://machinelearningmastery.com/types-of-classification-in-machine-learning/#:~:text= Machine%20learning%20is%20a%20field,examples%20from%20the%20problem%20d omain. Last Accessed 03 May 2022
20. Sauro, J.: Measuring usability with the system usability scale (SUS). https://measuringu.com/ sus/. Last Accessed 03 May 2022
21. Eklof, J., Podkorytova, O., Malova, A.: Linking customer satisfaction with financial performance: an empirical study of Scandinavian banks. Total Qual. Manag. Bus. Excell. **31**(4), 1–19 (2018)
22. Osman, A., Wong, J., Bagge, C.L., Freedenthal, S., Gutierrez, P.M., Lozano, G.: The depression anxiety stress scales-21 (DASS-21): further examination of dimensions, scale reliability, and correlates. J. Clin. Psychol. **68**(12), 1322–1338 (2012)
23. Lovibond, S.H., Lovibond, P.F.: Manual for the Depression Anxiety Stress Scales, 2nd edn. Psychology Foundation, Sydney (1995)
24. Creswell, J.W, Creswell, J.D.: Research Design, 5th edn. SAGE Publication (2017)
25. Sauro, J.: 5 ways to interpret a SUS score. https://measuringu.com/interpret-sus-score/. Last Accessed 03 May 2022
26. Porter, J.: Testing the three-click rule. https://articles.uie.com/three_click_rule/. Last Accessed 03 May 2022
27. Hassenzahl, M.: User experience (UX): Towards an experiential perspective on product quality. In: Proceedings of the 20th International Conference of the Association Francophone d'Interaction Homme-Machine on - IHM '08 (2008)
28. Hentati, A., Forsell, E., Ljótsson, B., Kaldo, V., Lindefors, N., Kraepelien, M.: The effect of user interface on treatment engagement in a self-guided digital problem-solving intervention: a randomized controlled trial. Internet Interv. **26**, 100448 (2021)
29. Low, D.M., Bentley, K.H., Ghosh, S.S.: Automated assessment of psychiatric disorders using speech: a systematic review. Laryngoscope Investigative Otolaryngology **5**(1), 96–116 (2020)
30. National Alliance on Mental Illness. Anosognosia. https://www.nami.org/About-Mental-Ill ness/Common-with-Mental-Illness/Anosognosia. Last Accessed 03 May 2022

Social Media and Well-being

Thinspiration Inspired by K-pop: A Comparison of K-pop Related Thinspiration Imagery and Texts to Regular Thinspiration Content on Tumblr

Linda Achilles[(✉)] ⓘ, Thomas Mandl ⓘ, and Christa Womser-Hacker ⓘ

Department of Information Science and Natural Language Processing, University of Hildesheim, Hildesheim, Germany
{achilles,mandl,womser}@uni-hildesheim.de

Abstract. The use of social media platforms can be related to body dissatisfaction and disordered eating habits. In online communities, users share common interests and discuss it. One trend has emerged around the hashtag Thinspiration, which refers to content that shall inspire consumers to be or become thin. One derivate is the K-pop Thinspiration. The research aim in information science is to explore how K-pop Thinspiration is different from the regular Thinspiration content on Tumblr. Therefore, images and texts of the posts are automatically analyzed by means of the calculation of colorfulness and emotional measures of the images, as well as a sentiment analysis and readability score calculation of the texts. In addition, a qualitative content analysis of 153 K-pop related Thinspiration posts is performed. Results show that the K-pop Thinspiration posts are closer to the ones of the control data set, than to regular Thinspiration posts.

Keywords: Social media · Image analysis · Text analysis · Content analysis · K-Pop · Thinspiration · Tumblr

1 Introduction

Research suggests a connection between body dissatisfaction, eating disorders and social media usage. Mabe et al. [18] could show with their experimental set of studies, that a typical Facebook use of 20 minutes in a laboratory setting, seems to support weight and shape concerns as well as state anxiety in young women, compared to a different internet activity. In addition, more frequent Facebook use was associated with greater disordered eating. Another study [23] investigated on the effect of 'Instagram vs. reality' imagery consumption on participants' body perception. Results show that watching the paired images (two photos of the same woman, one idealized version and one more natural depiction), as well as watching the natural picture causes less body dissatisfaction compared to watching the idealized photographs only. Holland and Tiggemann [15] confirmed in their systematic review of the impact of social media sites on body image and disordered eating that there is a connection between social networking platform usage and eating disorder symptoms.

H. Li et al. (Eds.): WIS 2022, CCIS 1626, pp. 63–77, 2022.
https://doi.org/10.1007/978-3-031-14832-3_5

Social media platforms have become a place where communities of different interests build around specific hashtags. *Thinspiration* has become the hashtag to share imagery of very thin body ideals as an inspiration for users to lose weight [4]. K-pop idols, with their extremely restrictive diet plans[1] also inspire their fans worldwide who share images of their idols under hashtags like *#K-pop Thinspiration* on social media. Although platforms like Tumblr formulate in their guidelines[2] that the promotion of harmful content, such as the glorification of disordered eating behavior, is forbidden, content must be reported by users to be removed. At the same time users who seek this content are not likely to report it and so it often remains on the platform.

This paper aims to investigate the K-pop Thinspiration content on Tumblr. This work contributes to the body of research in the following ways: 1) K-pop Thinspiration imagery is automatically analyzed based on colorfulness and emotional image measures, namely pleasure, arousal and dominance. 2) The text of K-pop Thinspiration posts is analyzed based on sentiments and readability. 3) A content analysis of a subset of K-pop Thinspiration posts reveals what these posts show on their images and discuss in their textual information. 4) A distinction between Thinspiration, K-pop Thinspiration and average Tumblr content is made, which helps understanding the difference between potential harmful content and simple fandom in social media. This insight can be beneficial to in the future automatically detecting posts that can endanger users of social networks. By understanding the differences of the Thinspiration contents, algorithms can help to provide supportive information to users with tendencies to eating disorders and prevent other users from being confronted with disturbing content when they expected to only see posts about their favorite music groups.

2   Related Work

Eating disorders (ED) are severe mental disorders affecting large portions of the general public. In the USA for instance, the National Eating Disorder Association (NEDA) reports that approximately 20 million women and 10 million men will suffer from an eating disorder at some point in their lives.[3] Hoek and van Hoeken [14] revealed that treatment for an ED only reaches one out of three people in general public that fulfill the diagnostic criteria. The most well-known form of an ED is anorexia nervosa, which is characterized by strict regulation of food intake to reduce body weight [1].

2.1   Thinspiration

On social media users often share content that is intended to inspire others to achieve e.g. a specific goal. The term *Thinspiration* or *Thinspo*, a pun combining the words thin and inspiration, shall inspire users to achieve a thin body. Typically, images depicting very skinny bodies or body parts, quotes or other weight loss techniques are shared

---

[1] https://www.allkpop.com/article/2018/09/8-K-pop-idol-diets-that-will-shock-you.

[2] Tumblr's Community Guidelines: https://www.tumblr.com/policy/en/community.

[3] NEDA: What are eating disorders? URL: https://www.nationaleatingdisorders.org/what-are-eating-disorders.

under the Thinspiration hashtag [4]. Furthermore, Thinspiration is strongly related to the pro-ana (= pro anorexia) movement on social media, a movement that glorifies eating disorders as a lifestyle of choice [5]. The exploration of Thinspiration content on social media was target of different previous studies. Ging and Garvey [12] retrieved posts from Instagram starting from three root hashtags relating to eating disorders (#ana, #starve and #fasting). They employed a content analysis of all in all 7,560 images and found nine content categories of which 'Thinspiration' was one of the most prominent ones and had a share of 25% of the whole data set. The images classified in this category showed underweight bodies, very thin female bodies and body parts with protruding hip and collarbones as well as thigh gaps. Another study [6] investigated the expression of eating disorder symptoms in Twitter tweets and found that the top three keywords contain besides #hipbones, the two variations #thinspiration and #thinspo. The posts discuss predominantly the concern about the body shape, including images in half of the writings. Talbot et al. [22] compared #fitspiration, #bonespiration and #thinspiration content on Twitter, Instagram and We Heart It and differentiate them from each other. They performed a content analysis on 734 images tagged with one of these hashtags and found that Thinspiration and bonespiration content shows more thin and objectified bodies when compared to fitspiration imagery, which contains more photos of muscular persons. Moreover, bonespiration, when compared to Thinspiration content, depicts more protruding bones and less muscles.

Thinspiration on Tumblr was also already studied [27]. The researchers qualitatively classified 222 image and text posts retrieved under the #thinspiration hashtag from Tumblr. They characterized the images as showing predominantly thin bodies, very few muscular people and curvy or overweight bodies only in before-after pictures. The vast majority of images shows culturally based beauty ideals, almost one third sexual objectification and 20.5% women in underwear. One quarter of the images shows people posing in a special way to appear thinner. They characterized the texts of the posts as predominately discussing dieting and losing weight. Other themes were, in descending order of popularity, food and body guilt, thin praise, fat stigma, only very rarely exercise for appearance and sexual objectification. This study's methodology was also applied in the work of this paper and further details are given in Sect. 3.4.

2.2 K-Pop

The Korean popular music industry evolved with strong influence from the Japanese idol system. The term *idol* in Korea refers to young pop singers who are strategically produced by big entertainment companies. Idols do appear in other media, like for instance drama series, but enter the entertainment industry traditionally by being a member of bands called idol groups [20].

The role of K-pop idols is to create desirable images for consumers as well as building intimacy to their fan base. While in earlier times of K-pop culture, entertainment companies tried to recruit trainees, who have talent in singing and dancing, the focus shifted in visual traits like beautiful faces. The idol groups are composed of different *types* of idols to address multiple groups within the audience. They are described as strategically produced commodities, with a strong focus on visual qualities. While plastic surgery is common among idols, before and after their debut, the visual perfection of the idols is gained by strict body control, so that body weighing belongs to the weekly schedule of trainees and idols, as well as the restriction of calorie intake per day. For instance, agencies also manifest discipline in eating and different other areas of life with a 'code of conduct': (1) punctuality at rehearsals, (2) no smoking, (3) a ninety-degree bow, (4) no cell phone use except during dinner, (5) no dating, (6) politeness during class, (7) no drinking, (8) no lateness or absence, (9) no food, and (10) staff members only in practice rooms [20].

2.3 Studies on Eating Disorders on Tumblr

The Thinspiration hashtag was also used to retrieve social media content and explore the pro-ana communities. One study analyzed Tumblr photo posts and tried to identify deviant content, that most likely is going to be banned my Tumblr's moderators. Thinspo and Thinspiration were the two most frequent tags in their data set for pro-ana content [7].

Another study also addressed the platform Tumblr to characterize anorexia on that social network. The results show that anorectic users differ from users of the control group e.g. by their contrasting tag usage or a stronger linguistic focus on the past [9].

Chancellor, Mitra and De Choudhury [8] explored the role and efficacy of Tumblr in regards to a sustained recovery from anorexia. They studied body image concerns, behavioral patterns, as well as cognitive and emotional factors of users who self-identify with anorexia. They found that only half of the studied cohort experiences recovery in the studied time period (four years).

A different study compared Tumblr and Twitter posts that discuss eating disorders and shows that aid organizations communicate more on Twitter, and if images are shared, they predominantly belong to Thinspiration content. On Tumblr authors post more anonymously and share more images than on Twitter, that mostly show (thin) bodies [5].

3 Research Methodology

3.1 Collection of Data

For the purpose of this study, three data sets were constructed: K-pop, Thinspo and Control.

To retrieve K-pop posts, a list of hashtags referring to K-pop Thinspiration content was manually assembled, by entering the first hashtag #k-pop thinspiration into the Tumblr search bar and filtering more related hashtags from the posts that were retrieved this way. Furthermore, K-pop band names were combined with the keywords 'Thinspiration' and 'Thinspo' to generate more hashtags. The 15 most popular K-pop bands[4] were used for this. Not all bands related Thinspo hashtags were included into the final list, since some were not used to create Thinspiration content at all. All hashtags were entered into the search bar, to make sure that they lead to posts. All tags that gave no results were

---

[4] According to this website: https://www.seventeen.com/celebrity/music/g38505052/best-K-pop-bands/.

excluded. Terms like 'K-pop Diet' and 'K-pop Body' were intentionally excluded to focus specifically on Thinspiration content. Table 1. shows the final 15 hashtags used for this study.

Next, the Tumblr Application Programming Interface (API)[5] was used to download posts that have one of these tags. The time period was the years 2017–2021 in the UTC time zone.

In addition to the K-pop specific data set a second one with *normal* Thinspiration content was built by using the hashtag 'Thinspiration' and downloading all posts of the year 2019. Those posts, that contained one of the K-pop related Thinspiration tags, were removed from this data set.

Besides, a collection of posts serving as control data set, showing *average* Tumblr content was created. A website for marketing purposes[6] was consulted to find most popular hashtags, that co-occur with #tumblr which resulted in the tag *love*. The #love posts of 2019 were downloaded and a subset of 4,000 was randomly selected as the control data set.

Next, all the images that were used within the posts were downloaded for each of the three data sets separately. Table 2. summarizes the basic descriptive statistics of the three data sets.

Table 1. Hashtags used to build the K-pop data set in alphabetical order.

blackpink thinspo	enhypen thinspo	kpop thinspo	kpopThinspo	thinspo kpop
bts thinspiration	k pop thinspo	k-pop thinspo	red velvet thinspo	twice thinspo
bts thinspo	kpop thinspiration	kpopThinspiration	thinspo blackpink	txt thinspo

3.2 Image Analysis

Branley and Covey [5] described in their work, that the Thinspiration content on Tumblr seemed to be gloomier and darker compared to other posts. Therefore, in this work images are analyzed based on their colorfulness and the corresponding colorfulness category. Wang et al. [26] used the emotional measures pleasure, arousal and dominance to distinguish self-harm related posts from regular social media content. For this paper, these measures shall be used for characterizing the eating disorder related posts.

The colorfulness measure was taken from Hasler and Süsstrunk [13] who conducted a study where they asked 20 participants to rate a set of 84 images and classify them into seven categories ranging from not colorful to extremely colorful. Through different experimental calculations they found a colorfulness measure that correlated to their empirical observations by 95.3%. This measure is derived from the opposing color spaces red, green and blue. Using these color spaces' mean and standard deviation they calculate their colorfulness measure C (see Eq. 1). The higher the value of C, the more

---

[5] Link to the Tumblr API: https://www.tumblr.com/docs/en/api/v2.

[6] https://displaypurposes.com/hashtags/hashtag/tumblr.

Table 2. Basic descriptive statistics of the three data sets. Numbers are rounded to two decimal places.

	K-Pop	Thinspiration	Control
Number of posts	431	3,707	4,000
Number of posts containing images	361 (83.76%)	1,493 (40.28%)	2,804 (70.1%)
Number of images	886	2,824	3,229
Mean number of images per image post	2.45	1.89	1.15
Number of notes on posts	52,046	310,318	203,290
Mean number of notes per post	120.76	83.71	50.82
Number of hashtags on posts	2,922	36,120	49,905
Mean number of hashtags per post	6.78	9.74	12.48
Number of unique users	162	1,121	2,975
Mean posts per users	2.66	3.31	1.34

colorful the image is. Table 3. depicts the colorfulness category and the corresponding C value.

$$C = \sigma_{rgyb} + 0,3 \cdot \mu_{rgyb} \tag{1}$$

Table 3. Relation between colorfulness category and colorfulness measure C as introduced by Hasler and Süsstrunk [13]. Numbers in brackets refers to the number of the category, that is used in Fig. 1.

Colorfulness category	C
Not colorful (1)	0
Slightly colorful (2)	15
Moderately colorful (3)	33
Averagely colorful (4)	45
Quite colorful (5)	59
Highly colorful (6)	82
Extremely colorful (7)	109

In addition, the emotional measures pleasure, arousal and dominance have been calculated. This can be done by combining the average saturation (S) and brightness (B) values of an image. These measures were introduced by Valdez and Mehrabian [25] and also derived from a series of empirical experiments showing that the saturation and brightness of colors have an emotional impact on the participants, as represented in the

Eqs. 2, 3 and 4.

$$\text{Pleasure} = 0.69 \cdot B + 0.22 \cdot S \tag{2}$$

$$\text{Arousal} = -0.31 \cdot B + 0.60 \cdot S \tag{3}$$

$$\text{Dominance} = -0.76 \cdot B + 0.32 \cdot S \tag{4}$$

Previous work on affective image analysis [19] as well as the understanding of self-harm content [26] utilized this method.

3.3 Text Analysis

For automatically analyzing the texts of the Tumblr posts two methods were chosen: A sentiment analysis and the calculation of the readability of the text. The sentiments of eating disorder social media posts were researched by Fettach and Benhiba [10] showing that topics such as Thinspiration are discussed differently, regarding the sentiment, depending on the community. For that reason, this measure was included into this work's study. The readability score was added to investigate on the assumption that posts from disordered people are less readable compared to regular content.

The sentiment analysis was performed using VADER [16], a lexicon and rule-based tool, that was especially designed to process social media content. For instance, it also analyzes elements such as emoticons, emojis or words written in capital letters and similar. The compound score, that VADER comes with, ranges between -1 and $+1$. Values between 0.05 and -0.05 are considered to be of neutral sentiment, while -1 is the most negative sentiment and $+1$ is the most positive one.[7] The sentiment analysis was applied at the post level, after removing any kind of markup language like HTML elements within the posts.

To evaluate the readability of a post, the Flesch Reading Ease score (FRES)[8] [17] was utilized. Equation 5 shows how FRES is composed.

$$206.835 - 1.015\left(\frac{\text{total words}}{\text{total sentences}}\right) - 84.6\left(\frac{\text{total syllables}}{\text{total words}}\right) \tag{5}$$

The measure has no minimum score, negative values are valid, and the maximum score is 121.22. Table 4. shows the relation between FRES value and readability [11].

3.4 Content Analysis

To perform the qualitative content analysis of the K-pop related Thinspiration posts, those posts from the K-pop data set were selected that have exactly one image and optional also a text. Depending on the type of post, text refers to captions of images or

---

[7] VADER on Pypi.org: https://pypi.org/project/vader-sentiment/.

[8] FRES score as part of the textstat package on Pypi.org: https://pypi.org/project/textstat/.

videos as well as longer written posts. This resulted in 153 posts. For the video posts, the thumbnail image of the video was analyzed.

The classification scheme for the content analysis was taken from a previous study on Thinspiration visual content on Tumblr [27]. It contains variables for image and text classification. The researchers selected these variables from prior work [2, 3] in a similar context. Table 5. shows the image and text variables as they were described by Wick and Harriger [27]. The variable descriptions are partly extended by K-pop specific explanations.

Two coders were rating the 153 Tumblr posts. Following the classification scheme, posts including images were coded for the images variables and posts combining text and image were coded with all variables. This way it is possible that one post contains different variables that are then coded with a '1'. If the post for example does not contain text, the text variables are all coded with a '0'. Both coders were participating in a discussion session prior to the rating process. An inter-rater agreement was calculated for each variable showing an overall good to nearly perfect agreement between the two raters. Cohen's Kappa ranged between 0.61 and 1.0 (see also Table 7.).

Table 4. Relation between FRES and reading difficulty according to Flesch [11].

Score	Reading difficulty
90–100	Very easy
80–89	Easy
70–79	Fairly easy
60–69	Standard
50–59	Fairly difficult
30–49	Difficult
0–29	Very confusing

4   Results

4.1   Automatic Analysis of Texts and Images

The visual analysis shows that in general the Thinspo data set contains images with lower values in all five measures colorfulness (and consequently the colorfulness category), pleasure, arousal and dominance. The K-pop data set has the highest values while the control images lie in between the two different Thinspiration image sets. The differences become most apparent in the colorfulness measures, which are related, as it is shown in Table 3.. A higher colorfulness score results in a higher colorfulness category. Figure 1 shows the results of the visual analysis by plotting the normalized means of each measure for each data set.

Figure 2 depicts the sentiment values and frequencies for all three data sets. It shows similar distributions at first sight. However, the control posts show less negative sentiments than positive ones. The extreme positives show a peak. The Thinspo posts seem to be more equally distributed when the positive and the negative sides are compared, while the K-pop posts have more writings with positive sentiments, especially in the mid-raged values.

Table 5. Description of text and image variables used to classify the K-pop posts. Taken from Wick and Harriger [27]

Variable	Description
Image Variables	
Thin	Showing very thin bodies, corresponding to Figs. 1 and 2 on Swami's photographic figure rating scale [21]
Muscular	Visible muscle tone
Curvy/Overweight	Corresponds to figures 6–10 on Swami's photographic figure rating scale [21]
Culturally Based Beauty Ideals	Shows persons with blemish free skin, neat and shiny hair, symmetrical features, white and straight teeth, lithe figure, supple breasts, or other culturally based beauty norms; For K-pop features like idols on stage or photo shooting pictures were also included into this category
Bathing Suits	Wearing only a bathing suit
Underwear	Wearing only underwear
Sexual Objectification	Wearing little clothing (including underwear or bathing suit) or displayed in a sexual context
Before/After	Before/after photo of the same person, demonstrating weight loss
Thin pose	Posed to appear smaller (e.g., angling body at 45°, putting hands on hips, crossing one leg over the other etc.)
Text Variables	
Sexual Objectification	Promotes a person as object of sexual pleasure
Fat Stigma	Implies negativity in regard to being overweight
Thin Praise	Implies positivity in regard to being thin
Exercise for Appearance	Encourages exercise for appearance related reasons
Food Guilt	Guilt-inducing messages about food
Dieting/Restraint	Discusses dieting or restraint around food
Losing Weight or Fat	Discusses losing weight or fat
Objectifying Messages	Encourages viewership to see the body as an observable object
Body/Weight Guilt	Guilt-inducing messages about body or weight

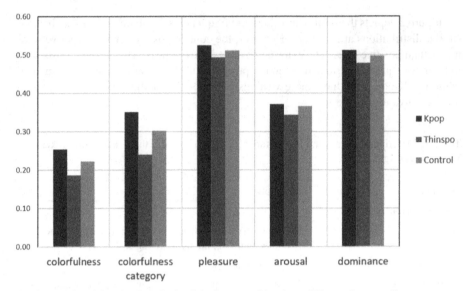

Fig. 1. Results of the visual analysis of the images of the three different data sets. Bars represent normalized means of the measures.

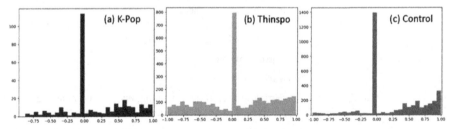

Fig. 2. Results of the sentiment analysis of the texts. X axis represents the sentiment compound value; Y axis shows the volume of posts.

All posts of all data sets have the highest peak in the neutral area, although the K-pop posts, as well as the control posts, have their peak on the negative side, while the Thinspo posts have it on the positive side.

The results of the readability analysis are shown in Table 6.. The majority of posts in all three data sets was classified as *very easy*. However, the control data reaches close to half of the posts (44.14%), while only a quarter of the Thinspo posts can be found in this category. Instead they are more equally distributed to the other *easy* categories. The K-pop posts seem to be the least confusing ones compared to those of the other data sets.

4.2   Content Analysis

All in all, there were 153 posts of the K-pop data set analyzed that contained an image, of which 81 were also composed of a text. Table 7. summarizes the frequencies for each variable as well as Cohen's Kappa for each. Most images (74.51%) show culturally based beauty ideals, very often K-pop idols, but also other (Korean) people who incorporate these beauty standards being promoted by the idols. Also prominent was the category *thin* (73.86%) while no images depicted curvy/overweight people, not even the before/after pictures. Before/after pictures showed in all cases a K-pop idol starting the career with a healthy body weight (before picture) and at a later point in time where they significantly lost weight (after picture). Uncommon among the K-pop posts were pictures showing people in bathing suits (0%) or underwear (3.27%). Only one image (0.65%) showed a picture of an idol where muscles were visible. About one third of the pictures (35.29%) showed people in *thin pose* and 15.03% were classified as *sexual objectification*. Another category was added since it did not correspond to the image variables of Wick and Harriger. It was called *other* and predominantly contained eating disorder related memes with a text on the image of a K-pop idol.

Table 6. Results of the readability analysis

	%	Frequency	%	Frequency	%	Frequency
Reading difficulty	**K-pop (304)**		**Thinspo (3,350)**		**Control (3,509)**	
Very easy	34.87	106	25.31	848	44.14	1,549
Easy	12.5	38	19.16	642	9.43	331
Fairly easy	19.08	58	19.04	638	11.94	419
Standard	10.53	32	13.22	443	7.24	254
Fairly difficult	9.87	30	9.64	323	5.9	207
Difficult	10.2	31	9.67	324	10.34	363
Very confusing	2.96	9	3.94	132	11	386

For the 81 text posts the most prominent variable (43.21%) was *thin praise* (e.g. "that little hint of thigh gap is EVERYTHING"), followed by 27.16% of posts addressing *losing fat or weight* (e.g. "i want to be 95 lbs/43 kg"). About one quarter of posts (25.93%) discussed dieting and restraint (e.g. "I aspire to be this[9] and if that means drinking water and one cup of coffee so be it"). 18.52% of the text posts were classified as *body/weight guilt* comprising posts like for instance "when your as tall as namjoon[10] but wanna be skinny as yoongi[11]". Food guilt appeared in 16.05% of posts (e.g. "when it's that point during dinner where you have to pretend you are actually eating so you just do 'the thing'[12] with the spoon hoping no one realizes"). The category *other* (16.05%) was chosen when the text did not fit in one of the other variables and usually contained

---

[9] Referring to the post's image.

[10] A Korean rapper.

[11] Another Korean rapper.

[12] Referring to the post's animated image where a K-pop idol drops the spoon into the soup and putting it back on the table without eating.

very few words referring to the post's image (e.g. "Hyuna[13] just gently killing me"). *Fat stigma* ("My scale: 89.8 lbs!! My brain: still fat. Where skinny?"), *exercise for appearance* ("Ngl[14] i feel proud i skateboarded today, i only did it for 30 min apparently if you skateboard it can keep ur legs slim and it burns 300–500 cals") and *objectifying message* ("I always shame her for her figure") only appeared rarely (8.64%, 4.94% and 3.7%) while there were no posts containing sexual objectifying texts.

Table 7. Summary of the results of the classified posts. Frequencies and corresponding percentages are the average of the annotators.

Variable	Percentage (%)	Frequency	Cohen's Kappa
Image Variables (153)			
Thin	73.86	113	0.83
Culturally Based Beauty Ideals	74.51	114	0.88
Sexual Objectification	15.03	23	0.61
Thin Pose	35.03	54	0.74
Underwear	3.27	5	1.0
Bathing Suit	0	0	–
Muscular	0.65	1	1.0
Curvy/Overweight	0	0	–
Before/After	3.27	5	1.0
Other	20.92	32	0.84
Text Variables (81)			
Dieting/Restraint	25.93	21	0.89
Losing Weight or Fat	27.16	22	0.71
Food Guilt	16.05	13	0.70
Body/Weight Guilt	18.52	15	0.73
Thin Praise	43.21	35	0.78
Objectifying Messages	3.7	3	0.79
Fat Stigma	8.64	7	0.76
Exercise for Appearance	4.94	4	1.0
Sexual Objectification	0	0	–
Other	16.05	13	0.91

---

[13] Korean singer.
[14] Colloquial: Not gonna lie.

5 Discussion

Regarding the relation of Thinspiration content to eating disorders, it is important to understand the different facets of Thinspiration on Tumblr or other social media platforms. When comparing the results of prior research on Thinspiration content on Tumblr [27] to the results of this study, it becomes obvious that there are similarities (predominantly thin people incorporating culturally based beauty ideals) but also significant differences. In the analyzed K-pop posts, only very few posts show people in underwear, while in *regular* Thinspiration content it is 20.5%. Also sexual objectification is depicted on approximately only half of the posts (15.03%) compared to the usual Thinspiration on Tumblr (31.8%). In the text variables it becomes clear, that dieting/restraint as well as loosing fat or weight are in both cases the most prominent categories, while K-pop Thinspo differs in the variables thin praise (K-pop 43.21%, regular Thinspo 20.8%) and also objectifying messages (K-pop 3.7%, regular Thinspo 19.8%) as well as fat stigma (K-pop 8.64%, regular Thinspo 16.7%). Hence, the K-pop Thinspiration seems to be less sexually depicting and objectifying. On the other hand, it is more thin praising, especially towards idols, and less fat shaming.

In relation to the visuals, we see that K-pop Thinspiration is closer to the pictures of the control data set than to the Thinspiration images. This is contradictory to findings by Wang et al. [26] who found that self-harm photos have lower values in pleasure, arousal and dominance, compared to normal social media content. Self-harm is related to disordered eating habits and over 70% of patients report that they engage in self-injuring behavior [24]. Knowing that, K-pop Thinspiration could be a first step into developing disordered eating habits spiraling downwards to comorbid illnesses such as self-harm. Also in regards to the sentiments, the K-pop data shows more similarities with normal content than with Thinspiration posts on Tumblr. The same can be seen in the readability scores. This contributes to making it more difficult to automatically detect potentially harmful content on social media.

The basic descriptive statistics (see Table 2.) suggests that the K-pop Thinspiration community on Tumblr is on the one hand a rather narrow group, because the mean number of hashtags per post is rather small (6.78) compared to the Thinspiration posts (9.74) and the control group's posts (12.48). At the same time the engagement, as expressed by the mean number of notes (rebloggs and likes) is much bigger within the K-pop group (120.76) than in the two other groups (Thinspo 83.72, control 50.82). The impact of K-pop idols behaviors and appearances on their fans was already described in the literature [20] and shows the big influence. Knowing that the Thinspiration content, that arose from this influence on Tumblr, stands out from normal social media content, by e.g. being more colorful imagery, makes it concerning in regards to young fans who might be negatively influence towards eating disorders by consuming K-pop Thinspiration.

6 Conclusion

Regarding the differences among Thinspiration on Tumblr and the similarities of K-pop Thinspo to normal content, more research is needed to better understand what makes content potentially harmful and what is only fandom towards idols. It is important to better understand when content, in regards to eating disorders, becomes problematic. This study investigated K-pop Thinspiration content on Tumblr and compared it to regular Thinspiration posts as well as content with no eating disorder relation and found that K-pop Thinspiration is closer to the data of the control data set than to the Thinspiration posts. This shows that potentially dangerous content, especially for a young audience, may look and read as simple harmless posts about one's favourite music groups, while actually eating disorder related messages are already transported. It would be beneficial to also focus on other social media platforms to verify the results of this study in future research and learn to better distinguish between the different faces of Thinspiration online.

References

1. American Psychiatric Association: Diagnostic and Statistical Manual of Mental Disorders: DSM-5, 5th edn. American Psychiatric Association Arlington, VA (2013)
2. Boepple, L., Ata, R.N., Rum, R., Thompson, J.K.: Strong is the new skinny: a content analysis of fitspiration websites. Body Image 17, 132–135 (2016)
3. Boepple, L., Thompson, J.K.: A content analytic comparison of fitspiration and thinspiration websites. Int. J. Eat. Disord. 49(1), 98–101 (2016)
4. Boero, N., Pascoe, C.J.: Pro-anorexia Communities and online interaction: bringing the pro-ana body online. Body Soc. 18(2), 27–57 (2012)
5. Branley, D.B., Covey, J.: Pro-ana versus pro-recovery: a content analytic comparison of social media users' communication about eating disorders on twitter and Tumblr. Front. Psychol. 8, 1356 (2017)
6. Cavazos-Rehg, P.A., et al.: "I just want to be skinny.": a Content analysis of tweets expressing eating disorder symptoms. PloS ONE 14(1), e0207506 (2019)
7. Chancellor, S., Kalantidis, Y., Pater, J.A., De Choudhury, M., Shamma, D.A.: Multimodal classification of moderated online pro-eating disorder content. In: Mark, G., Fussell, S.R., Lampe, C., Schraefel, M.C., Hourcade, J.P., Appert, C., Wigdor, D. (eds.) Proceedings of the 2017 CHI Conference on Human Factors in Computing Systems, Denver, CO, USA, May 06–11, 2017, pp. 3213–3226. ACM (2017). https://doi.org/10.1145/3025453.3025985
8. Chancellor, S., Mitra, T., De Choudhury, M.: Recovery amid pro-anorexia: analysis of recovery in social media. In: Kaye, J., Druin, A., Lampe, C., Morris, D., Hourcade, J.P. (eds.) Proceedings of the 2016 CHI Conference on Human Factors in Computing Systems, San Jose, CA, USA, May 7–12, 2016, pp. 2111–2123. ACM (2016). https://doi.org/10.1145/2858036.2858246
9. De Choudhury, M.: Anorexia on Tumblr: a characterization study. In: Kostkova, P., Grasso, F. (eds.) Proceedings of the 5th International Conference on Digital Health 2015, Florence, Italy, May 18–20, 2015, pp. 43–50. ACM (2015). https://doi.org/10.1145/2750511.2750515
10. Fettach, Y., Benhiba, L.: Pro-eating disorders and pro-recovery communities on Reddit: text and network comparative analyses. In: Proceedings of the 21st International Conference on Information Integration and Web-based Applications and Services, iiWAS 2019, Munich, Germany, December 2–4, 2019, pp. 277–286. ACM (2019). https://doi.org/10.1145/3366030.3366058
11. Flesch, R.: How to write plain English: a book for lawyers and consumers. Harper and Row. https://books.google.de/books?id=-kpZAAAAMAAJ (1979)
12. Ging, D., Garvey, S.: 'Written in these scars are the stories I can't explain': a content analysis of pro-ana and thinspiration image sharing on instagram. New Media Soc. 20(3), 1181–1200 (2018)

13. Hasler, D., Süsstrunk, S.: Measuring colorfulness in natural images. In: Rogowitz, B.E., Pappas, T.N. (eds.) Human Vision and Electronic Imaging VIII, Santa Clara, CA, USA, January 20, 2003. SPIE Proceedings, vol. 5007, pp. 87–95. SPIE (2003). https://doi.org/10.1117/12.477378
14. Hoek, H.W., van Hoeken, D.: Review of the prevalence and incidence of eating disorders. Int. J. Eat. Disord. **34**, 838–396 (2003)
15. Holland, G., Tiggemann, M.: A Systematic Review of the Impact of the Use of Social Networking Sites on Body Image and Disordered Eating Outcomes. Body Image **17**, 100–110 (2016)
16. Hutto, C.J., Gilbert, E.: VADER: a parsimonious rule-based model for sentiment analysis of social media text. In: Adar, E., Resnick, P., Choudhury, M.D., Hogan, B., Oh, A.H. (eds.) Proceedings of the 8th International Conference on Weblogs and Social Media, ICWSM 2014, Ann Arbor, Michigan, USA, June 1–4, 2014. The AAAI Press. http://www.aaai.org/ocs/index.php/ICWSM/ICWSM14/paper/view/8109 (2014)
17. Kincaid, J.P., Fishburne Jr, R.P., Rogers, R.L., Chissom, B.S.: Derivation of new Readability Formulas (Automated Readability Index, Fog Count and Flesch Reading Ease Formula) for Navy Enlisted Personnel. Tech. rep., Naval Technical Training Command Millington TN Research Branch (1975)
18. Mabe, A.G., Forney, K.J., Keel, P.K.: Do you "like" my photo? facebook use maintains eating disorder risk. International Journal of Eating Disorders **47**(5), 516–523 (2014). https://doi.org/10.1002/eat.22254
19. Machajdik, J., Hanbury, A.: Affective image classification using features inspired by psychology and art theory. In: Bimbo, A.D., Chang, S., Smeulders, A.W.M. (eds.) Proceedings of the 18th International Conference on Multimedia 2010, Firenze, Italy, October 25–29, 2010, pp. 83–92. ACM (2010). https://doi.org/10.1145/1873951.1873965
20. Oh, Y.: Pop City: Korean Popular Culture and the Selling of Place. Cornell University Press (2018)
21. Swami, V., Salem, N., Furnham, A., Tovée, M.J.: Initial examination of the validity and reliability of the female photographic figure rating scale for body image assessment. Personality Individ. Differ. **44**(8), 1752–1761 (2008)
22. Talbot, C.V., Gavin, J., Van Steen, T., Morey, Y.: A content analysis of thinspiration, fitspiration, and bonespiration imagery on social media. J. Eat. Disord. **5**(1), 1–8 (2017)
23. Tiggemann, M., Anderberg, I.: Social Media is not real: the effect of 'instagram vs reality' images on women's social comparison and body image. New Media Soc. **22**(12), 2183–2199 (2020)
24. Turner, B.J., Yiu, A., Layden, B.K., Claes, L., Zaitsoff, S., Chapman, A.L.: Temporal associations between disordered eating and nonsuicidal self-injury: examining symptom overlap over 1 year. Behav. Ther. **46**(1), 125–138 (2015)
25. Valdez, P., Mehrabian, A.: Effects of color on emotions. J. Exp. Psychol. Gen. **123**(4), 394 (1994)
26. Wang, Y., et al.: Understanding and discovering deliberate self-harm content in social media. In: Barrett, R., Cummings, R., Agichtein, E., Gabrilovich, E. (eds.) Proceedings of the 26th International Conference on World Wide Web, pp. 93–102. ACM (2017). https://doi.org/10.1145/3038912.3052555
27. Wick, M.R., Harriger, J.A.: A content analysis of thinspiration images and text posts on Tumblr. Body Image **24**, 13–16 (2018). https://doi.org/10.1016/j.bodyim.2017.11.005

Mental Health Communication on Social Media in India: Current Status and Predictors

Sairaj Patki$^{(\boxtimes)}$ and Anika Iyer

FLAME University, Pune, Maharashtra, India
{sairaj.patki,anika.iyer}@flame.edu.in

Abstract. Social media is emerging as a popular platform for health communication and has gained an even stronger impetus since the COVID-19 pandemic. With conversations about mental health slowly building momentum in recent times even in developing countries like India, this study sought to understand the current status of mental health communication on social media in the country. The factors predicting these communication behaviours were explored as well. The data comprised 421 participants (Mean age = 28.26 years) hailing from metros, urban and semi-urban areas. Almost 64% of participants reported having used social media for mental health communication. The extent of mental health knowledge and empathy emerged as the most consistent predictors of indulging in mental health communication behaviours on social media. Almost 92% of participants reported that they observed an increase in these communication behaviours among people, as a result of the pandemic.

Keywords: Mental-health · Health communication · Social media

1 Introduction

1.1 Health Communication

Health communication has emerged as a prominent and specialized domain in communication study, that is constantly evolving progressively across public health in government sectors as well as the non-profit and commercial sectors. Its multidisciplinary nature has resulted in a wide variety of definitions. However, despite the differences in definitions, they all point towards the common goal of advocating and refining individual or public health outcomes. There are certain phrases and keywords that have been used time and again, which can be identified as the most common attributes of health communication. "Sharing meanings or information," "influencing individuals or communities," "informing," "motivating target audiences," "exchanging information," and "changing behaviours" are some of these. The definition by the Centers for Disease Control and Prevention (CDC) of the United States, is one of the most popular and comprehensive ones and includes these common attributes. It conceptualizes health communication as the study and use of communication strategies, with the aim of informing and influencing health-enhancing decisions of individuals and communities [1].

H. Li et al. (Eds.): WIS 2022, CCIS 1626, pp. 78–93, 2022.
https://doi.org/10.1007/978-3-031-14832-3_6

1.2 Health Communication Behaviours and Social Media

Social media is being considered an effective medium for spreading a large amount of information across the masses in a short period of time. In the health communication sector, there is a widespread assumption that recent advances in Internet technologies, particularly the participative Internet (popularly known as social media), have transformed the pattern of communication, including health-related communications [2]. There is an increasing research interest in assessing the relationship between social media and health.

Evidence suggests that there is ample social support information, that sharing is more patient-controlled and that social media has become one of the most successful platforms for communication. The COVID-19 pandemic led to a massive surge of seeking information and updates from the public, and the governments of all countries met these demands in an unparalleled communicative effort. News media, probably the most effective source of information, direct communications from political and health leaders through live press conferences and social media posts have become invaluable tools in the direct transmission of life-saving information to an attentive public [3]. Social media platforms, have thus become an integral mediator in transferring information about the pandemic and health in general, from the government to citizens.

Social media can give users all the data on what information needs to be updated in general, and also when one wants specific information about a particular health condition or health-related aspect. Through social media, one can also get the answers to health-related queries and clarification at one's fingertips, as social media is not focused on one-to-one communication, but rather on a more informative, group reception-focused orientation. By facilitating dialogue between patients and professionals, a great deal can be accomplished and obtained. Data collected on patient experiences, thoughts and opinions across health-related topics can be used further in the fields of health intervention, health promotion and health education. Last, but not least, it helps reduce stigma and prejudice around the various issues of health.

1.3 Social Media and Mental Health Communication

Studies conducted especially in the last decade, have explored the potential of social media in directly and indirectly supporting efforts to promote mental health. For instance, a study [4] discussed how people with mental illnesses turn to social media for peer support. The study identified four benefits of using social media that motivated the users. It helped reduce the sense of isolation they experienced and provided them hope, it helped them experience support when peers exchanged information and reciprocated with their experiences, it helped them identify coping strategies for dealing with the challenges of everyday life and finally it became a source of practical and factual information related to use of medication use and seeking mental health care. Naslund and colleagues [5] suggest that through social media, people with serious mental illness who otherwise fail to receive support in their immediate real environment can connect with others on social media, who are facing the same challenges. Such connections, termed peer-to-peer support, could advance efforts to promote physical and emotional well-being in the groups. This support also helps to challenge stigma by sharing personal stories, which also helps build confidence and personal empowerment in such individuals. They could also learn about important mental health behaviours and decisions. A qualitative study [6] using focus group discussions, explored the perspectives of youth receiving web and mobile-based mental health information, services and support. The results highlighted the value perceived by the participants in accessing mental health information and support online. A more recent study spread across 10 countries, further established the preference of participants with self-identified mental health conditions for using social media as a means of intervention, promotion of overall health and wellbeing and coping with their symptoms [7].

The COVID-19 pandemic posed a mammoth mental health challenge for developing countries like India where trained mental health professionals were already struggling to meet the supply–demand gap between practitioners and clients. According to a pre-pandemic report published by the WHO, India had only 0.29 psychiatrists, 0.07 psychologists, and 0.36 other mental health workers per 1,00,000 citizens [8]. Besides the scarcity of mental health practitioners, many others factors have been identified that further increase the challenges faced by those seeking help. For some individuals, the feeling of being stigmatized, discriminated and socially isolated becomes a hurdle in accessing mental health care [9]. The time and expenses involved in travel to clinics, expenses of the therapy itself and extended waiting period for appointments of therapists are other barriers that may dissuade people from seeking help [10]. These barriers get magnified when considering the taboo associated historically with mental health issues in a collectivistic country like India.

While dealing with the above-mentioned challenges would require sustained efforts on all fronts for a significant amount of time, starting and supporting conversations around topics related to mental health, spreading necessary information and awareness, reducing the taboo and sharing of resources and experiences to build a supportive community are initial supportive measures to create an ecology that favours mental health in the society in a more organic way. Social media could act as a prominent platform for serving this purpose. The rapidly increasing presence of digital communication in the country supports this proposition. India had 1.10 billion mobile phone connections by January 2021, amounting to 79% of the total population of the country, as a result of 23 million new connections compared to the previous year [11]. In January 2022, there were 467 million social media users, 19 million more than in 2021 [12].

1.4 The Present Study

Existing literature abundantly explains the role of social media in impacting mental health or as a platform for delivering mental health-based interventions. The study of social media as a platform for health communication, especially mental health-based communication is receiving more impetus only recently, with the pandemic playing an important role in this context. The actual experiences, perspectives and observations of the general population, too are crucial in understanding the current status of mental health communication on social media in the country and the related predictors. The present study thus aimed to explore this area which has received very little attention.

The peer-to-peer support phenomenon described in the previous section and the social media ecology model provided a foundation for determining the variables of the present study. We have considered the definition of social media as given by Naslund and colleagues, who describe it as an online and mobile-based platform, that is interactive, and that allows individuals and groups to discover, share, co-create, or exchange information, in the form of ideas, photos, or videos with others in their virtual network [5].

The social media ecology model is a honeycomb framework of seven building blocks that are configured by various social media platforms. These building blocks are – identity: the extent to which users reveal themselves, conversations: the extent to which users communicate with each other, sharing: the extent to which users exchange, distribute and receive content, and presence: the extent to which users know if others are available, relationships: the extent to which users relate to each other, reputation: the extent to which users know the social standing of others and content, and lastly groups: the extent to which users are ordered or form communities [13] (Fig. 1).

Fig. 1 The motivation needs mapped across the elements of the honeycomb model of social media [14]

Through the present study, we intended to focus on health communication in India using social media exclusively in the context of mental health. The study used the more generic perspective of health communication for this purpose, conceptualizing mental health communication on social media as a set of behaviours that use communication strategies as supported by the platform, with the aim of discussing, spreading awareness, and potentially also influencing health beliefs and decisions of individuals and communities with respect to mental health and related issues. Communication is seen as being more democratic and horizontal and driven by the masses rather than a top-down channel wherein information is disseminated unidirectionally by governments, policymakers, experts, corporations, or media houses.

2 Method

2.1 Participants

The study implemented convenience sampling technique by using social media platforms to reach out to potential participants. While this non-probability technique poses certain inherent limitations, it was thought to be the most suitable and practical approach in the context of the given study, given the inclusion criteria, and also to help reach out to a wide sample. The inclusion criteria for the study specified that participants must have completed 18 years of age, must have completed education at least till grade twelve, must hail from metro cities, urban or semi-urban areas and must have access to social media. Sampling bias was reduced due to the anonymous nature of the survey. The final sample comprised 421 participants (Mean age = 28.26 years), hailing from various regions across India. In terms of social media usage, WhatsApp was the most widely used platform among the participants closely followed by Instagram. Facebook and Twitter came next and were followed by Reddit (Table 1).

Table 1. Distribution of sociodemographic characteristics of the participants.

Characteristic	n	%
Age (in years)		
18–25	240	57.0
26–33	58	13.8
34–41	67	15.9
42–49	35	8.3
50–57	16	3.8
58–65	5	1.2
Gender		
Women	283	67.2
Men	133	31.6
Non-binary	2	0.5
Undisclosed	3	0.7
Education		
12th Grade	144	34.2
Diploma	24	5.7
Graduation	134	31.8
Postgraduation	83	19.7
Professional degree	32	7.6

(continued)

Table 1. (*continued*)

Characteristic	n	%
Doctoral degree	4	1.0
Annual income in lacs		
Less than 2.5	23	5.5
2.5–5	38	9.0
5–7.5	43	10.2
7.5–10	35	8.3
10–12.5	37	8.8
12.5–15	39	9.3
Above 15	206	48.9
Residence		
Semi-urban	30	7.1
Urban	182	43.2
Metro	209	49.6

2.2 Tool

A survey questionnaire was developed for the study with the aim of understanding the behaviours, experiences, perceptions, and pandemic associated changes in mental health communication and related behaviours of the general population. The entire survey required approximately 15 min to be completed.

The resulting anonymous online survey included a section on sociodemographic details of the participants including age, gender, educational qualification, annual income (based on formal ranges used by the Government for the taxation brackets based on annual income), and residence (metro, urban, and semi-urban). Social media platforms used, time spent daily on social media, and the general extent of knowledge about mental health were recorded next.

The following section required participants to report mental health communication behaviours that they themselves displayed and those that they observed others displaying on social media. For the present study, mental health communication was operationalized as including four behaviours on social media in the context of mental health-seeking information, forwarding messages/posts/reels/videos/posters/memes etc., creating and sharing messages/posts/reels/videos/posters/memes etc. and sharing personal experiences.

The survey also included a section dedicated to understanding the perspectives of the participants about various reasons for the usage of social media for mental health communication. There were 22 statements in this section implementing a five-point Likert type scale response pattern with two statements each for 11 motivational needs. A pilot study conducted earlier [15] on a comparative sample of 81 participants was the source for these statements. These eleven motivational needs were – empathy, catharsis, concern, reassurance, sharing of personal experiences, spreading awareness, seeking information, recommending suggestions, tangible help, glamourization/trend and peer pressure (the last two needs reflected a negative attitude towards the use of social media for mental health communication). Confirmatory factor analysis using the principal axis factoring extraction method and oblimin rotation with Kaiser normalization was performed and it supported this dichotomy. The pattern matrix revealed that the 18 statements related to the motivation needs, depicting a positive attitude towards the use of social media for mental health communication loaded on one factor. The four statements related to glamourization/trend and peer pressure, depicting a negative attitude, loaded on a second factor. Cronbach's alpha reliability coefficients were computed for this 22-item section on a representative sample of 377 participants. The obtained coefficient value ($r = 0.90$) demonstrated good internal consistency, following the rules of thumb regarding acceptable and necessary reliability coefficients [16].

The last section of the survey asked participants about any quantitative change that they have observed in themselves and others with reference to the use of social media for mental health communication after the pandemic. The reason for capturing the observations of others' behaviours along with the self-report of one's own behaviour, was that participants may provide valuable data on these behaviours even though they may not perform the behaviours themselves. Participants noted their observation in terms of there being no change, there being an increase in usage or there being a decrease in usage. An additional option was provided to identify those who had never used social media for mental health communication.

2.3 Procedure

Data collection for the study commenced after receiving the ethics approval from the University's Internal Review Board (IRB) (Approval number: 2022/02/04/EXP). Data collection was carried out through the month of March, 2022. At this point, India had seen a drastic reduction in the number of new COVID-19 cases (with daily cases being around 6,500 at the beginning of the month and further reduced to about 2,500 towards the end of the data collection), compared to the third wave that hit the country around mid-January, 2022 (when the count of new cases per day had reached almost 3.5 lakhs). Participation in the study was voluntary and completely anonymous with no identifiable data like name, email address, contact number or address being recorded. The online survey questionnaire link was forwarded to prospective participants through personal contacts, University students, professional and personal networks and social media platforms. Data obtained was then cleaned for responses from participants that did not meet the inclusion criteria. The final data was coded and then further put through statistical analysis.

2.4 Analysis

The study followed a quantitative exploratory analysis approach. Descriptive statistics were calculated for understanding the contemporary state of mental health-related social media communication. For further inferential statistics, the total data ($n = 421$) was split into two groups based on the usage of social media for mental health communication ($n = 270$ for users and $n = 151$ for non-users). While participant age and extent of knowledge about mental health were originally continuous scalar variables, the categorical variables including educational qualification, annual income and time spent on social media daily were encoded and converted to numerical data for analysis. After studying the correlation matrix and verifying the absence of multicollinearity, multiple linear regression analyses were performed for the significant relationships, to identify the predictors of mental health communication behaviours in this group of users. The entire data analysis was performed using SPSS Ver. 22.

3   Results

The study was aimed at understanding the current status of the general population with respect to mental health-related communication on social media in India especially as impacted by the pandemic and to explore the crucial determinants of these communication behaviours.

3.1   Current Status of Mental Health Communication in India

In this section, we present the descriptive statistics depicting mental health communication in the country along with the impact that the pandemic was perceived to have in this context.

Table 2. Descriptive statistics for mental health communication behaviours.

Behaviour	M	SD
Displayed by oneself		
iInfo	2.95	1.28
iForward	2.94	1.23
iCreate	2.13	1.23
iShare	2.24	1.23
Observed behaviours		
oInfo	3.19	1.26
oForward	3.26	1.28
oCreate	2.93	1.38
oShare	2.98	1.33
Impact of the pandemic	n	$\%$
On one's behaviours		
Increase	169	40.1
Decrease	14	3.3

(continued)

Table 2. (*continued*)

Behaviour	M	SD
No change	87	20.7
Never used for mental health	151	35.9
On others' behaviours		
Increase	386	91.7
Decrease	2	0.47
No change	33	7.8

Note. iInfo = Health communication behaviour involving searching for mental health-related information on social media, iForward = Health communication behaviour involving forwarding of mental health-related information on social media, iCreate = Health communication behaviour involving the creation of content for spreading awareness about mental health on social media, iShare = Health communication behaviour involving sharing one's own personal mental health experiences with others on social media. oInfo = Others' health communication behaviour involving searching for mental health-related information on social media as observed by the participant, oForward = Others' health communication behaviour involving forwarding of mental health-related information on social media as observed by the participant, oCreate = Others' health communication behaviour involving creating content for spreading awareness about mental health on social media as observed by the participant and oShare = Others' health communication behaviour involving sharing their own mental health-related experiences on social media as observed by the participant.

As observed in Table 2, the mean frequency of mental health communication behaviours was found to be less for the participant's self-report as compared to what they observed. Among those displayed by oneself as well as by others, searching for information and forwarding mental health information were the most frequent behaviours. Content creation was observed to have the most variability. With reference to the perceived impact of the pandemic, while almost 36% of participants reported never using social media for mental health communication, among the others, over 40% of participants reported witnessing an increase in their mental health communication since the onset of the pandemic. On the other hand, for observed usage of social media, almost 92% of participants reported noticing an increase since the onset of the pandemic.

3.2 Factors Relevant to Mental-Health Communication on Social Media

In this section we present the summary of the analysis performed for the group of participants using social media for mental health communication ($n = 270$), to identify the significant predictors of mental health communication on social media in this group.

Sociodemographic Characteristics, Usage, Knowledge and Mental Health Communication. Pearson's product-moment correlation followed by multiple linear regression analysis was performed to identify the role of sociodemographic participant characteristics, time spent on social media and extent of knowledge of mental health issues in predicting mental health communication on social media.

Table 3. Summary of correlation coefficients for sociodemographic characteristics, time spent on social media, knowledge and mental health communication.

Variable	1	2	3	4	5
1. Age	–				
2. Education	0.57**	–			
3. Income	−0.05	−0.04	–		
4. Usage[a]	−0.19**	−0.19**	0.08	–	
5. Knowledge	−0.22**	−0.11	0.09	0.09	–
iInfo	−0.24**	−0.07	0.03	0.16**	0.41**
iForward	−0.30**	−0.15*	0.01	0.16**	0.37**
iCreate	−0.12	−0.03	−0.07	0.11	0.38**
iShare	−0.07	−0.08	−0.01	0.04	0.27**

[a] Usage refers to the time spent on social media by the participant on a daily basis
*$p < 0.05$. **$p < 0.01$.

Following the results of the correlation analysis as seen in Table 3, a multiple regression analysis was performed for the significant relationships. The first model with age, time spent on social media daily and extent of mental health knowledge collectively predicted searching for information communication behaviour, ($F_{(3, 266)} = 22.14$, $p < 0.001$, $R^2 = 0.20$). The individual predictors were examined further and indicated that age ($t = -2.52$, $p = 0.012$) and knowledge ($t = 6.52$, $p = 0.001$) were significant predictors in the model. The second model tested with age, educational qualification, time spent on social media daily and extent of mental health knowledge collectively predicted forwarding information communication behaviour, ($F_{(4, 265)} = 16.48$, $p < 0.001$, $R^2 = 0.20$). Age ($t = -3.46$, $p = 0.001$) and knowledge ($t = 5.62$, $p = 0.001$) again emerged as significant predictors in the model. The next model tested extent of mental health knowledge as a predictor of creating content, ($F_{(1, 268)} = 44.21$, $p < 0.001$, $R^2 = 0.14$). Extent of mental health knowledge ($t = 6.45$, $p = 0.001$) emerged as a significant predictor in the model. The last model tested the extent of mental health knowledge as a predictor of the communication behaviour of sharing personal mental health experiences, ($F_{(1, 268)} = 21.19$, $p < 0.001$, $R^2 = 0.07$). The extent of mental health knowledge ($t = 4.60$, $p = 0.001$) emerged as a significant predictor in the model. The extent of mental health knowledge of the participants thus significantly predicted each of the four communication behaviours.

Motivational Needs and Mental Health Communication. In this section, we present the analysis performed to identify the role of the 11 motivational needs in predicting mental health communication on social media.

Following the results as seen in Table 4 and Table 5, empathy was shown to have relationships of moderate strength with the behaviours, whereas the negative motivational needs of glamour/trend and peer pressure showed no significant relationships throughout with the behaviours. Multiple regression analysis was then performed for

Table 4. Summary of correlation coefficients for the positive motivational needs and mental health communication.

Variable	1	2	3	4	5	6	7	8	9
1. Emp	–	–	–	–	–	–	–	–	–
2. Cath	0.56**	–	–	–	–	–	–	–	–
3. Cncrn	0.61**	0.60**	–	–	–	–	–	–	–
4. Reass	0.60**	0.55**	0.60**	–	–	–	–	–	–
5. Share	0.63**	0.56**	0.66**	0.58**	–	–	–	–	–
6. Aware	0.60**	0.41**	0.57**	0.52**	0.68**	–	–	–	–
7. Info	0.50**	0.45**	0.56**	0.41**	0.52**	0.48**	–	–	–
8. Reco	0.56**	0.51**	0.59**	0.46**	0.61**	0.58**	0.59**	–	–
9. Help	0.48**	0.51**	0.55**	0.40**	0.51**	0.54**	0.54**	0.64**	–
iInfo	0.24**	0.14*	0.08	0.17**	0.12	0.05	0.07	0.10	0.20**
iForward	0.28**	0.24**	0.16**	0.23**	0.22**	0.23**	0.14*	0.11	0.13*
iCreate	0.24**	0.13*	0.06	0.10	0.11	0.09	0.14*	0.10	0.20**
iShare	0.25**	0.17**	0.14*	0.20**	0.16**	0.09	0.17**	0.15*	0.14*

Note. Emp = Empathy, Cath = Catharsis, Cncrn = Concern, Reass = Reassurance, Share = Sharing of personal experiences, Aware = Spreading awareness, Info = Seeking information, Reco = Recommending suggestions, Help = Tangible help
*$p < 0.05$. **$p < 0.01$.

Table 5. Summary of correlation coefficients for the negative motivational needs and mental health communication.

Variable	1	2
1. Glam	–	
2. Peer	0.54**	–
iInfo	−0.08	−0.03
iForward	−0.09	−0.04
iCreate	−0.03	0.08
iShare	−0.02	0.01

Note. Glam = Glamour/trend, Peer = Peer pressure
**$p < 0.01$.

the significant relationships. The first model with empathy, catharsis, reassurance and help motivational needs and searching for information emerged significant, ($F(4, 265) = 4.23$, $p < 0.01$, $R^2 = 0.06$). Among the individual predictors, only empathy ($t = 2.70$, $p = 0.007$) significantly predicted the communication behaviour of searching for mental health information on social media. The next model tested empathy, concern, catharsis, reassurance, help, sharing, awareness and information as predictors of forwarding information, and emerged as significant, $(F(8, 261) = 3.88, p < 0.001, R^2 = 0.11)$. Among the motivational needs only empathy $(t = 1.99, p = 0.048)$ emerged as a significant predictor of forwarding mental health information on social media. The third regression model assessing the creating content communication behaviour as predicted by empathy, catharsis and information emerged significant, $(F(3, 266) = 5.30, p < 0.001, R^2 = 0.06)$. Again, empathy emerged as the sole significant predictor $(t = 2.96, p = 0.003)$. The final model tested the motivational needs of empathy, concern, catharsis, reassurance, help, sharing, information and recommendation as predictors of the communication behaviour of sharing personal experiences about mental health on social media. This model was overall significant, $(F(8, 261) = 2.56, p < 0.05, R^2 = 0.07)$. As in the earlier model, empathy was the only significant individual predictor $(t = 2.25, p = 0.025)$.

4 Discussion

4.1 Current Status of Mental Health Communication on Social Media in India

The results suggested that the use of social media for mental health communication is quite prevalent in the sample for the study that hailed from Indian metro, urban and semi-urban areas, with only about 36% of participants reporting that they never used social media for this purpose. This could be attributed to the social media usage and the extent of mental health awareness levels in this section of society. Moreover, theorists and researchers have identified that the advantages of social media as a platform for mental health communication, outweigh its limitations like lack of reliability of the information or the possibility of compromised privacy. Apart from peer-to-peer support, social media also helps spread knowledge within the general society. Through this, it also helps others identify mental health concerns and be more proactive towards them and one's own mental health as well. An additional benefit could be that social media enhances opportunities to augment existing mental health services and programs and supply the same support to those facing similar issues [7].

Secondly, the study revealed that the use of social media for searching for information related to mental health and forwarding such information were behaviours that were both more frequently displayed and observed by the participants. These were followed by creating content and sharing personal experiences which were comparatively less frequently displayed and observed. These differences can be expected, considering the greater amount of time, effort and technical skills required for content creation on social media and considering the taboo associated with sharing personal mental health experiences, especially on a more public platform like social media.

The study also clearly demonstrated the effect of the pandemic on the usage of social media for mental health communication in the sample studied. Across the total sample of the study $(n = 421)$, almost 92% of participants reported that they observed an increase in mental health communication by others on social media, since the pandemic. Among those who used social media for mental health communication themselves $(n = 270)$, 169 participants (62.6%) reported an increase in their own behaviours owing to the pandemic. This increase reflects the ease of the platform to connect to others for support and information, especially during such challenging times. For instance, a study conducted in Indonesia [17] that explored the role of social media in health communication during the first phase of the pandemic outbreak, supports this notion. The study revealed that a vast majority of participants benefited from using social media for health communication and demonstrated a positive attitude towards it because it allowed them to seek social support from online networks as well as from offline friends, relatives and colleagues.

4.2 Predictors of Mental Health Communication on Social Media in India

The younger the participants and the more knowledgeable they were about mental health, the more likely they were to use social media for searching information about mental health and forward such information on social media. Likewise, mental health knowledge predicted content creation and sharing of personal experiences in the sample studied. This can be explained using Everett Rogers' Diffusion of Innovation theory which talks about how new concepts, ideas and practices can spread within a community. The theory proposes five subgroups classified based on the nature of the audience and characteristics to adopt innovation – innovators, early adopters, early majority, late majority and laggards [1]. The time spent by the younger adults on social media, their technical skills of using the platform and the extent of awareness about mental health-related topics make them innovators, early adopters and early majority while the elder ones may be categorized into the remaining two categories.

With reference to the 11 motivational needs as predictors, only empathy emerged as a significant predictor of mental health communication on social media in the sample studied. Empathy is the basic human value needed to be sensitive to the needs of oneself as well as others and thus individuals with higher empathy can be expected to express this concern even in the context of mental health. To understand how all these factors come together to predict mental health communication on social media, we use the Precede-Proceed Model developed by Lawrence Green and Marshall Kreuter. This model analyses three key categories that influence behavioural change – pre-disposing factors, enabling factors and reinforcing factors [1]. Young empathetic individuals, with the necessary access to social media and usage skills, would use the platform for mental health communication. The positive reactions and support to these acts by the online community especially post the pandemic would further reinforce their behaviours.

Consequently, social media fosters a global form of communication, as people get to know others outside of their community, empower them to talk about health more and provide a platform for conversations that certain topics need [18]. This can ultimately lead to people seeking out help, online consulting and spreading extensive awareness about it. Some of the other benefits include increased interactions with others, increase in the quantity of information, tailored and shared information, increased accessibility and widened access, peer/emotional/social support, public health surveillance and potential to influence health policies [13].

4.3 Limitations, Conclusions and Implications

While we attempted to obtain a representative sample of the typical urban Indian population, the sample for the study comprised 57% of young adults and 30% of participants falling in the middle adulthood category. While this sample may represent the age group of the most active social media users, more data from participants belonging to the elder age groups could have aided the understanding of their social media usage for mental health communication as well. Likewise, participants belonging to the middle and low-income groups (as categorized by national level taxation brackets) were underrepresented in the study, and further studies and conscious efforts to include these groups would give a more holistic understanding of the status of mental health communication on social media in the country. Post hoc power analysis for the effect sizes obtained for the regression analyses was found to be above 0.90 in all instances. However, since the study used convenience sampling, the findings may not be directly generalized to the entire population. Lastly, while we have focussed on the potential of social media to foster mental health, one cannot ignore the limitations and hazards that may emerge from blind reliance on these platforms. Misinformation, fake news, and fraudulent accounts are some of the common pitfalls in the path of establishing a healthy and safe social community on the Internet. Social media should be considered a complementary intervention strategy and cannot replace professional aid or expertise.

Despite the above-mentioned limitations, the study highlighted the potential of social media to be harnessed as a platform for supporting efforts to foster mental health communication. As a country that is only recently witnessing an increase in awareness about mental health and that has a tremendous deficit of mental health practitioners on one hand and millions of social media users on the other, the findings of our study hold a promise for developing social media-based interventions for propagating mental health. By building on the capacity of this platform to reach across the length and breadth of the country, mental health awareness can spread wider and faster, unlike the traditional health communication mediums. The broad findings of the study may also have implications for other developing countries facing similar mental health-related challenges.

Secondly, the findings elicited the importance of the extent of mental health awareness among the participants in predicting their actual behaviours related to mental health communication on social media. Moreover, considering the fact that such behaviours on social media are elicited more frequently by young adults, interventions focused on this age group for spreading awareness about mental health through experts will ensure the wider and more effective dissemination of accurate information about mental health issues. Simultaneously, efforts ought to be made to build the necessary technical skills for the elderly to equip them for using social media platforms in the context of mental health-related needs. On-going traditional mental health awareness programs and drives can receive a boost by getting such social media influencers on board.

The study also revealed that the major motivational need driving mental health communication behaviours on social media was empathy. The vital role of this core human virtue implies that these behaviours are not merely trends and are not performed for any direct incentives. This could have long term implications for the organic growth of this phenomenon on social media. Especially considering the impact of the pandemic on both mental health and social media usage, both quantitative and qualitative developments in pro-mental health-related dialogue on social media can be expected.

Acknowledgements. The authors would like to thank Dr Moulika Mandal, Assistant Professor of Psychology and the entire batch of students registered for the course of Abnormal Psychology at FLAME University for assisting in the data collection process.

Conflict of Interests. The authors declare that there is no conflict of interest. The study did not receive any funding and was conducted independently.

References

1. Schiavo, R.: Health Communication: From Theory to Practice. Jossey-Bass, San Francisco (2007)
2. Chou, S.Y., Hunt, Y.M., Beckjord, E.B., Moser, R.P., Hesse, B.W.: Social media use in the united states: implications for health communication. J Med. Internet Res. 11(4), e48 (2009)
3. Teichmann, L., et al.: Public Health Communication and Engagement on Social Media during the COVID-19 Pandemic (2020). https://www.mediatechdemocracy.com/work/meo-public-health-communication-and-engagement-on-social-media-during-the-covid-19-pandemic. Last accessed 23 Mar 2022
4. Naslund, J.A., Grande, S.W., Aschbrenner, K.A., Elwyn, G.: Naturally occurring peer support through social media: the experiences of individuals with severe mental illness using YouTube. PLOS ONE 9(10), e110171 (2014)
5. Naslund, J.A., Aschbrenner, K.A., Marsch, L.A., Bartels, S.J.: The future of mental health care: Peer-to-peer support and social media. Epidemiol. Psychiatr. 2, 113–22 (2016). https://doi.org/10.1017/S2045796015001067
6. Lal, S., Nguyen, V., Theriault, J.: Seeking mental health information and support online: experiences and perspectives of young people receiving treatment for first-episode psychosis. Early Interv. Psychiatry 12(3), 324–330 (2018)
7. Naslund, J.A., Aschbrenner, K.A., McHugo, G.J., Unützer, J., Marsch, L.A., Bartels, S.J.: Exploring opportunities to support mental health care using social media: a survey of social media users with mental illness. Early Interv. Psychiatry 13(3), 405–413 (2019)
8. World Health Organization: Mental Health ATLAS 2017. https://www.who.int/mental_health/evidence/atlas/profiles-2017/IND.pdf?ua=1 (2018). Last accessed 27 Mar 2022
9. Thornicroft, G.: Stigma and discrimination limit access to mental health care. Epidemiol. Psychiatr. Soc. 17(1), 14–19 (2008)
10. Hert, M.D., et al.: Physical illness in patients with severe mental disorders. II. Barriers to care, monitoring and treatment guidelines, plus recommendations at the system and individual level. World Psychiatry 10(2), 138–151 (2011)
11. DataReportal: Digital 2021: India. https://datareportal.com/reports/digital-2021-india (2021). Last accessed 27 Mar 2022
12. DataReportal: Digital 2022: India. https://datareportal.com/reports/digital-2022-india (2022). Last accessed 27 Mar 2022
13. Moorhead, S.A., Hazlett, D.E., Harrison, L., Carroll, J.K., Irwin, A., Hoving, C.: A new dimension of health care: Systematic review of the uses, benefits, and limitations of social media for health communication. J. Med. Internet Res. 15(4), e85 (2013)

14. Kietzmann, J.H., Hermkens, K., McCarthy, I.P., Silvestre, B.S.: Social media? get serious! Understanding the functional building blocks of social media. Bus. Horiz. **54**(3), 241–251 (2011). https://doi.org/10.1016/j.bushor.2011.01.005

15. Patki, S.M., Namjoshi, S.: Hashtag illness: illness beliefs and behaviours in the context of social media. In: Srivastava, S.K., Sharma, K. (eds.) Health care challenges in India: Psycho-social perspectives, 1st edn., pp. 230–245. Global Vision Publishing House, New Delhi (IND) (2020)

16. Nunnally, J.C., Bernstein, I.H.: Psychometric Theory, 3rd edn. McGraw-Hill, New York (1994)

17. Saud, M., Mashud, M.I., Ida, R.: Usage of social media during the pandemic: Seeking support and awareness about COVID-19 through social media platforms. J. Public Aff. **20**(4), e2417 (2020). https://doi.org/10.1002/pa.2417

18. Steele, R.: Social media, mobile devices and sensors: categorizing new techniques for health communication. In: 2011 Fifth International Conference on Sensing Technology, pp. 187–192 (2011)

Understanding University Students' Health Information Seeking Behaviours on Social Media During the COVID-19 Pandemic: A Developing Country Perspective

Aung Pyae[1]([⊠]) [iD] and Shahrokh Nikou[2] [iD]

[1] ISE, Faculty of Engineering, Chulalongkorn University, Bangkok, Thailand
aung.p@chula.ac.th
[2] Faculty of Social Sciences, Business and Economics, Åbo Akademi, Turku, Finland
shahrokh.nikou@abo.fi

Abstract. According to the World Health Organization (WHO), the COVID-19 pandemic is considered the worst global health crisis in the 21st century that caused unprecedented disruption to many sectors around the world (e.g. education, business, and tourism). Misinformation on social media is one of the major issues during the COVID-19 pandemic, which must be carefully considered. To address this issue, people's health information-seeking behaviours play an important role to access accurate and reliable information on social media. In this study, we conducted a questionnaire-based study in Myanmar, which is one of the developing countries according to the United Nations to understand university students' health information-seeking behaviours on social media during the COVID-19 pandemic. The findings suggest that social media plays a vital role to spread reliable and accurate information during the pandemic. The role of governments and authorities is also important to effectively use social media platforms (e.g. Facebook) to reach out to the public so that they can spread timely and accurate information during the COVID-19 pandemic. Lastly, users need to assess and verify the credibility of information related to pandemics on social media when they seek health-related information. This study suggests opportunities for further research in health information seeking on social media.

Keywords: COVID-19 pandemic · Health information-seeking Behaviour · Social media

1 Introduction

Since the beginning of 2020, the world has experienced the COVID-19 pandemic caused by a new coronavirus (SARS-CoV-2). It became the worst global health crisis since 1918 [1, 2]. According to WHO [3], the COVID-19 pandemic has become a severe global threat and caused unprecedented disruptions and damages to many sectors and activities including education, business (e.g. work from home), social (e.g. stay-at-home), health-related activities (e.g. restrictions on on-site health visit), and tourism (e.g. closures of

H. Li et al. (Eds.): WIS 2022, CCIS 1626, pp. 94–111, 2022.
https://doi.org/10.1007/978-3-031-14832-3_7

hotels and restaurants). Moreover, most universities and schools around the world had to temporarily stop their onsite and face-to-face educational activities and moved to online platforms (e.g. using Zoom or MSTeam). Since the beginning of the COVID-19 pandemic, which has cost the lives of millions of people worldwide [4], people have sought health-related information (e.g. daily infection rates, mortality rate, and COVID-19 disease symptoms) from various sources including print media (e.g. television, radio, or social media channels) and online platforms (e.g. health-related websites and social media).

According to the existing literature, the ways people seek information about their health such as risks, symptoms, illnesses, treatment, and health-protective behaviours can be referred as '*Health Information-Seeking Behaviour*' (HISB) [5, 6]. For instance, people use various platforms (e.g. newspapers, online media, TV, and radio) to seek, obtain, and verify health-related information to deal with their health problems. Generally, HISB refers to the individual's discretionary actions to seek, obtain, and verify health-related information, as well as sources of information they use. Some discretionary actions of information seeking include reading (e.g. blogs), browsing (e.g. websites), listening (e.g. health talks), direct questioning (e.g. forum), asking for clarifications (e.g. chatbot), discussion (e.g. forum), and exchanging information with others (e.g. social media) [7–14].

Concerning people's health-related information-seeking behaviours, the existing literature shows that the internet, particularly social media, is the primary source for users to seek, obtain, and verify health-related information in order to make decisions on their health-related issues [15]. Furthermore, in recent years, social media platforms (e.g. Facebook and Twitter) have become a vital communication tool for people to identify health-related data. For instance, people seek information related to the outbreaks of infectious diseases and daily mortality rates during the COVID-19 pandemic. Furthermore, they analyse, verify, and interpret such health information on social media when they share it with others (e.g. friends on social media) [16–19]. The literature also points out that people usually seek health-related information mostly on social media to understand a particular health problem (e.g. symptoms and treatments). Furthermore, they use social media to assess and verify the credibility of health-related information (e.g. effectiveness of different vaccines for COVID-19). Most people have become reliant on social media for health information-seeking because it can provide immediate access to information seekers to have access to a large amount of health information, and the various perspectives on different health topics [20]. Not only do people want to engage in health-seeking from professional medical websites but they may also want to contribute to online health communities [22, 23]. For instance, they write, share, and post COVID-19-related information on social media during the pandemic. As described in [21, 22], among online health information seekers, 16% tried to seek others who may share similar health concerns with them, 30% consulted online health-related reviews or rankings of health care services or treatments, and 26% of them read or watched someone else's experience about health or medical issues. The existing literature also confirms that regarding seeking health information behaviours and resources, social media plays a dominating role, which can empower users in terms of improvements in making decisions and ultimately fostering better public health outcomes.

In the past decade, people have been frequently seeking information on social media including Facebook, Twitter, WeChat, and Weibo [24]. During the recent pandemic, as people were forced to stay under lockdowns and nationwide restrictions, their health-related information-seeking behaviours and activities had moved to the internet, particularly on social media. For instance, during the pandemic, people shared, exchanged, and acquired COVID-19 health-related information on social media platforms including Facebook and Twitter. Not only do they use social media to obtain up-to-date information, but they also use social media to assess and verify the credibility of COVID-19-related information. Hence, social media had also become an alternative for a personal visit to hospitals and medical centers, as well as face-to-face consultations with health practitioners [25]. In addition, the existing literature also confirms that social media has become the most common platform for users during the COVID-19 pandemic [24, 26]. It is not surprising that over 3.8 billion people are utilizing social media around the world; hence, the vast volume of information that people received through social media has an impact on how they interpret and respond to the current COVID-19 pandemic [27, 28]. During the pandemic, the WHO stated that the largest number of COVID-related talks on Twitter in one day was 548,152,410. Furthermore, COVID-19 was mentioned 40.2 million times on social media between May 12th and May 18th, 2020, according to the online social media tracking platform TalkWalkerTM [29, 30].

More importantly, the literature has also highlighted that misinformation related to the COVID-19 pandemic has caused a major threat to public health [31]. According to [37], misinformation is false or inaccurate information, which is deliberately created, as well as is propagated with or without intention. From the science and health point of view, misinformation is defined as information that is contrary to the epistemic consensus of the scientific community regarding a phenomenon [38, p.434]. Furthermore, the spread of such misinformation about COVID-19 is associated with people's health information-seeking behaviours on social media [32]. In 2020, the WHO announced that the COVID-19 pandemic was accompanied by a contemporary challenge called the '*infodemic*' of misinformation [33]. Furthermore, to properly address rapidly spreading rumours and questions from the public obtained on social media during the COVID-19 pandemic [34], the WHO has used search optimization strategies within the social media platforms to guide questions about the pandemic by redirecting them to reliable sources.

Although the existing research highlights the importance of people's health information-seeking behaviours and the challenge of misinformation being spread on social media during the pandemic, there is limited research on the Covid-19-related information-seeking behaviour of university students, who are known as the largest user group of social networking sites according to [35]. Furthermore, the research is limited to the health information-seeking behaviours of university students particularly in developing countries during the COVID-19 pandemic. To be able to bridge the gaps, this research is important to conduct as the findings from this study can be useful for researchers in health informatics to understand students' information-seeking behaviours on social media during a health crisis (e.g. COVID-19). Hence, in this paper, we aimed to conduct empirical research and perform questionnaire-based research to investigate the HISB of university students in Myanmar. The main objectives of the study are:

- To understand university students' social media usage and their social media self-efficacy during the COVID-19 pandemic,
- To understand their HISB during the COVID-19 pandemic in terms of their trustworthiness, assessment of information credibility, and their fear of COVID-19, and
- To understand how they verify misinformation related to COVID-19 on social media

2 Method

2.1 Participants Recruitment

Regarding the recruitment of participants in this study, we defined the inclusion criteria. For instance, participants must age between 18 and 25 years, as well as they must belong to a particular program (e.g. undergraduate or graduate) in a local university in Myanmar. The participants were recruited through the Myanmar University Network including social media platforms (e.g. Facebook) and instant messaging tools (e.g. Viber). We recruited participants who were interested in voluntarily participating in the study. Upon the participants' agreement, we shared the questionnaire link with the participants via email. The data collection took place for 30 days. The research was conducted according to the university's ethical guidelines.

2.2 Approach and Instruments

In this study, we conducted a web-based questionnaire research to understand university students' HISB on social media (e.g. Facebook and Twitter). Particularly, we were interested in their behaviours in terms of seeking, verifying, and acquiring the COVID-19 related health information on social media during the pandemic. First, we developed an online questionnaire based on the research objectives and the concepts discussed above. The questionnaires consisted of demographic questions (e.g. age, gender, and education background), followed by participants' social media usage. Regarding participants' social media self-efficacy, which was adapted from [34], it focuses on participants' perceived social media skills, their confidence in finding information on social media successfully, social media content production (e.g. writing a post), and consumption of such information (e.g. read a post).

Moreover, we were interested in participants' HISB in social media in terms of their trustworthiness in the credibility of COVID-19 information. Hence, we adopted the questionnaire 'Social Media Trustworthiness' from [34]. The questionnaire focuses on participants' trustworthiness in COVID-19 information shared by different sources. We were also interested in participants' assessment of the credibility of COVID-19-related information, particularly on social media. Thus, we adopted the 'Social Credibility Assessment' questionnaire from [34], assessing how much the participants believe in COVID-19-related information posted by people on social media (e.g. friends, non-friends, unknown sources, and governmental pages). In addition, we used the questionnaire for measuring 'Social Media Verification' by [34] to investigate how participants used social media platforms to verify misinformation related to COVID-19. For instance, the questionnaire asked if participants considered others' opinions when they verified COVID-19 information, as well as when they decided whether it is false or inaccurate information. Also, we used the Fear of COVID-19 questionnaire developed by [35] to understand participants' fear of getting contracted COVID-19. Lastly, we used open-ended questions to understand participants' perspectives on COVID-19 information-seeking behaviours on social media platforms. We used the *Google Form* to create the online questionnaires. For all questionnaire items, we used a 5-point Likert scale (Strongly Disagree '*1*' to Strongly Agree '*5*').

3 Results

3.1 Demographic Data Analysis

In this research, we distributed a total of 250 invitation links to participants via email to respond to the online questionnaire form. By the deadline, we received 200 responses, of which, 199 responses were qualified while one response was rejected due to the incomplete data. According to the responses to the questionnaire, we found that all participants are currently university students at local universities in Myanmar. Among these participants, there was 124 female (62.31%) and 74 male (37.19%) participants. There were 184 undergraduate students (92.45%), 10 graduate students (5.03%), and 5 others (2.61%). Regarding the participants' age, there were 178 participants aged between 18 and 29 years (92.46%), 17 participants aged between 30 and 49 years (8.54%), and 4 participants aged between 50 and 59 years (2.01%) respectively. Regarding social media platforms use, it was found that 196 participants use Facebook, followed by 73 participants who also use Instagram, 28 participants use Twitter, 7 participants use YouTube, and 14 participants use other social media platforms (e.g. Weibo) respectively. About their HISB related to COVID-19, 175 participants used different social media platforms including Facebook, followed by 85 participants who used TV or radio, 68 participants used social communication applications such as WhatsApp, WeChat, and Messenger, and only 3 participants used Google search engine.

Regarding the participants' social media usage, 141 participants (70.85%) responded that they used '*several times a day*', while 44 participants (22.11%) mentioned that they used '*once a day*', 10 participants (5.03%) answered that they used '*a few times a week*', and 4 participants (2.01%) used '*a few times a month*' respectively. Regarding the duration of social media usage, 76 participants (38.19%) responded that they used approximately 30 min every time they used a social media application, while 71 participants (35.68%) used approximately two hours each time they used social media. Furthermore, 21 participants (10.55%) used less than 15 min, 19 participants (9.55%) used approximately 4 h, and 12 participants (6.03%) used more than 4 h of social media usage every time they used it.

3.2 Social Media Self-efficacy

In this study, the participants' self-efficacy in using social media platforms was assessed (see Table 1). First, we found that the participants were skillful in using social media platforms (M = 3.41, SD = 0.74). Second, they were good at finding information on social media platforms (M = 3.51, SD = 0.74). Third, they contributed to social media in terms of posts, comments, shares, and like (M = 3.01, SD = 0.89). Lastly, they searched for information on social media such as reading posts and comments (M = 3.5, SD = 0.92) respectively. The overall self-efficacy of the participants in using social media platforms was (M = 3.4, SD = 0.2).

Table 1. Participants' self-efficacy on social media.

Self-efficacy questionnaire	M	SD
1. How skillful are you in using social media platforms?	3.41	0.74
2. How good are you at finding information on social media platforms?	3.51	0.74
3. How often do you contribute to social media (e.g. post, comment, share, and like)?	3.01	0.89
4. How often do you obtain/look for information on social media (e.g. read posts and comments, watch videos, visit the shared links, and save posts)?	3.5	0.92

3.3 Trustworthiness

Regarding the participant's trustworthiness in COVID-19-related information shared on social media, we found that their trust in information shared by friends on social media was merely above average (M = 2.77, SD = 0.60). Concerning their trustworthiness in COVID-19-related information shared by non-friends on social media, their trust in such information (M = 2.32, SD = 0.81) was below average. Furthermore, they had the least trustworthiness in COVID-19-related information shared by unknown sources on social media (M = 1.88, SD = 0.82). Lastly, they had the highest trust in COVID-19-related information shared by reliable and credible sources such as the government's website and international organizations (e.g. WHO) (M = 3.66, SD = 0.80) on social media. Table 2 shows the participants' trustworthiness in COVID-19 information on social media.

Table 2. Participants' trustworthiness in COVID-19 information on social media.

Social media trustworthiness questionnaire	M	SD
1. How much do you trust information related to COVID-19 posted/shared by friends on social media?	2.77	0.60
2. How much do you trust information related to COVID-19 posted/shared by others (not in your friends' list) on social media?	2.32	0.81
3. How much do you trust information related to COVID-19 from unknown sources on social media?	1.88	0.82
4. How much do you trust information related to COVID-19 from known sources on social media (e.g. WHO, media, and local authorities)?	3.66	0.80

According to Table 3, the participants' trust in COVID-19 information shared by their friends on social media was mostly neutral. However, it can be seen that they did not trust the COVID-19 information shared by non-friends on social media. Apparently,

Table 3. Participants' trustworthiness in COVID-19 information on social media in percentages

Social media trustworthiness questionnaire	Not at all (%)	Not so much (%)	Neutral (%)	Very much (%)	Extremely very much (%)
1. How much do you trust information related to COVID-19 posted/shared by friends on social media?	2.51	24.62	65.83	7.04	0.00
2. How much do you trust information related to COVID-19 posted/shared by others (not in your friends' list) on social media?	17.59	36.68	42.21	3.02	0.50
3. How much do you trust information related to COVID-19 from unknown sources on social media?	38.69	36.18	23.62	1.51	0.00
4. How much do you trust information related to COVID-19 from known sources on social media (e.g. WHO, media, and local authorities)?	0.00	6.03	36.68	42.21	15.08

the results also show that the majority of the participants had the least trust in COVID-19-related information shared by unknown and unreliable sources on social media. On the contrary, most participants trusted COVID-19 information shared by reliable and credible sources on social media.

3.4 Information Credibility Assessment

We also investigated the participants' assessment of the credibility of COVID-19-related information on social media. First, when the participants sought COVID-19-related information on social media, they believed the credibility of particular information just because their friends on social media shared it (M = 2.66, SD = 0.69), which was above average. The mean score was below average (M = 2.26, SD = 0.80) for the credibility of information shared by non-friends on social media. Also, the results show that the COVID-19-related information shared by unknown sources on social media was the least credible (M = 1.91, SD = 0.89). Lastly, the COVID-19-related information shared by reliable sources and people such as the government's websites and international organizations (e.g. WHO) was the most credible (M = 3.64, SD = 0.80). Table 4 shows the participants' assessment of the credibility of COVID-19 information on social media.

Table 4. Participants' assessment on the credibility of COVID-19 information on social media.

Social credibility assessment questionnaire	Mean (M)	Standard deviation (SD)
1. When looking at information related to COVID-19 on social media, how often do you believe the information because your friends on social media also believe it?	2.66	0.69
2. When looking at information related to COVID-19 on social media, how often do you believe the information because other people (not on your friends' list) on social media also believe it?	2.26	0.80
3. When looking at information related to COVID-19 on social media, how often do you believe the information because unknown sources on social media also believe it?	1.91	0.89
4. When looking at information related to COVID-19 on social media, how often do you believe the information because known sources on social media also believe it (e.g. WHO, media, and local authorities)?	3.64	0.80

According to Table 5, most participants mentioned that the credibility of COVID-19 information shared by friends on social media was '*neutral*'. The results also highlighted that such information shared by non-friends on social media was '*not so much credible*'. Apparently, most of them did not believe the credibility of such information shared by unknown and unreliable sources on social media. In contrast, the majority of the participants believed the credibility of COVID-19 information shared by reliable and credible sources on social media.

Table 5. Credibility assessment of COVID-19 information in social media in percentages

Social media credibility assessment questionnaire	Not at all (%)	Not so much (%)	Neutral (%)	Very much (%)	Extremely very much (%)
1. When looking at information related to COVID-19 on social media, how often do you believe the information because your friends on social media also believe it?	5.03	31.16	56.28	7.54	0.00
2. When looking at information related to COVID-19 on social media, how often do you believe the information because other people (not on your friends' list) on social media also believe it?	19.10	39.20	38.19	3.52	0.00
3. When looking at information related to COVID-19 on social media, how often do you believe the information because unknown sources on social media also believe it?	40.70	31.16	24.62	3.52	0.00
4. When looking at information related to COVID-19 on social media, how often do you believe the information because known sources on social media also believe it (e.g. WHO, media, and local authorities)?	1.01	5.03	35.18	46.73	12.06

3.5 The Use of Social Media for Misinformation Verification

We also investigated the participants' HISB in terms of the way they verified misinformation related to COVID-19 on social media. First, the question asking, '*How likely are you to check the updates from your friends on social media to make sure the information you received is believable?*' had a mean score (M = 2.93, SD = 0.97), which was above average, indicating that the participants believe and trust more on the information provided by their friends. Second, the question asking, '*How likely are you to check the updates from others (who are not on your friends' list) on social media to make sure the information you received is believable?*', had a below-average score (M = 2.42, SD

= 1.15), indicating that there is lack of trust and believe on information provided by non-friends on social media. Third, the question asking, '*How likely are you to check the updates from unknown sources on social media to make sure the information you received is believable?*', had the least mean score among others (M = 2.36, SD = 1.20), indicating that the participants had the least trust in information shared by unknown or unreliable sources on social media. Lastly, the question asking, '*How likely are you to check the updates from known sources on social media (e.g. WHO, media, and local authorities) to make sure the information you received is believable?*', has the highest mean score among others (M = 3.45, SD = 0.99), which was expected as apparently, the participant find the information provided by the officials more trustful. Table 6 shows the participants' HISB in terms of their verification of such information on social media.

Table 6. Participants' verification of COVID-19 misinformation on social media.

Social media trustworthiness questionnaire	Mean (M)	Standard deviation (SD)
1. How likely are you to check the updates from your friends on social media to make sure the information you received is believable?	2.93	0.97
2. How likely are you to check the updates from others (who are not on your friends' list) on social media to make sure the information you received is believable?	2.42	1.15
3. How likely are you to check the updates from unknown sources on social media to make sure the information you received is believable?	2.36	1.20
4. How likely are you to check the updates from known sources on social media (e.g. WHO, media, and local authorities) to make sure the information you received is believable?	3.46	0.99

According to Table 7, most participants mentioned that when they checked the falsehood of COVID-19-related information with the updated news or information (e.g. posts) on social media, they tended to believe such information if it was also shared by their friends on social media. However, most participants had less trust in information shared by non-friends because it was unreliable to check the falsehood of information related to COVID-19. Apparently, most of them did not check or use the updated news from unknown and unreliable sources on social media to verify if the information they received was false and inaccurate. In contrast, the majority of them checked the updated information from reliable and credible sources on social media to verify the reliability and accuracy of COVID-19 information.

3.6 Fear of COVID-19

We also investigated the participants' fear of COVID-19 based on the information that they obtained from social media platforms. First and in general, the participants were

Table 7. Participants' verification of COVID-19 misinformation on social media in percentages

Social media verification questionnaire	Not at all (%)	Not so much (%)	Neutral (%)	Very much (%)	Extremely very much (%)
1. How likely are you to check the updates from your friends on social media to make sure the information you received is believable?	7.04	24.62	41.71	21.61	5.03
2. How likely are you to check the updates from others (who are not on your friends' list) on social media to make sure the information you received is believable?	30.65	18.09	32.66	16.08	2.51
3. How likely are you to check the updates from unknown sources on social media to make sure the information you received is believable?	35.68	14.07	32.66	14.07	3.52
4. How likely are you to check the updates from known sources on social media (e.g. WHO, media, and local authorities) to make sure the information you received is believable?	5.53	6.53	37.69	37.19	13.07

most afraid of COVID-19 (M = 3.31, SD = 1.01). Second, when the participants thought that COVID-19-related information on social media could make them uncomfortable (M = 3.27, SD = 0.97). When they thought about COVID-19-related information on social media, they thought that their hands became clammy (M = 2.15, SD = 1.04). They also mentioned that they were afraid of losing lives due to COVID-19-related information on social media (M = 3.01, SD = 0.99). They also pointed out that when watching news and stories about COVID-19 on social media, they became nervous and anxious (M = 3.01, SD = 0.99). Furthermore, they stated that they could not sleep because they were worried about getting COVID-19 after seeking such information on social media (M = 2.03, SD = 1.04). Lastly, they mentioned that their heart raced when they thought about getting COVID-19 after they had obtained such information on social media (M = 2.37, SD = 1.15) respectively. Table 8 shows the participants' fear of COVID-19, and Table 9 also shows that most of the participants responded 'neutral' concerning their fear of COVID-19.

Table 8. Participants' fear of COVID-19.

Social media trustworthiness questionnaire	Mean (M)	Standard deviation (SD)
1. I am most afraid of COVID-19	3.31	1.01
2. It makes me uncomfortable to think about COVID-19	3.27	0.97
3. My hands become clammy when I think about COVID-19	2.15	1.04
4. I am afraid of losing my life because of COVID-19	3.25	1.08
5. When watching news and stories about COVID-19 on social media, I become nervous and anxious	3.01	0.99
6. I cannot sleep because I'm worried about getting COVID-19	2.03	1.04
7. My heart races or palpitates when I think about getting COVID-19	2.37	1.15

Table 9. Participants' fear of COVID-19 in percentages

Social media trustworthiness questionnaire	Not at all (%)	Not so much (%)	Neutral (%)	Very much (%)	Extremely very much (%)
1. I am most afraid of COVID-19	4.52	12.56	45.23	23.12	14.57
2. It makes me uncomfortable to think about COVID-19	4.52	12.56	45.23	26.63	11.06
3. My hands become clammy when I think about COVID-19	31.66	33.67	26.13	5.03	3.52
4. I am afraid of losing my life because of COVID-19	7.54	14.07	36.68	29.15	12.56
5. When watching news and stories about COVID-19 on social media, I become nervous and anxious	8.54	17.09	46.23	21.61	6.53
6. I cannot sleep because I'm worried about getting COVID-19	39.20	30.65	21.11	6.53	2.51
7. My heart races or palpitates when I think about getting COVID-19	30.65	22.11	30.15	13.57	3.52

4   Discussion

The current research examined and investigated the participants' health information-seeking behaviour during the COVID-19 pandemic. All participants were university students and the majority of them were undergraduate students at various universities in Myanmar. We found that the participants mainly and extensively use Facebook as a social media platform to seek information related to COVID-19. This finding is consistent with the findings that they used Facebook as a health information-seeking tool to search, verify, and obtain COVID-19-related information during the pandemic [39]. The findings also pointed out that most of them were active in using social media platforms in their daily routines, using the platforms daily for between 30 and 120 min. Hence, it can be said that the participants were active users of social media platforms, particularly Facebook, and they have had extensive experience in using such a tool. Regarding their self-efficacy in using social media platforms, we found that the participants were confident in their abilities in using social media platforms. For instance, they were skillful in using social media platforms, as well as they were good at finding information on social media. These findings are consistent with their social media usage patterns. They usually contributed to social media platforms in terms of writing posts, comments, and sharing. In addition, they often looked for information on social media such as by reading posts, comments, and videos. These findings also support that the participants used social media platforms for seeking, verifying, and obtaining information during the COVID-19 pandemic [40]. In addition, they shared health-related information (e.g. COVID-19) on social media platforms, particularly on Facebook.

Concerning the participants' HISB on social media, the findings suggest that when they sought COVID-19-related information on social media, they mainly trusted known and credible sources such as the official Facebook Page of WHO or the government's Facebook pages. For instance, if either WHO or the government's social media page announced or shared COVID-19 daily rates, they tended to trust such information because it was shared by a credible and reliable source. They used such reliable sources to search, verify, and obtain COVID-19 information. The results show that although they took opinions about COVID-19 from their friends on social media, they did not take it seriously, and their trustworthiness was mostly neutral. As an example, when they read the Covid-19 outbreak information shared by their friends on social media, they would neither believe nor reject it. However, the participants' trustworthiness was low in COVID-19 information shared by non-friends on social media. For example, if they saw particular information about the COVID-19 outbreak shared by non-friends on social media, they did not tend to believe it. As most of the participants in this research were experienced users of social media, we could assume that they could easily distinguish who to trust and what to trust when they sought COVID-19-related information on social media. For instance, they did not trust the information concerning COVID-19 treatment or vaccine effectiveness shared by unreliable sources on social media. It means that such unreliable sources may easily spread misinformation about COVID-19 that is likely to alleviate individual and public concerns about COVID-19 information.

According to the findings, the participant's behaviours in the assessment of the credibility of COVID-19 show that official and known sources on social media (e.g. WHO or government pages) were the most reliable. For example, when they sought COVID-19 symptoms on social media, they tended to believe the credibility of information by WHO or the government's social media pages because the information was shared by reliable sources. In contrast, they did not believe in the credibility of information shared by unreliable sources on social media because it was hard to verify how credible such information was, as well as the transparency and accountability of such information were not clear. As seen in the previous discussion, the participants had a similar 'neutral' view toward the credibility of COVID-19 information shared by friends on social media. However, they believed that the COVID-19 information shared by non-friends on social media was less credible compared to the information shared by friends. For instance, when a friend on social media shares COVID-19 new variants (e.g. Coronavirus Delta variant), they tended to believe that it was credible, whereas they did not believe if it was shared by non-friends on social media. These findings are supported by the existing literature that public trust plays a key role to control the Covid-19 pandemic, as well as to provide effective crisis information during the pandemic [41].

When the participants checked the falsehood of the COVID-19 information they received, as expected, they used the updated information from reliable sources on social media (e.g. the government's official Facebook pages). For instance, if they doubted the credibility of the COVID-19 information (e.g. vaccine), they used the official's social media page to confirm; whereas they had no trust in the information shared by unreliable and unknown sources on social media. To a certain extent, they believed and used their friends' updated information on social media to check the accuracy and reliability of COVID-19 information. For example, if a friend on social media shares the symptoms of COVID-19, the participants tended to believe and use such information to verify the information they received; however, they had low trust in the information shared by non-friends on social media. These findings are supported by the existing literature that as misinformation on social media tends to be more popular than accurate information, fact-checking or filtering is important for users so that they can receive reliable information [42].

Lastly, about the participants' fear of COVID-19 information, we found that they had concerns about being contracted or getting infected with such disease. However, their level of fear was found to be average. It can be related to their information-seeking behaviours on social media, or it can also be related to their high self-efficacy in using social media platforms. For instance, they were skillful in using social media platforms; hence, they were confident to seek, verify, and obtain reliability in social media. They also sought COVID-19-related information mostly from reliable and credible sources, as well as they trusted such information shared by their friends on the same social media platform. Furthermore, they always considered the opinions from credible sources before they decided to believe a piece of information about COVID-19. Hence, it can be said that most information they trusted was credible and trustworthy. Furthermore, they also verified such information by checking reliable and credible sources.

Based on the findings from the study, we summarise that social media, particularly Facebook in the context of the current research, plays an important role for university students in developing countries in terms of seeking, verifying, obtaining, and judging the credibility of related information during the COVID-19 pandemic. Furthermore, users' HISB on social media is also important when they seek health-related information such as COVID-19. In addition, the existing literature shows the issues of misinformation during the COVID-19 pandemic [36]. To solve such issues, users need to assess the credibility of health information and verify its sources and make a judgment on whether they should believe such information or not. The findings from this paper show that such users' HISBs are important so that they can obtain accurate and reliable health-related information. For instance, users need to assess and verify the credibility of COVID-19-related information (e.g. vaccine effectiveness or new COVID-19 variant) before making a judgment about such information. They need to assess and verify the credibility of such information in terms of what the source of the information is and how credible such information is. Unless users assess and verify it, unreliable information (aka misinformation or disinformation) can influence people's views on COVID-19 (e.g. adherence to social distancing), as well as it may cause disturbances to authorities' actions in fighting for COVID-19. Finally, the findings clearly show that the role of governments and authorized organizations (e.g. WHO) plays a vital role to spread credible and reliable information related to COVID-19, particularly on social media. The findings from this study can be insightful for researchers, practitioners, and policymakers particularly in educating misinformation or disinformation related to COVID-19 disease and pandemic. Furthermore, the study creates opportunities for researchers to further investigate the role of social media in controlling misinformation. The limitation of the research includes a small sample size, duration of data collection, and research method (i.e. this study used only a quantitative approach); hence, further inquiry into this research is recommended.

5 Conclusion

Information particularly those provided through social media is one of the major issues during the COVID-19 pandemic. People's health information-seeking behaviours play an important role in finding relevant and accurate information on social media during COVID-19. Hence, in this research, we conducted a questionnaire-based study to investigate and understand university students' HISBs during the recent global COVID-19 pandemic. This research focuses on university students particularly in Myanmar, which is a developing country. Based on the findings from the study, most university students in Myanmar greatly relied on Facebook as a social media tool to seek COVID-19-related information during the pandemic. The findings show that they mostly believed in COVID-19 information shared by reliable and credible sources (e.g. government's social media pages), whereas they did not trust the information shared by unreliable sources. They had a neutral view of the credibility of information shared by friends or non-friends on social media. This research suggests that the source of information plays an important role in terms of the credibility of such information. Furthermore, users need to assess and verify the credibility of information on social media when seeking COVID-19-related information so that they can avoid misinformation or rumours on social media. Lastly, the role of governments and authorities is vital to use social media as a platform to spread trustworthy and credible health-related information to users during the COVID-19 pandemic. This study suggests opportunities for researchers to investigate the role of social media in fighting health-related misinformation. This study contributes to making public health policies, practices, and actions on social media, especially for governments and authorities in terms of spreading accurate and reliable health-related information and fighting against misinformation related to COVID-19.

References

1. Ángeles, M., Fuentes-Lara, C., Navarro, C.: Covid-19 communication management in Spain: exploring the effect of information-seeking behavior and message reception in public evaluation. El profesional de la Información **29**(4), e290402 (2020)
2. Cheung, E.: Wuhan pneumonia: Thailand confirms the first case of the Wuhan virus outside China. South China Morning Post. https://www.scmp.com/news/hong-kong/health-env ironment/article/3045902/wuhan-pneumonia-thailand-confirms-first-case. Last accessed 11 Apr 2022
3. World Health Organization: Coronavirus disease (COVID-19). https://www.who.int/health-topics/coronavirus#tab=tab_1. Last accessed 11 Apr 2022
4. Masip, P., Aran-Ramspott, S., Ruiz-Caballero, C., Suasu, J., Almenar, E., Puertas-Graell, D.: Consumo informativo y cobertura mediática durante el confinamiento por el Covid-19: sobre-información, sesgo ideológico y sensacionalismo. El profesional de la información **29**(3), e290312 (2020)
5. Lambert, S.D., Loiselle, C.: Health information-seeking behavior. Qual. Health Res. **17**(8), 1006–1019 (2007)
6. Mills, A., Todorova, N.: An integrated perspective on factors influencing online health-information seeking behaviors. In: Australasian Conference on Information Systems 2016 Proceedings. 83. (2016)
7. Borgers, R., et al.: The information-seeking behavior of cancer outpatients: a description of the situation. Patient Educ. Couns. **22**(1), 35–46 (1993)
8. Brashers, D.E., Goldsmith, D.J., Hsieh, E.: Information seeking and avoiding in health contexts. Hum. Commun. Res. **28**(2), 258–271 (2002)
9. Feltwell, A.K., Rees, C.E.: The information-seeking behaviours of partners of men with prostate cancer: a qualitative pilot study. Patient Educ. Couns. **54**(2), 179–185 (2004)
10. Johnson, J.D.: Cancer-related information-seeking. Hampton, Cresskill, NJ (1997)
11. Beisecker, A.E., Beisecker, T.D.: Patient information-seeking behaviours when communicating with doctors. Med. Care **28**(1), 19–28 (1990)
12. Friis, L.S., Elverdam, B., Schmidt, K.G.: The patient's perspective. Support. Care Cancer **11**, 162–170 (2003)
13. Matthews, A.K., Sellergren, S.A., Manfredi, C., Williams, M.: Factors influencing medical information-seeking among African American cancer patients. J. Health Commun. **7**(3), 205–219 (2002)
14. Brereton, L., Nolan, M.: "Seeking": a key activity for new family carers of stroke survivors. J. Clin. Nurs. **11**(1), 22–31 (2002)
15. Miller, L.M.S., Bell, R.A.: Online health information seeking: the influence of age, information trustworthiness, and search challenges. J. Aging Health **24**(3), 525–541 (2012)
16. Jordan, S.E., Hovet, S.E., Fung, I.C., Liang, H., Fu, K., Tsem, Z.T.H.: Using Twitter for public health surveillance from monitoring and prediction to public response. Data **4**(1), 6 (2018)
17. Shah, Z., Surian, D., Dyda, A., Coiera, E., Mandl, K.D., Dunn, A.G.: Automatically appraising the credibility of vaccine-related web pages shared on social media: a Twitter surveillance study. J. Med. Internet Res. **21**(11), e14007 (2019)
18. Sinnenberg, L., Buttenheim, A.M., Padrez, K., Mancheno, C., Ungar, L., Merchant, R.M.: Twitter as a tool for health research: a systematic review. Am. J. Public Health **107**(1), e1–e8 (2017)

19. Steffens, M.S., Dunn, A.G., Wiley, K.E., Leask, J.: How organizations promoting vaccination respond to misinformation on social media: a qualitative investigation. BMC Public Health **19**, 1348 (2019)

20. Li, Y., Wang, X., Lin, X., Hajli, M.: Seeking and sharing health information on social media: a net valence model and cross-cultural comparison. Technol. Forecast. Soc. Chang. **126**, 28–40 (2016)

21. Pew Research Center: The Internet and Health. https://www.pewresearch.org/internet/2013/02/12/the-internet-and-health/. Last accessed 2022

22. Zhao, Y., Zhang, J.: Consumer health information seeking in social media: a literature review. Health Info. Libr. J. **34**(4), 268–283 (2017)

23. Keselman, A., Browne, A.C., Kaufman, D.R.: Consumer health information seeking as hypothesis testing. J. Am. Med. Inform. Assoc.: JAMIA **15**(4), 484–495 (2008)

24. Hitlin, P., Olmstead, K.: The science people see on social media. https://www.pewresearch.org/science/2018/03/21/the-science-people-see-on-social-media/. Last access 20 Apr 2022

25. Hsu, W.C.: Undergraduate students' online health information-seeking behavior during the COVID-19 pandemic. Int. J. Environ. Res. Public Health **18**(24), 13250 (2021)

26. Gupta, L., Gasparyan, A.Y., Misra, D.P., Agarwal, V., Zimba, O., Yessirkepov, M.: Information and misinformation on COVID-19: a cross-sectional survey study. J. Korean Med. Sci. **35**(27), e256 (2020)

27. Social Media Users: DataReportal. https://datareportal.com/social-media-users. Last Accessed 30 Apr 2022

28. Jurkowitz, M., Mitchell, A.: Americans who primarily get news through social media are least likely to follow COVID-19 coverage, and most likely to report seeing made-up news. Pew Research Center. https://www.pewresearch.org/journalism/2020/03/25/americans-who-primarily-get-news-through-social-media-are-least-likely-to-follow-covid-19-coverage-most-likely-to-report-seeing-made-up-news/. Last accessed 3 March 2022

29. Brooks, I., Agostino, M.D.: Analysis of social media data about COVID-19 in the Americas. https://cdn.who.int/media/docs/default-source/epi-win/presentations-of-all-speeches/webinar-18-sgs-ib-8-april-2020.pdf?sfvrsn=db304bde_2. Last accessed 30 Apr 2022

30. Gottlieb, M., Dyer, S.: Information and disinformation: social media in the COVID-19 crisis. Acad. Emerg. Med. **27**(7), 640–641 (2020)

31. Roozenbeek, J., et al.: Susceptibility to misinformation about COVID-19 around the world. R. Soc. Open Sci. **7**(10), 201199 (2020)

32. Wu, L., Morstatter, F., Carley, K.M., Liu, H.: Misinformation in social media: Definition, manipulation, and detection. ACM SIGKDD Explor. Newsl. **21**(2), 80–90 (2019)

33. Swire-Thompson, B., Lazer, D.: Public health and online misinformation: challenges and recommendations. Annu. Rev. Public Health **41**, 433–451 (2020)

34. Tasnim, S., Hossain, M., Mazumder, H.: Impact of rumors and misinformation on Covid-19 in Social Media. J. Prev. Med. Public Health **53**(3), 171–174 (2020)

35. WHO Novel Coronavirus (2019-nCoV) Situation Report – 13, https://www.who.int/docs/default-source/coronaviruse/situation-reports/20200202-sitrep-13-ncov-v3.pdf. Last accessed 16 Apr 22

36. Hocevar, K.P., Flanagin, A.J., Metzger, M.J.: Social media self-efficacy and information evaluation online. Comput. Hum. Behav. **39**, 254–262 (2014)

37. Ahorsu, D.K., Lin, C.-Y., Imani, V., Saffari, M., Griffiths, M.D., Pakpour, A.H.: The fear of COVID-19 scale: development and initial validation. Int. J. Ment. Health Addict. **20**(3), 1537–1545 (2020)

38. Yang, K.-C., et al.: The COVID-19 infodemic: twitter versus facebook. Big Data & Soc. **8**, 205395172110138 (2021)

39. Yu, M., Li, Z., Yu, Z., He, J., Zhou, J.: Communication related health crisis on social media: a case of COVID-19 outbreak. Curr. Issue Tour. **24**(19), 2699–2705 (2021)
40. MacKay, M., Colangeli, T., Gillis, D., McWhirter, J., Papadopoulos, A.: Examining social media crisis communication during early COVID-19 from public health and news media for quality, content, and corresponding public sentiment. Int. J. Environ. Res. Pub. Health **18**(15), 7986 (2021)
41. Wang, Y., McKee, M., Torbica, A., Stuckler, D.: Systematic review on the spread of health-related misinformation on social media. Soc. Sci. Med. **240**, 112552 (2019)
42. WHO Infodemic: https://www.who.int/health-topics/infodemic/understanding-the-infodemic-and-misinformation-in-the-fight-against-covid-19#tab=tab_1. Last accessed 26 Apr 22

Innovative Solution for Well-being in the Information Society

Classification of Healthcare Robots

Rong Huang[✉] [ID]

University of Turku, Rehtorinpellonkatu 3, Turku, Finland
rong.r.huang@utu.fi

Abstract. With the advancement of artificial intelligence, robots have entered the healthcare field and provided various intelligent services. Compared to the growing number of use cases for healthcare robots, conceptual, and theoretical research on healthcare robots is still in its infancy. There is a need to explore how healthcare robots play different roles in society with the improvement of AI technology. To fill in this research gap, we provide a conceptualization of healthcare robots and a summary of main categories of healthcare robots in previous research. This study provides a classification of healthcare robots according to their service roles and discusses their differences in different dimensions, including appearance, presence, AI and automation ability, and social ability. Finally, we propose future research directions based on the discussion to provide insights into the conceptualization of healthcare robots. This study contributes to IS literature by providing a comprehensive knowledge base for further theory-building processes of AI-based healthcare robots and providing design guidance to robotic designers in specific healthcare fields.

Keywords: Healthcare robots · Artificial intelligence · Classification · Service roles

1 Introduction

The potential impact of robotics combined with artificial intelligence and machine learning on front-line workers in various industries is of great concern to business practitioners. Robots are often thought to perform human-like tasks, and they rely on the success of information technology in artificial intelligence to accomplish these pursuits [1]. In healthcare, robots are helping patients, healthcare professionals, and healthcare systems in various ways to improve people's health and well-being [2, 3]. In the early days, robotic systems in healthcare were commonly used for surgical assistance, diagnosis, prosthetics, and nursing assistance [4]. Advances in the field of artificial intelligence have transformed robotics from passive entities to active entities and agents. Especially since the outbreak of COVID-19, the service role of health robots is rapidly being re-evaluated, starting to be used in more expansive fields such as disinfection, telemedicine, psychotherapy, and companionship [5]. It can be seen that the co-evolution of artificial intelligence will make healthcare robots more integrated into the real world and provide complex services to people. However, there are still many obstacles to be overcome before they can successfully integrate into society.

H. Li et al. (Eds.): WIS 2022, CCIS 1626, pp. 115–123, 2022.
https://doi.org/10.1007/978-3-031-14832-3_8

Studies on healthcare robots have been continuously increasing in the past couple of years. Some studies have investigated how healthcare robots can enhance the health and well-being of consumers [6, 7], their effectiveness [8, 9], and users' perception regarding different healthcare robots [10, 11]. Compared to the growing number of use cases for healthcare robots, conceptual and theoretical research on healthcare robots is still in its infancy. With the continuous development of artificial intelligence technology, how healthcare robots play different roles in society with the improvement of artificial intelligence capabilities has not been fully explored.

To fill in this research gap, we provide a conceptualization of healthcare robots and their main categories with the development of artificial intelligence. Specifically, we classify healthcare robots into three categories based on their service roles in healthcare contexts: healthcare robots as functional tools, healthcare robots as service assistants, and healthcare robots as social colleagues. Then we discussed the differences between the three kinds of healthcare robots from the dimensions of appearance, presence, AI and automation ability, and social ability. This study hopes to provide some insights into the theoretical research of healthcare robots in the context of artificial intelligence and help healthcare managers, designers and employees better understand the design features and service roles of different healthcare robots to adopt and utilize specific healthcare robots.

This paper is organized as follows. The definitions and classifications of healthcare robots in the literature are presented in the background section. Then a classification of healthcare robots is proposed based on social roles in Sect. 3. Finally, the contribution and limitations of this study are highlighted.

2 Background

2.1 Definitions of Healthcare Robots in Literature

The term "robot" has been widely discussed in the research. From a technical perspective, robots are defined as machines capable of performing a complex series of actions, they can make autonomous decisions and adapt to their environment based on data received from various sensors and other sources. With the advancement of artificial intelligence, the development of robots is further encouraged. The Ministry for Health, Labour, and Welfare (MHLW) defines a robot as an intelligent mechanical system with three technical elements of perception, judgment and operation. Perception represents the sensor system, judgment represents the control system, and operation represents the driving system [12]. From a service perspective, a robot is defined in the service industry context as a relatively autonomous physical device capable of moving and performing services. As robots' service roles continue to extend, robots are considered human agents acting in real-world environments [13]. Software agents may be included in some definitions [14].

When robotics enters the healthcare field, various applications and research continue to emerge. Academics are beginning to define healthcare robots in their research. Table 1 summarizes the definitions of healthcare robots in the literature. Some common synonyms for healthcare robots are carebots and nursing robots. It can be seen that the current research mainly discusses the definition of a healthcare robot from two perspectives: function and role. From the functional perspective, a healthcare robot is defined as a robot that can enhance and detect health and assist various tasks related to health [4]. From the perspective of the role, health robots are considered nursing devices that can be used to support users' self-reliance or reduce the burden on caregivers [15].

Considering the complex functions of healthcare robots and various application contexts, we believe that a more flexible definition of healthcare robots is given. In this paper, we define healthcare robots as autonomous or semi-autonomous machines with a certain degree of intelligence that performs various complex tasks in various healthcare contexts.

Table 1. Definitions of healthcare robots in literature.

Definition	Source
A healthcare robot is a robot with the aim of promoting or monitoring health, assisting with tasks that are difficult to perform due to health problems, or preventing further health decline. Health in this sense encompasses not just physical but mental, emotional, and psychosocial problems	[12]
Robots have been proposed as one form of assistive device that can help bridge the widening gap between the need and supply of healthcare services	[13]
Carebots are robots designed for use in homes, hospitals, or other settings to assist, support, or provide care for the sick, disabled, young, elderly, or otherwise vulnerable persons	[14]
Systems are able to perform coordinated mechatronic actions (force or movement exertions) based on processing information acquired through sensor technology to support the functioning of impaired individuals, medical interventions, care, and rehabilitation of patients, and also individuals in prevention programs	[15]
Robots used within the field of healthcare encompass varying degrees of autonomy and broadly include affiliated technology, including sensor systems, algorithms for processing data, and cloud services	[16]
A nursing robot is defined as nursing equipment that has these elements and can be used to support the user to be self-reliant or to reduce the burden of the carer	[17]

2.2 Classifications of Healthcare Robots in Literature

Some taxonomies have been proposed in research to differentiate and classify healthcare robots. Table 2 summarizes some commonly used classifications of healthcare robots in literature. Healthcare robots can be classified according to various dimensions, such as function, task, context, and target users. Given all this evidence, there seems to be no gold standard or taxonomy for which technologies and robotics applications can be included in a particular field of healthcare robotics. Moreover, with the combination of artificial intelligence and robots in healthcare, the service functions, roles, and scenarios of robots in healthcare continue to expand. It is necessary to continuously update and create the classification of healthcare robots based on service perspectives.

Table 2. Classifications of healthcare robots in literature.

Dimension	Category	Source
Function	(a) rehabilitation robots; (b) social robots (service type robots or companionship robots)	[12]
	(a) therapy robots; (b) mental commitment robots; (c) socially assistive robots; (d) surgical assistance robots; (e) robot-assisted telesurgery; (f) rehabilitation robot; (g) robots to aid elderly	[18]
	(a) surgical robots; (b) assistive robots (socially assistive robots or physically assistive robots); (c) healthcare service robots	[19]
Tasks	(a) surgical robots; (b) robots that aid with rehabilitation therapy, help the disabled and cognitively impaired maintain their independence, and motivate people to exercise and lose weight; (c) robots used for telemedicine; (d) robots that deliver meals, medication and laundry in hospitals	[13]
	(a) rehabilitation/prosthetic robots; (b) patient support robots; (c) surgical robots; (d) imaging and navigation robots; (e) decision making robots; (f) bionic robots; (g) automated pharmacy robots	[20]
Target users	(a) doctor healthcare robots; (b) nurse healthcare robots; (c) home healthcare robots	[21]
Medical context	(a) clinical robots; (b) nonclinical robots	[22]

3   The Proposed Classification of Healthcare Robots

Drawing on the recent literature on healthcare robots and the need for robotic service roles in the current healthcare environment, we can develop a classification in which healthcare robots can be differentiated according to different types of service roles. In this paper, we conceptualize healthcare robots as three distinct types: healthcare robots as functional tools, healthcare robots as service assistants, and healthcare robots as social colleagues. This classification attempt to capture the design, technology, and application characteristics of different types of healthcare robots from multiple dimensions, such as appearance, presence, AI and automation capabilities, and social capabilities. Table 3 summarizes the main characteristics of the three kinds of healthcare robots.

3.1   Healthcare Robots as Functional Tools

Healthcare robots as functional tools are the first and most widely used healthcare robots. Robots in this category refer to robots consisting of mechanical aspects used to accomplish some given medical task [23]. At work, they can be in the same physical space as the user, also considered copresence. At the same time, those proxies that appear on a screen or projection as a live video feed are also considered "telepresence" [24]. In terms of AI capabilities, healthcare robots as functional tools are usually non-AI autonomous robots that are programmed to perform repetitive actions to achieve the user's goals until they are deactivated [25]. The decisions they make do not contain uncertainty because

Table 3. The proposed classification of healthcare robots

Type	Healthcare robots as functional tools	Healthcare robots as service assistants	Healthcare robots as social colleagues
Appearance	Mechanical	Mechanical/Humanoid/Animal-like	Humanoid/Animalization/virtual
Presence	Copresence/Telepresence	Copresence	Copresence/Virtual agents
AI and autonomy capability	Non-AI autonomy	AI semi-autonomy	AI pseudo-autonomy
Social capability	Non	Low/mediate	High
Examples	The neuroArm robotic system, the Rex (Robot Exoskeleton)	Healthbot, Charlie	Paro, Pepper, Alice

they are used in a known environment. These robots usually can control their execution entirely autonomously, and the tasks they perform are not complex, so they do not have the ability to learn, reason, and interact [26]. That is to say, this type of robot cannot participate in and maintain various complex social interactions.

Examples include surgical robots, cleaning robots, robotic skeletons, and medication dispensing robots. For example, the neuroArm robotic system has been successfully used in hospitals. It is used in conjunction with real-time magnetic resonance imaging (MRI) to provide surgeons with unprecedented detail and control, allowing them to manipulate tools at the microscopic scale [27]. The robotic system includes two robotic arms, each with six degrees of freedom, and the third arm with two cameras that provide a 3D stereoscopic view. Introduced in 2010 by Rex Bionics, New Zealand, the Rex (Robot Exoskeleton) is a pair of robotic legs that allow users to stand and walk freely, move sideways, turn around, and move their feet up and down, designed to overcome wheelchair movement by restoring the user's ability to walk limit [28]. As robotics becomes more sophisticated and responsive, the use of such robots in the healthcare field continues to increase.

3.2 Healthcare Robots as Service Assistants

This category of healthcare robots refers to robots that act as human assistants to assist in performing various tasks and provide health services in a healthcare environment [13, 29]. AI semi-autonomous healthcare robots can react to their environment and operate without constant supervision to perform more complex tasks [30]. They can change execution according to the context within the set predefined limits to a certain extent. Artificial intelligence provides a mechanism for integrating human-like reasoning and computing power into control systems. They can adjust goal setting within a range, and the types of decisions they make contain low levels of uncertainty because they are context-aware and learn to improve to a certain extent from their experience and user feedback [31]. They can identify, process relevant information about the situation, and make sensible decisions about what to do.

Research has shown an intricate relationship between the anthropomorphic image of a machine and the perceived service value. Healthcare robots of this type are primarily co-occurring while developing from a mechanical appearance to a human-like appearance. For example, some assistive service robots are helping healthcare staff focus on other essential aspects of the hospital by helping patients walk or monitoring their health [32]. Before artificial intelligence and robotics advent, tasks such as helping patients walk, assisting with patient examinations, and taking patient medical histories were manual and time-consuming [33]. Today, however, these tasks can be easily automated and performed quickly by machines. In such situations, staff is often eager to assist the patient rather than perform other tasks. As a result, those assistive robots can aid with activities of daily living (such as heavy lifting and logistics, monitoring, mobility, and safety detection) and basic nursing tasks (such as vital signs measuring and fall detection). At the same time, humans spend more time with patients [34]. With the advancement of technologies such as machine learning, data analysis, and artificial intelligence, healthcare robots will develop as assistants in the service field to complete tasks more autonomously, efficiently, and accurately.

3.3   Healthcare Robots as Social Colleagues

In addition to functional tools and service assistants, there are also healthcare robots as social colleagues. This type of healthcare robot is designed to attempt to act as a healthcare professional colleague, providing services to end-users in the roles of doctor, therapist, navigator, personal caregiver, and friend [35, 36]. They serve users in a healthcare setting by engaging and maintaining social interactions with humans. They can interact with humans and the physical environment in a virtual or copresence manner [34]. A high degree of humanization and animalization is a trend, and some virtual agents are also included. Such AI pseudo-autonomy robots can self-organize, that is, construct their means and laws of operation to achieve satisfactory performance without experience and compensate for system failures without external control [34]. They assume interactive elements in non-deterministic systems and are able to interact with other objects, process information, evaluate alternatives, and thus make decisions on their own [37].

This type of healthcare robot is mainly in the research and development stage. These AI-based intelligent robots can perform operations and augment the work of physicians with specific diagnostics and treatment methods, reduce cost and time, and improve response time to patient needs when healthcare personnel is unavailable [38]. For example, the humanoid robot Zora has been used in public elderly care services in Lahti, Finland, for rehabilitation and recreational assistance with exercise, playing music, performing dances, story-telling, and playing interactive memory and guessing games [39]. Patients suffering from depression and other mental illnesses have gained comfort, pleasure, calmness, and approachability in the robotic experience [40]. In dementia treatment, an animal-like robot called Paro could alleviate the behavioral and psychological symptoms of dementia like anxiety, agitation, and depression and provide distraction and interrupt problematic behaviors [41]. Therefore, healthcare services are no longer an isolated silo of healthcare personnel. The advancement of artificial intelligence will significantly expand the application of robots in different healthcare contexts. This trend is expected to accelerate in the future.

4 Conclusion

With the advancement of artificial intelligence, a large number of healthcare robots have been invented and entered the market. However, only a few of these devices are widely accepted to coexist in the human environment. In this paper, we classify healthcare robots according to their service roles and clarify the differences in design character- istics between the different categories identified, adding to the existing knowledge and conceptual understanding of different types of healthcare robots. This classification can provide a comprehensive knowledge base for further theory-building processes of AI- based healthcare robots and provide design guidance to robotic designers in specific healthcare fields. At the same time, in terms of practical contribution, this classifica- tion may help practitioners understand the status quo of the development of healthcare robots and promote the development of healthcare robots in specific fields. In our future research, we hope to build a clearer and more consistent conceptual framework con- sidering the robot's design features, functions, technology, service scenarios, and other aspects.

This paper discusses the limited characteristics of healthcare robots that may limit our comprehensive understanding of healthcare robots. It is necessary to consider different dimensions such as the design features, functions, technologies, and service scenarios of robots to build a clearer and more consistent conceptual framework. At the same time, advances in AI technology are breaking down the boundaries of healthcare, well- being, and life itself [37]. In the future, a comprehensive conceptual understanding of intelligent health robots should be constructed from a more comprehensive and dynamic perspective.

References

1. Balistreri, M., Casile, F.: Care Robots: From Tools of Care to Training Opportunities. Moral Considerations, vol. 1008, pp. 18–25. Springer Verlag, Department of Philosophy and Educational Sciences, University of Turin, Turin, Italy (2020)
2. Bogue, R.: Robots in healthcare. Industrial Robot **38**, 218–223 (2011)
3. Kriegel, J., Rissbacher, C., Reckwitz, L., Tuttle-Weidinger, L.: The requirements and appli- cations of autonomous mobile robotics (AMR) in hospitals from the perspective of nursing officers. Int. J. Healthcare Manag. **15**, 204–210 (2021)
4. Holland, J., et al.: Service robots in the healthcare sector. Robotics **10**, 1–47 (2021)
5. Freeman, W.D., et al.: Robotics in simulated COVID-19 patient room for health care worker effector tasks: preliminary, feasibility experiments. Mayo Clin. Proc. Innov. Qual. Outcomes **5**, 161–170 (2021)
6. González-González, C.S., Violant-Holz, V., Gil-Iranzo, R.M.: Social robots in hospitals: a systematic review. Appl. Sci. (Switzerland) **11** (2021)
7. Sciarretta, E., Alimenti, L.: Wellbeing Technology: Beyond Chatbots, vol. 1034, pp. 514–519. Springer Verlag, Link Campus University, Via del Casale di S. Pio V, 44, Rome, 00165, Italy (2019)

8. Manca, M., Paternò, F., Santoro, C., Zedda, E., Braschi, C., Franco, R., Sale, A.: The impact of serious games with humanoid robots on mild cognitive impairment older adults. Int. J. Human Comput. Stud. **145**, 1–21 (2021)
9. Achit, H., et al.: Cost-effectiveness of four living-donor nephrectomy techniques from a hospital perspective. Nephrol. Dial. Transplant. **35**, 2004–2012 (2020)
10. Scerri, A., Sammut, R., Scerri, C.: Formal caregivers' perceptions and experiences of using pet robots for persons living with dementia in long-term care: a meta-ethnography. J. Adv. Nurs. **77**, 83–97 (2021)
11. Alimardani, M., Qurashi, S.: Mind Perception of a Sociable Humanoid Robot: A Comparison Between Elderly and Young Adults, vol. 1093 AISC, pp. 96–108. Springer, Department of Cognitive Science and AI, Tilburg University, Tilburg, Netherlands (2020)
12. Robinson, H., MacDonald, B.A., Broadbent, E.: The role of healthcare robots for older people at home: a review. Int. J. Soc. Robot. **6**, 575–591 (2014)
13. Broadbent, E., Stafford, R., MacDonald, B.: Acceptance of healthcare robots for the older population: review and future directions. Int. J. Soc. Robot. **1**, 319–330 (2009)
14. Vallor, S.: Carebots and caregivers: sustaining the ethical ideal of care in the twenty-first century. Philos. Technol. **24**, 251–268 (2011)
15. Fosch-Villaronga, E., Felzmann, H., Ramos-Montero, M., Mahler, T.: Cloud services for robotic nurses? Assessing legal and ethical issues in the use of cloud services for healthcare robots. In: 2018 IEEE/RSJ International Conference on Intelligent Robots and Systems (IROS), pp. 290–296. IEEE (2018)
16. Riek, L.D.: Healthcare robotics. Commun. ACM **60**, 68–78 (2017)
17. Yasuhara, Y., et al.: Potential legal issues when caring healthcare robot with communication in caring functions are used for older adult care. Enferm. Clin. **30**(Suppl 1), 54–59 (2020)
18. Khan, A., Anwar, Y.: Robots in healthcare: a survey. In: Science and Information Conference, pp. 280–292. Springer (2019)
19. Fosch-Villaronga, E., Drukarch, H.: On healthcare robots: concepts, definitions, and considerations for healthcare robot governance. arXiv preprint arXiv:2106.03468 (2021)
20. Schweikard, A., Ernst, F.: Medical Robotics. Springer (2015)
21. Hughes, R.: Patient Safety and Quality: An Evidence-Based Handbook for Nurses (2008)
22. Mettler, T., Sprenger, M., Winter, R.: Service robots in hospitals: new perspectives on niche evolution and technology affordances. Eur. J. Inf. Syst. **26**, 451–468 (2017)
23. Chien, W.t., Chong, Y.y., Tse, M.k., Chien, C.w., Cheng, H.y.: Robot-assisted therapy for upper-limb rehabilitation in subacute stroke patients: a systematic review and meta-analysis. Brain Behav. **10**, 1–16 (2020)
24. Li, J.: The benefit of being physically present: a survey of experimental works comparing copresent robots, telepresent robots and virtual agents. Int. J. Human Comput. Stud. **77**, 23–37 (2015)
25. Gade, V.R., Soni, A., Rajaram, B., Seth, D.: Semi-Autonomous Collaborative Mobile Platform with Pre-diagnostics for Hospitals, vol. 12198, LNCS, pp. 402–414. Springer, Mahindra Ecole Centrale, 1A, Survey No: 62, Bahadurpally, Hyderabad, Telangana 500043, India (2020)
26. Parisi, G.I., Wermter, S.: A Neurocognitive Robot Assistant for Robust Event Detection, vol. 633, pp. 1–27. Springer Verlag, Department of Informatics, Knowledge Technology, University of Hamburg, Vogt-Koelln-Strasse 30, Hamburg, 22527, Germany (2016)
27. Bogue, R.: Robot ethics and law: part one: ethics. Industrial Robot **41**, 335–339 (2014)
28. Hall, A.K., et al.: Acceptance and perceived usefulness of robots to assist with activities of daily living and healthcare tasks. Assist. Technol. Official J. RESNA **31**, 133–140 (2019)
29. Nestorov, N., Stone, E., Lehane, P., Eibrand, R.: Aspects of socially assistive robots design for dementia care. In: 27th IEEE International Symposium on Computer-Based Medical Systems, pp. 396–400. Institute of Electrical and Electronics Engineers Inc. (2014)

30. Shafi, P.M., Jawalkar, G.S., Kadam, M.A., Ambawale, R.R., Bankar, S.V.: AI—Assisted Chatbot for E-Commerce to Address Selection of Products from Multiple Products, vol. 266, pp. 57–80. Springer, Department of Computer Engineering, Smt. Kashibai Navale College of Engineering, Pune, India (2020)

31. Preum, S.M.M., et al.: A review of cognitive assistants for healthcare: trends, prospects, and future directions. ACM Comput. Surv. **53** (2021)

32. Saadatzi, M.N.M.N., et al.: Acceptability of using a robotic nursing assistant in health care environments: experimental pilot study. J. Med. Internet Res. **22**, 1–7 (2020)

33. Rantanen, T., Lehto, P., Vuorinen, P., Coco, K.: The adoption of care robots in home care—A survey on the attitudes of Finnish home care personnel. J. Clin. Nurs. **27**, 1846–1859 (2018)

34. Pee, L.G., Pan, S.L., Cui, L.: Artificial intelligence in healthcare robots: a social informatics study of knowledge embodiment. J. Assoc. Inf. Sci. Technol. **70**, 351–369 (2019)

35. Rossi, S., Dell'Aquila, E., Bucci, B.: Evaluating the emotional valence of affective sounds for child-robot interaction. In: Salichs, M.A., et al. (eds.) ICSR 2019. LNAI, vol. 11876, pp. 505–514. Springer, Cham (2019). https://doi.org/10.1007/978-3-030-35888-4_47

36. Martinez-Martin, E., Escalona, F., Cazorla, M.: Socially assistive robots for older adults and people with autism: an overview. Electronics **9**(2) (2020)

37. Yoon, S.N., Lee, D.: Artificial intelligence and robots in healthcare: what are the success factors for technology-based service encounters? Int. J. Health. Manag. **12**, 218–225 (2019)

38. Murphy, K., et al.: Artificial intelligence for good health: a scoping review of the ethics literature. BMC Med. Ethics **22**, 14–14 (2021)

39. Kort, H., Huisman, C.: Care robot ZORA in Dutch nursing homes; an evaluation study. Stud. Health Technol. Inform. **242**, 527–534 (2017)

40. Cheng, Y., Jiang, H.: AI-Powered mental health chatbots: examining users' motivations, active communicative action and engagement after mass-shooting disasters. J. Conting. Crisis Manag. **28**, 339–354 (2020)

41. Wagemaker, E., Dekkers, T.J., Agelink van Rentergem, J.A., Volkers, K.M., Huizenga, H.M.: Advances in mental health care: five N = 1 studies on the effects of the robot seal Paro in adults with severe intellectual disabilities. J. Ment. Health Res. Intellect. Disabil. **10**, 309–320 (2017)

Digital Solutions for the Marginalised in Society: A Review of Systems to Address Homelessness and Avenues for Further Research

Michael Oduor[1,2](✉) 🆔

[1] Institute of Rehabilitation, JAMK University of Applied Sciences, Jyväskylä, Finland
`michael.oduor@oulu.fi`, `michael.oduor@jamk.fi`
[2] OASIS Research Unit, Faculty of Information Technology and Electronic Engineering, University of Oulu, Oulu, Finland

Abstract. The use of technology to access information and other services is increasingly seen as an integral element to enhance participation in society. Recent years have seen an increase in research focusing on information and communication technologies for marginalised groups such as those experiencing homelessness. With reports of increasing levels of homelessness in Europe and beyond, an understanding of the current literature exploring how information and communication technologies are used to address homelessness and how this may impact the well-being of the homeless is of relevance to policymakers and social service organisations. This research aims to address this by investigating the use of digital solutions to serve those experiencing homelessness. The study explored and synthesised peer-reviewed literature to understand the use of technology to address homelessness. Preliminary findings highlight perceptions and use of various technologies among homeless people and the communication patterns of the homeless. Overall, the research shows how technology enables the homeless to access information and services and why it is important for vulnerable groups to be socially and digitally connected.

Keywords: Marginalisation · Homelessness · Digital inclusion · Information and communication technologies

1 Introduction

The marginalised are those whose position in the society is weak, are drawn towards the dark sides of society and are excluded from everyday societal interactions which limits their access to economic, social and political resources [1]. These could include the homeless, low-income communities, those living in underserved areas amongst others as outlined in the special issue discussing the role of information and communication technology (ICT) in addressing major societal challenges [2]. Those in marginalised situations face significant barriers and inequities in entitlement as they go through unfamiliar environments and situations in which they need to construct meaningful lives [3, 4]. Communication difficulties, low health literacy, lack of social support and other

H. Li et al. (Eds.): WIS 2022, CCIS 1626, pp. 124–139, 2022.
https://doi.org/10.1007/978-3-031-14832-3_9

forms of socioeconomic problems adversely affect the capacity of the marginalised to successfully navigate complex and changing health and social care systems [4]. The use of ICT by marginalised groups provides an opportunity to study how certain ICT-mediated activities can contribute to their social inclusion. Not being able to access, interpret, and use relevant informational resources may exclude them and push them further to the margins of society [3].

The advancement of ICT has led to a hyperconnected world characterized by immediate access to information, institutions, and people. The multi-modality of technology–the ability to combine text, image, audio and video–not only satisfies the communication needs of marginalised groups, but is also useful for establishing and promoting a sense of community [5, 6]. Digital solutions have become effective means to create opportunities for all, to further individual autonomy and individual ability to use technology to access public services. Digital solutions have the potential to improve people's lives and achieving a more inclusive information society is one of the key ambitions of information society policy. A society that is open, inclusive and accessible to all citizens [7, 8]. The central place of IT in this digital world creates a need to investigate the part IT plays in determining the extent to which people can participate in a hyperconnected society [5].

There is already sufficient confirmation of societal disparities, which could perhaps be ameliorated by the use of ICTs [1, 2, 9]. This requires the scientific community and other stakeholders to investigate ways to empower citizens by developing the tools and approaches to bridge the gap between civil society and decision-makers [8, 10]. Becoming empowered can be a big step for people who have been constantly devalued. Changing their state of affairs and fueling their willingness to act requires development of initiatives focused on promoting users' resources for participation [11].

This preliminary research aims to address this by investigating the use of digital solutions to address the needs of the homeless. There has been an increase in research focusing on homelessness and technology (see [12, 13]). And with the number of homeless increasing,[1] there is a pressing need for more research on how housing policies supported by ICT can be used to address short and long-term challenges of homelessness. This research has the following underpinnings: the increasing problem of homelessness represents a unique, urgent, and poorly understood challenge with the potential for many technological solutions. There needs to be an in-depth understanding of the unique design challenges posed by those who are homeless [12]. Especially, as the information needs of the marginalised in society are multi-faceted, difficult to ascertain, and much more complex than assumed by stakeholders [14]. Therefore, the main research question is: *What kinds of digital solutions are used to address the challenges the homeless face?* This question seeks to understand the use of technology to address some of the challenges the homeless face in the context of information systems.

The rest of the paper is organized as follows. First, we present the theoretical background about the homeless and use of digital solutions for homelessness. Second, we outline the review process. Third, the results of the review are presented. Lastly, we present the conclusion and avenues for further research.

---

[1] Here's how Finland solved its homelessness problem.

2 Background

2.1 Defining Homelessness

How homelessness should be defined is a fundamental and persistent problem and it remains an enduring social issue which has been analysed and interpreted from a wide range of theoretical and practical disciplines [15, 16]. A robust definition of homelessness is necessary to produce meaningful statistics on the size and characteristics of homeless populations, which are of critical importance for informed policymaking. The definition is useful if it allows for accurate and reliable identification and classification of homeless people so that policies can be developed to respond to different manifestations of homelessness and monitor the effectiveness of such interventions [15].

There is a general consensus within the literature that being homeless is more than just being without a home. It is a consequence of a set of individual, systematic and structural factors that impact those affected [17, 18]. Homelessness can be characterized by marginalisation, social exclusion and a lack of opportunity for meaningful activity [18]. People who experience homelessness are profoundly impacted by social exclusion. Homelessness may be understood "*as a set of consequences that arise when social exclusion occurs in a context within which little or no assistance is given to those who experience it*" and individuals are left to fend for themselves in an environment that does little to support them [17]. Homelessness represents a lack of access to adequate housing and there are different degrees of homelessness, including rough sleeping (primary homelessness); living in temporary or transitional accommodation with uncertain tenancy (secondary homelessness); and marginal housing with poor amenities or over-crowding (tertiary homelessness) [18].

2.2 Digital Solutions for Homelessness

Within a context where our societies are increasingly and rapidly digitalised, access to services and goods will transform, thus affecting our societies.[2] As ICTs are seen as having the potential to alter how social, political, and economic relations are played out, they are a useful resource to promote participation in society [3, 9]. The concept of exclusion also features prominently in the information society discourse where access to and knowledge of ICTs are portrayed as either exacerbating exclusion or seen as a platform to create inclusiveness [9]. Access to digital resources can promote social inclusion, and digital inclusion for all is tasked with creating opportunities for everyone and enhancing individual autonomy and capability. The main objective is to remove obstacles in the widest sense for equitable participation in society [7, 8].

A growing body of work in information systems, human computer interaction and social sciences research is calling for an in-depth understanding of the needs of people who are homeless or at risk of becoming homeless (see the list of reviewed articles in Table 2). Recent research also suggests that the homeless are increasingly tech-savvy and technologies are becoming ubiquitous element in the lives of individuals experiencing homelessness [12, 13, 19].

---

[2] FEANTSA – Digital Inclusion and Homelessness.

In a study investigating mobile phone use among the homeless, Eyrich-Garg [19], found that a significant proportion of the sample they interviewed had a mobile phone. Mobile phones make communication and access to one's social support network easier for homeless individuals which could, in turn, lead to better health outcomes. Technology could also be used to enhance communication between the homeless and healthcare providers [19]. And the research by Eyrich-Garg [19] suggests that service providers and researchers should consider incorporating mobile phones into their prevention, intervention, aftercare, and data collection efforts as electronic connectivity could be important in addressing the challenges faced by this vulnerable population.

Sala and Mignone [13] found a positive relationship between ICT use among individuals experiencing homelessness and health outcomes. Greater access to information and social connectedness supposedly gained through ICTs may improve the health and social outcomes of individuals experiencing homelessness. However, the evidence was inconclusive, and little is known about the ways in which these populations utilise or leverage ICTs for their own benefit. In the analysis of users' perceptions of an application designed for the homeless, Burrows et al. [12], found seven themes relevant for the design of technology for those experiencing homelessness. These included: empowerment and control, hopefulness, assurance, cared for, identify and belonging, clarity and being unashamed. That is, the extent to which technology supported individuals to access critical services, to develop a sense of belonging, gain a sense of clarity, feel empowered, appreciated and independent [12]. These are similar to the main themes that emerged from Sala and Mignone's [13] review: social connectedness, identity management and instrumental purposes.

3   Research Method

Using technology to access information and other services is increasingly seen as an integral element to enhance participation in society and to address social exclusion [3, 9]. As digital solutions have become increasingly ubiquitous mechanisms for maintaining and building social relationships, and for instrumental purposes, the relevance of ICTs and the benefits or potential harms of their use is a subject area of increasing interest [13]. Thus, the present article aims to investigate use of digital solutions to address the endemic problem of homelessness. The main question is: *What kinds of digital solutions are used to address the challenges the homeless face?* To answer this question, the author undertook a search of peer reviewed literature to understand how ICT is being used to address these challenges.

Literature reviews are an appropriate method to systematically and critically assess the state of research on a particular topic and they help to understand the phenomenon as a whole, its meaning and its relationships [20]. The review process is driven by scholars' need to report progress in a particular area of research. There are reviews on mature topics and those on emerging issues that would benefit from exposure to new theoretical foundations to develop agendas for future research [21]. The present review focused on the latter. The study maps out and categorises existing literature about digital solutions to address homelessness [22].

Even though the search was broad, the focus was on studies that examined use of technology by the homeless themselves, those technologies that are/could be used by service providers to address the needs of the homeless and/or both. As in [13], no specific typologies of homelessness were examined in this study. Publications which only mentioned homeless as a term amongst others, often without context or relation to technology use, were excluded from further review. The review focused on primary studies that were published in peer-reviewed academic journals and conference proceedings, excluding, for example, editorials, reviews, white papers, books, (unpublished) dissertations, and working papers. This was done to ensure consistency between the studies.

To identify relevant academic sources, we conducted electronic searches for the years between 2006 and 2019 in several academic databases (ProQuest, EBSCOhost (Academic Search Ultimate), ACM, ScienceDirect, Springer and Web of Science). The search was conducted using combinations of the following search terms:

(homeless*) AND (technolog* OR communication technolog*) OR.
("digital inclusion" OR e-inclusion).

Applying the criteria above, the search resulted in 198 articles. After removing duplicates, the author selected publications based on their relevance by reading the titles and abstract. This resulted in 32 articles presented in Table 1.

Table 1. Results of literature search

Database	Hits	Relevant	References
ProQuest	3	0	n/a
EBSCOhost	36	8	[23–30]
ACM	47	12	[31–43]
ScienceDirect	21	5	[44–49]
Springer	62	2	[50, 51]
Web of Science	29	5	[51–55]

4   Results

In the retrieved articles, digital solutions for homelessness were applied to different user groups and in different environments. The articles identified the widespread use of ICTs amongst homeless populations as in [13] and [19]. Overall, the articles analysed access to ICT, perceptions and use of various ICTs among homeless people, compared technology

Table 2. Summary of analysed articles

Author(s), objective	Method, subjects	Findings
[23], Investigate the association between social media use and HIV risk behaviours among homeless youth	Survey conducted in 4 waves, N = 1,046	Reinforced earlier studies that found homeless youth actively use social media to communicate about a range of issues
[24], Empower women by engaging them into a self-learning model	Interviews and observations, women (16–60) at a shelter home	Access to the learning system shaped the participants' interests towards using computers
[25], Examine the potential of mHealth interventions among homeless youth to improve access to health information and services	Mixed method, focus group, N = 52, structured survey, N = 41	Mobile coverage was high, but many had challenges in maintaining connectivity. Mobile phones were useful in obtaining social support
[26], Explore the engagement of homeless drug users (HDUs) with ICT	Qualitative (Interviews) longitudinal, initial N = 30, follow-up N = 22	HDUs often had access to ICTs, used ICTs, and wanted to engage with them more
[27], Improve outcomes for homeless individuals by producing research to enhance homeless services delivery	Case study of university-community partnership that implement a homeless management IS	The study demonstrates how partnerships, innovative technology delivery and social work research can reduce homelessness
[28], Investigate the impact of including technology into operations for a program addressing chronic homelessness	Case study, interviews, N = 133	By adding technology enhancement, the program was also able to expand its ability to provide reliable and responsive support

(*continued*)

Table 2. (*continued*)

Author(s), objective	Method, subjects	Findings
[29, 30, 34, 35, 37, 45, 54, 55] Analyse access to and perceptions of technology and use of various ICTs among homeless people in Madrid [29] and youths in different cities in the United States [48], compare technology use between college students and young homeless adults [52], Identify and reveal the digital communication patterns and experiences of the homeless	Structured interview, N = 188 [29]. Retrospective interview, N = 100 [30]. Participant observation, semi-structured interviews, N = 39 [34]. Observation and interviews N = 34 (Age 13–25) [35]. Qualitative (photo elicitation interview, and Interviews), N = 13 [37]. Interview, N = 100 [45]. Survey, N = 303, [48]. Mixed methods, N = 65 [52]. Survey, N = 201 [54]	Reinforce the importance of mobile phones when homeless. ICTs are used to varying degree among the homeless. Technology use is linked to collaborative practices, social connectedness, business purposes (job and housing search), and for leisure. Digital divide has a negative impact on some marginalised populations, and it is important to bridge the gap between what people know and what they need to know
[31], Investigate housing assignment among homeless youth. [33], to devise an optimal strategy to minimise violence among the youth	Develop and test an algorithm for assigning youth to housing programs. Develop a model to capture non-progressive diffusion of violence N = n/a	The algorithm was effective in assigning youth to housing and it can be deployed as a core algorithm for an intelligent agent, studies indicated the strategy outperformed those based on centrality measures
[32], Investigate how the challenges associated with homelessness impact security and privacy practices and needs	Semi-structured interviews, N = 18	Based on themes from interviews, provided a framework to support the homeless and other marginalised groups
[36], Examine challenges faced in deployment of two agents for social influence maximization, which assist service providers in maximizing HIV awareness in real-world homeless-youth social network	Pilot study (survey for analysis), N = 173	Instructive challenges and proposed solutions for assisting the deployment of agents to assist service providers in optimising their intervention strategies

(*continued*)

Table 2. (*continued*)

Author(s), objective	Method, subjects	Findings
[38], Report on the adoption and use of a community resource manager for staff and residents at a shelter for homeless mothers	Qualitative (focus groups, interviews) and ethnographic observation, N = 25	Innovative technologies can open new lines of communication between the homeless and their care providers, leading to more efficient and frequent communications, better coordination, and improved awareness of resources and needs
[39], Explore issues of technology adoption and coordination in non-profit homeless outreach centres	Qualitative (observations = 53 h, interviews), N = 15	Non-profit organisations that can develop better integration of ICTs and a strong community of practice are better positioned to provide coordinated care to some of the most vulnerable members of society
[40], Study and compare the value expression in Tweets by the homeless. [43], examine patterns of follow relationships on Twitter	Quantitative content analysis, N = 32 [40] Quantitative content analysis (cluster analysis and visualisation), N = 476 [43]	Values are expressed both implicitly and explicitly through opinions, judgments, and sarcastic statements and a broad range of individuals used Twitter for self-advocacy and connectedness as they experienced homelessness
[41], Explores how to support the homeless and other marginalised communities to connect with each other and social services online	Quantitative content analysis, N = 32	Methods for identifying values and several implications for considering values in online communities as a first step in the design of ICTs

(*continued*)

Table 2. (*continued*)

Author(s), objective	Method, subjects	Findings
[42], To reflect on fieldwork from case studies of severe life disruptions such as homelessness and share sketches that depict the lived reality of finding a "new normal"	Case studies	Extend existing understanding of technology use during the performance of daily living and show how technology can be used to mitigate the consequences of disruptive life events
[44], Understand how technology may be used to better engage homeless youth in case management	4 interviews (baseline, 1-week, 6-week, and 3-month follow-up), N = 97 (Age 18–21)	Technology holds promising implications for effectively engaging and retaining homeless youth in case management services
[46] Report on the development and findings of a curriculum to develop homeless youth's life skills for technology and digital media	Descriptive case study, N >75	Education in information technology and digital media can create an engaging setting for learning skills and building relationships useful for escaping homelessness
[47], Investigate the feasibility of using cell phones to collect ecological momentary assessment (EMA) data with homeless crack cocaine-addicted adults treated in an intensive outpatient treatment program	Quantitative (survey), N = 30 Participants received automated calls daily for 14 consecutive days	The usefulness of EMA as potential intervention and suitability of mobile phones as a reliable survey tool
[49], Investigate where sustainable financial resource for ICT programs can be obtained and address key elements affecting the adoption of the Internet by the homeless and underserved in Taiwan	Descriptive case study	Practical solutions for financial problems and a foundation for comparative analyses of the relevance of organizational structures to integrate people at the bottom of the pyramid into e-society and reduce poverty

(*continued*)

Table 2. (*continued*)

Author(s), objective	Method, subjects	Findings
[50], Understand the meaning, experience, and design of ICTs to improve the welfare of young homeless people	Design research	Precautions and suggestions of how and when to intervene with ICT when addressing problems caused by homelessness
[51] Examine the implications for Australians experiencing homelessness of data use necessitated by large-scale digitisation of government services and other everyday interactions	Multiple triangulation study	Digital inclusion approaches have not sufficiently addressed the digital harms that come about through digital participation, and there is a need to focus on exposing and countering these
[53] To investigate how socio-technical systems help homeless young people to succeed broadly in employment	Value-sensitive design, focus groups, N = 28	Barrier and possible solutions to employment for homeless young people. Design insights for a socio-technical system for job search

use between the homeless and other groups in the population and the communication patterns of the homeless (Table 2).

The articles addressed how technology could support the concerns of homeless women [42], the youth [30, 54] those suffering from HIV [33, 36], and how algorithms could be deployed to autonomously manage household assignments of youths subject to resource constraints [31] amongst other related topics addressing the challenges of homelessness.

Seven of the studies highlighted the importance of mobile communication and reported on the levels of mobile phone usage by the homeless. In the study by Massimi et al. [42] investigating the role of technology in life disruptions, they learned that a staff shelter for homeless mothers could extend their reach by providing facilities to encourage mobile communication as the shelter was only open at night. The homeless mothers were already coping with information overload and helping them restore order and timing to the information they received would help them make better use of resources [42]. Dependence on smartphones for access to information and communication when homeless, in combination with the design and regulation of urban spaces, structures the mobilities of homeless young people, resulting in distinctive connectivity needs and barriers [51]. The research by Humphry [51] revealed how those experiencing homelessness are resourceful at getting their digital needs meet.

Le Dantec et al. [37] reported 76% of participants owned a mobile phone in their study investigating the use of a system that integrated a shared display, the Web and mobile phones to help the residents and staff at a shelter stay connected. The system became a stable medium for sharing information that helped the staff be more effective and helped the residents feel more connected. As a summary regarding the use of mobile technologies among the homeless, they are an essential means for maintaining contact with peers and they open up new lines of communication with their care providers leading to more efficient and frequent communications, better coordination, and improved awareness of resources and needs [38].

Other articles investigated the expression of values through opinions, judgements and sarcastic comments and self-identity in online social networks [40, 41, 55]. This research highlighted the range of homelessness characteristics displayed in online biographies and the perception of users on helpfulness (as it relates to social connectedness [19]) and wealth. Although these studies focused on online social environments, they resulted in similar themes as those in [12, 13] which studied user values and emotions. The studies also highlighted the importance of online social networks as avenues for social participation for the homeless that helps them to develop and maintain social ties and stave away their sense of alienation from society [55].

The nature of ICT utilization by individuals experiencing homelessness is often dependent on individual factors such as mental health, addiction histories, pre-existing social factors, and time spent homeless [13, 35, 37]. Although mostly beneficial, increasingly digitalized societies also bare challenges and can negatively affect people's lives. Digital engagement brings both a cost and responsibility shift to citizens, especially those already on the fringes of society, who face unique, urgent and poorly understood problems that some do not have the resources or skills to address [56, 57]. Some of these challenges, associated with financial security, can limit the inclusivity of technology design [32]. Therefore, developers of technology need to understand that digital inclusion of the vulnerable may take time and prioritize the issues that can limit inclusion [32].

5 Conclusions and Further Research

The use of technology to tackle societal challenges has been receiving increased attention, however, there is still a need for research on how technology can be used to benefit different marginalised groups. The concrete measures that effectively promote social inclusion and what the marginalised are actually able to do and achieve with ICTs [3, 6]. To this end, the author reviewed the literature to understand the research on digital inclusion for those experiencing homelessness.

Due to its preliminary nature, this research has a few limitations. First, forward, and backward searches were not conducted, thereby limiting the scope of the research. It also lacks the synthesis and analysis of a structured review [22]. Second, the review results are only up to date as of December 2019. Third, more information systems literature on digital and social inclusion and ICT4D should be covered in more detail. However, this might be challenging due to the multidisciplinary research question posed in the current study and the multidisciplinary nature of information systems [21]. There are plans to carry out more in-depth reviews of literature that covers the key goals of ICT, stakeholder requirements, outcomes of interventions and the effectiveness of ICT in supporting integration processes, which the retrieved articles did not adequately address.

Additional research is also needed to identify and compare the effects and outcomes ICT tools may have in bridging the gap for digital and social inclusion among homeless people and other vulnerable groups.[3] There are further plans to conduct surveys and interviews to better understand stakeholders' concerns and their perceptions of digital solutions for inclusion.

After getting a clearer understanding of the stakeholders' needs, existing digital interventions and defining the key goals of these interventions, the research will propose concrete solutions for implementing digital solutions to serve the needs of the homeless and other marginalised groups. The proposed solutions will highlight the following issues:

1. That the addressed problems apply to the marginalised
2. Development of the intervention(s) involves the marginalised
3. The marginalised have the capabilities to use these interventions and
4. The interventions have a beneficial effect on the livelihoods of the marginalised

Acknowledgements. The author acknowledges grant support from KAUTE Foundation and thanks Dr. Rachel Burrows for preliminary discussions that inspired this article.

References

1. Sam, S.: Exploring mobile internet use among marginalised young people in post-conflict Sierra Leone. Electron. J. Inf. Syst. Dev. Countries. **66**, 1–20 (2015). https://doi.org/10.1002/j.1681-4835.2015.tb00475.x
2. Majchrzark, A., Markus, M.L., Wareham, J.: Designing for digital transformation: lessons for information systems research from the study of ICT and societal challenges. MIS Q. **40**, 267–278 (2016)
3. Andrade, A.D., Doolin, B.: Information and communication technology and the social inclusion of refugees. MIS Q. **40**, 405–416 (2016). https://doi.org/10.25300/MISQ/2016/40.2.06.
4. O'Donnell, C.A., et al.: Reducing the health care burden for marginalised migrants: the potential role for primary care in Europe. Health Pol. **120**, 495–508 (2016). https://doi.org/10.1016/j.healthpol.2016.03.012
5. Carter, M., Armstrong, D.J., Lee, A.S., Loiacono, E.T., Thatcher, J.B.: Social inclusion in a hyperconnected world. In: 19th Americas Conference on Information Systems, AMCIS 2013 – Hyperconnected World: Anything, Anywhere, Anytime, vol. 4, pp. 3011–3013 (2013)

---

[3] FEANTSA.

6. AbuJarour, S., Krasnova, H.: Understanding the role of ICTs in promoting social inclusion: the case of Syrian refugees in Germany. In: Proceedings of the 25th European Conference on Information Systems, ECIS 2017, pp. 1792–1806 (2017)
7. Almuwil, A., Weerakkody, V., El-Haddadeh, R.: A conceptaul study of the factors influencing e-inclusion. In: Proceedings of the European, Mediterranean and Middle Eastern Conference on Information Systems – Informing Responsible Management: Sustainability in Emerging Economies, EMCIS 2011, pp. 198–209 (2011)
8. Weerakkody, V., Dwivedi, Y.K., El-Haddadeh, R., Almuwil, A., Ghoneim, A.: Conceptualizing e-inclusion in Europe: an explanatory study. Inf. Syst. Manag. **29**, 305–320 (2012). https://doi.org/10.1080/10580530.2012.716992
9. Trauth, E.M., Howcroft, D.: Social inclusion and the information systems field: why now? IFIP Int. Federation Inf. Process. **208**, 3–12 (2006). https://doi.org/10.1007/0-387-34588-4_1
10. Wolske, M., Williams, N.S., Johnson, E.O., Noble, S.U., Duple, R.Y.: Effective ICT Use for Social Inclusion. iConference 2010 (2010)
11. de Freitas, C., Martin, G.: Inclusive public participation in health: policy, practice and theoretical contributions to promote the involvement of marginalised groups in healthcare. Soc. Sci. Med. **135**, 31–39 (2015). https://doi.org/10.1016/j.socscimed.2015.04.019
12. Burrows, R., Mendoza, A., Sterling, L., Miller, T., Pedell, S.: Evaluating ask Izzy: a mobile web app for people experiencing homelessness. In: Proceedings of the 17th European Conference on Computer-Supported Cooperative Work: The International Venue on Practice-centred Computing and the Design of Cooperation Technologies - Exploratory Papers, Reports of the European Society for Socially Embedde (2019). https://doi.org/10.18420/ecscw2019_ep17
13. Sala, A., Mignone, J.: The benefits of information communication technology use by the homeless: a narrative synthesis review. J. Soc. Distress Homeless. **23**, 51–67 (2014). https://doi.org/10.1179/1573658x14y.0000000006
14. Mervyn, K., Simon, A., Allen, D.K.: Digital inclusion and social inclusion: a tale of two cities. Inf. Commun. Soc. **17**, 1086–1104 (2014). https://doi.org/10.1080/1369118X.2013.877952
15. Amore, K., Baker, M., Howden-Chapman, P.: The ETHOS definition and classification of homelessness: an analysis. Eur. J. Homelessness. **5**, 19–37 (2011)
16. Anderson, I., Filipovič Hrast, M., Finnerty, J.: Researching homelessness: challenging exclusion? Soc. Incl. **4**, 1–4 (2016). https://doi.org/10.17645/si.v4i4.774
17. Pauly, B., Wallace, B., Perkin, K.: Approaches to evaluation of homelessness interventions. Hous. Care Support. **17**, 177–187 (2014). https://doi.org/10.1108/HCS-07-2014-0017
18. Neale, K., Buultjens, J., Evans, T.: Integrating service delivery in a regional homelessness service system. Aust. J. Soc. Issues. **47**, 243–261 (2012). https://doi.org/10.1002/j.1839-4655.2012.tb00245.x
19. Eyrich-Garg, K.M.: Mobile phone technology: a new paradigm for the prevention, treatment, and research of the non-sheltered "street" homeless? J. Urban Health. **87**, 365–380 (2010). https://doi.org/10.1007/s11524-010-9456-2
20. Rowe, F.: What literature review is not: diversity, boundaries and recommendations. Eur. J. Inf. Syst. **23**, 241–255 (2014)
21. Webster, J., Watson, R.T.: Analyzing the past to prepare for the future: writing a literature review. MIS Q. **26**, xiii–xxiii (2002)
22. Grant, M.J., Booth, A.: A typology of reviews: an analysis of 14 review types and associated methodologies. Health Info. Libr. J. **26**, 91–108 (2009). https://doi.org/10.1111/j.1471-1842.2009.00848.x
23. Barman-Adhikari, A., Rice, E., Bender, K., Lengnick-Hall, R., Yoshioka-Maxwell, A., Rhoades, H.: Social networking technology use and engagement in HIV-related risk and protective behaviors among homeless youth. J. Health Commun. **21**, 809–817 (2016). https://doi.org/10.1080/10810730.2016.1177139

24. Dangwal, R., Sharma, K.: Impact of HiWEL learning stations on women living in shelter homes. Br. J. Educ. Technol. **44**, 26–31 (2013). https://doi.org/10.1111/j.1467-8535.2012.01353.x

25. Jennings, L., et al.: U.S. Minority Homeless Youth's access to and use of mobile phones: implications for mHealth intervention design. J. Health Commun. **21**, 725–733 (2016). https://doi.org/10.1080/10810730.2015.1103331

26. Neale, J., Stevenson, C.: Homeless drug users and information technology: a qualitative study with potential implications for recovery from drug dependence. Subst. Use Misuse **49**, 1465–1472 (2014). https://doi.org/10.3109/10826084.2014.912231

27. Patterson, D.A., Cronley, C., West, S., Lantz, J.: Social justice manifest: a university-community partnership to promote the individual right to housing. J. Soc. Work Educ. **50**, 234–246 (2014). https://doi.org/10.1080/10437797.2014.885244

28. Stefancic, A., Henwood, B.F., Melton, H., Shin, S.M., Lawrence-Gomez, R., Tsemberis, S.: Implementing housing first in rural areas: pathways vermont. Am. J. Pub. Health **103**, 206–210 (2013). https://doi.org/10.2105/AJPH.2013.301606

29. Vázquez, J.J., Panadero, S., Martín, R., del Val Diaz-Pescador, M.: Access to new information and communication technologies among homeless people in Madrid (Spain). J. Commun. Psychol. **43**, 338–347 (2015). https://doi.org/10.1002/jcop.21682

30. Pollio, D.E., Batey, D.S., Bender, K., Ferguson, K., Thompson, S.: Technology use among emerging adult homeless in two U.S. cities. Social Work (United States) **58**, 173–175 (2013). https://doi.org/10.1093/sw/swt006

31. Chan, H., Tran-Thanh, L., Wilder, B., Rice, E., Vayanos, P., Tambe, M.: Utilizing housing resources for homeless youth through the lens of multiple multi-dimensional knapsacks. In: AIES 2018 – Proceedings of the 2018 AAAI/ACM Conference on AI, Ethics, and Society, pp. 41–47 (2018). https://doi.org/10.1145/3278721.3278757

32. Sleeper, M., et al.: Tough times at transitional homeless shelters: considering the impact of financial insecurity on digital security and privacy. In: Proceedings of the 2019 CHI Conference on Human Factors in Computing Systems. Association for Computing Machinery, New York, NY, USA (2019). https://doi.org/10.1145/3290605.3300319

33. Srivastava, A., Petering, R., Kannan, R., Rice, E., Prasanna, V.K.: How to stop violence among homeless: Extension of voter model and intervention strategies. In: Proceedings of the 2018 IEEE/ACM International Conference on Advances in Social Networks Analysis and Mining, ASONAM 2018, pp. 83–86 (2018). https://doi.org/10.1109/ASONAM.2018.8508641

34. Roberson, J., Nardi, B.: Survival needs and social inclusion: technology use among the homeless. In: Proceedings of the 2010 ACM Conference on Computer Supported Cooperative Work, pp. 445–448. Association for Computing Machinery, New York, NY, USA (2010). https://doi.org/10.1145/1718918.1718993

35. Woelfer, J.P., Hendry, D.G.: Homeless young people's experiences with information systems: life and work in a community technology center. Conf. Human Fact. Comput. Syst. Proc. **2**, 1291–1300 (2010). https://doi.org/10.1145/1753326.1753520

36. Yadav, A., et al.: Influence maximization in the field: the arduous journey from emerging to deployed application. In: Proceedings of the International Joint Conference on Autonomous Agents and Multiagent Systems, AAMAS, vol. 1, pp. 150–158 (2017). https://doi.org/10.1017/9781108669016.005

37. Le Dantec, C.A., Edwards, W.K.: Designs on dignity: perceptions of technology among the homeless. In: Proceedings of the SIGCHI Conference on Human Factors in Computing Systems, pp. 627–636. Association for Computing Machinery, New York, NY, USA (2008). https://doi.org/10.1145/1357054.1357155

38. Le Dantec, C.A., et al.: Publics in practice: ubiquitous computing at a shelter for homeless mothers. In: Conference on Human Factors in Computing Systems – Proceedings, pp. 1687–1696 (2011). https://doi.org/10.1145/1978942.1979189

39. Le Dantec, C.A., Edwards, W.K.: The view from the trenches: ofrganization, power, and technology at two nonprofit homeless outreach centers. In: Proceedings of the ACM Conference on Computer Supported Cooperative Work, CSCW, pp. 589–598 (2008). https://doi.org/10.1145/1460563.1460656
40. Koepfler, J.A., Fleischmann, K.R.: Studying the values of hard-to-reach populations: content analysis of tweets by the 21st century homeless. In: ACM International Conference Proceeding Series, pp. 48–55 (2012). https://doi.org/10.1145/2132176.2132183
41. Koepfler, J.A., Shilton, K., Fleischmann, K.R.: A stake in the issue of homelessness: Identifying values of interest for design in online communities. ACM International Conference Proceeding Series. 36–45 (2013). https://doi.org/10.1145/2482991.2482994.
42. Massimi, M., Dimond, J.P., Le Dantec, C.A.: Finding a new normal: the role of technology in life disruptions. In: Proceedings of the ACM Conference on Computer Supported Cooperative Work, CSCW, pp. 719–728 (2012). https://doi.org/10.1145/2145204.2145314
43. Koepfler, J.A., Hansen, D.L.: We are visible: technology-mediated social participation in a Twitter network for the homeless. In: Proceedings of the 2012 IConference. pp. 492–493. Association for Computing Machinery, New York, NY, USA (2012). https://doi.org/10.1145/2132176.2132261
44. Bender, K., Schau, N., Begun, S., Haffejee, B., Barman-Adhikari, A., Hathaway, J.: Electronic case management with homeless youth. Eval. Prog. Plann. 50, 36–42 (2015). https://doi.org/10.1016/j.evalprogplan.2015.02.002
45. Eyrich-Garg, K.M.: Sheltered in cyberspace? Computer use among the unsheltered 'street' homeless. Comput. Human Behav. 27, 296–303 (2011). https://doi.org/10.1016/j.chb.2010.08.007
46. Hendry, D.G., Woelfer, J.P., Harper, R., Bauer, T., Fitzer, B., Champagne, M.: How to integrate digital media into a drop-in for homeless young people for deepening relationships between youth and adults. Child. Youth Serv. Rev. 33, 774–782 (2011). https://doi.org/10.1016/j.childyouth.2010.11.024
47. Freedman, M.J., Lester, K.M., McNamara, C., Milby, J.B., Schumacher, J.E.: Cell phones for ecological momentary assessment with cocaine-addicted homeless patients in treatment. J. Subst. Abuse Treat. 30, 105–111 (2006). https://doi.org/10.1016/j.jsat.2005.10.005
48. Guadagno, R.E., Muscanell, N.L., Pollio, D.E.: The homeless use Facebook?! Similarities of social network use between college students and homeless young adults. Comput. Human Behav. 29, 86–89 (2013). https://doi.org/10.1016/j.chb.2012.07.019
49. Huang, S.C., Cox, J.L.: Establishing a social entrepreneurial system to bridge the digital divide for the poor: a case study for Taiwan. Univ. Access Inf. Soc. 15, 219–236 (2016). https://doi.org/10.1007/s10209-014-0379-7
50. Woelfer, J.P., Hendry, D.G.: Designing ubiquitous information systems for a community of homeless young people: precaution and a way forward. Pers. Ubiquitous Comput. 15, 565–573 (2011). https://doi.org/10.1007/s00779-010-0341-5
51. Humphry, J.: 'Digital First': homelessness and data use in an online service environment. Commun. Res. Pract. 5, 172–187 (2019). https://doi.org/10.1080/22041451.2019.1601418
52. Humphry, J.: Looking for Wi-Fi: youth homelessness and mobile connectivity in the city. Inf. Commun. Soc. (2019). https://doi.org/10.1080/1369118X.2019.1670227
53. Hendry, D.G., Woelfer, J.P., Duong, T.: U-District Job Co-op: constructing a future vision for homeless young people and employment. Inf. Technol. People 30, 602–628 (2017). https://doi.org/10.1108/ITP-05-2015-0117
54. Rice, E., Barman-Adhikari, A.: Internet and social media use as a resource among homeless youth. J. Comput. Mediated Commun. 19, 232–247 (2014). https://doi.org/10.1111/jcc4.12038
55. Taylor, P.-F., Narayan, B.: Homeless but at home in cyberspace. Inf. Res. Int. Electr. J. 21 (2016)

56. Foster, C., Heeks, R.: Conceptualising inclusive innovation: modifying systems of innovation frameworks to understand diffusion of new technology to low-income consumers. Eur. J. Dev. Res. **25**, 333–355 (2013). https://doi.org/10.1057/ejdr.2013.7

57. McLean, R., Cushman, M.: Exclusion, inclusion and changing the face of information systems research. Inf. Technol. People. **21**, 213–221 (2008). https://doi.org/10.1108/095938408108 95993

Investigating Students' Engagement, Enjoyment, and Sociability in Virtual Reality-Based Systems: A Comparative Usability Study of Spatial.io, Gather.town, and Zoom

Summa Sriworapong, Aung Pyae$^{(\boxtimes)}$ ⓘ, Arin Thirasawasd, and Wasin Keereewan

International School of Engineering, Faculty of Engineering, Chulalongkorn University, Bangkok, Thailand
aung.p@chula.ac.th

Abstract. The COVID-19 pandemic has impacted globally on many industries worldwide (e.g., business and tourism). It has also caused unprecedented disruption to Thailand's educational system. For instance, regular face-to-face classrooms had been temporarily stopped and moved to full-time online learning in which educators and students have used commercially available e-learning platforms (e.g., Moodle) and conferencing tools (e.g., Zoom). Although e-learning platforms and conferencing tools have shown benefits for both educators and learners, social interaction is limited on such platforms. Alternative solutions such as Virtual Reality (VR) technologies have shown promise to solve these challenges; however, research is limited in using such VR technologies in higher education in Thailand. To fill these gaps, we conducted a comparative usability study of three different learning platforms (three-dimensional VR – Spatial.io, two-dimensional VR – Gather.town, and Zoom application) to understand differences in usability and user experiences in terms of students' engagement, enjoyment, and their sociability in learning. Findings suggest that due to its game-like environment and user-friendly features and user interface, Gather.town is the most promising alternative for online learning in higher education in Thailand. This study suggests opportunities for using game-like virtual classrooms for students to improve their engagement in learning.

Keywords: Virtual reality · Usability · User experience · Engagement · E-learning

1 Introduction

Virtual Reality (VR) is a computer-generated environment that allows users to be immersed using digital entities and objects (e.g., 3D images) to simulate the real-world experience [1]. Through a VR platform (e.g., Second Life), users can experience immersion and presence in a simulated environment to perform some tasks (e.g., virtual cycling). To have an immersive experience in such a virtual platform, users need to use a head-mounted display (HMD) such as Oculus and Samsung Gear. For some VR

H. Li et al. (Eds.): WIS 2022, CCIS 1626, pp. 140–157, 2022.
https://doi.org/10.1007/978-3-031-14832-3_10

applications, it is possible that users can experience VR by using a personal computer where immersive experience can be limited. In recent decades, VR has been used in industry, commercial, and research such as architecture and civil engineering [2] and medical training [3]. Over the few years, VR has become largely popular in other fields including education. The existing research shows that VR technologies are promising to be used as an alternative solution or supplementary tool in education [4, 5].

Technology plays a vital role for learning and education in the 21st century. For instance, online learning or e-learning has been widely adopted by both educators and students due to its convenience, flexibility, and accessibility [6]. The role of technology in education has become prominent in recent years during the COVID-10 pandemic, which has largely disrupted the educational sector of many countries in the world. As this virus could be contagious, individuals including students and teachers were suggested to study at home and work from home. Consequently, educational activities have been all pushed online as opposed to traditional onsite or face-to-face learning. For instance, since the beginning of the pandemic, all educational activities including lectures, presentations, and students' group activities have been conducted through online platforms (e.g., Zoom). Although online learning has proven positive benefits such as flexibility for students, there have been many challenges for both educators and students. For instance, particularly during the COVID-19 pandemic, students have struggled to concentrate in lectures and feel a lack of interactivity or connectivity between peers due to the limited social features in the existing tools (e.g., Zoom) [7]. These limitations and challenges of online learning had led to our study as an opportunity to discover feasible alternative solutions for online learning particularly for higher education in Thailand.

Not only are these opportunities derived from the limitations and challenges of existing online learning, but there is a limited study on using VR technologies for education in higher education in Thailand. Hence, we are interested in investigating if commercial VR platforms can be a feasible alternative for online learning in higher education in Thailand. Using two commercially available VR platforms that can simulate the real-world learning environments (e.g., classrooms or labs), we conducted a comparative usability of Spatial.io, Gather.town, and Zoom application. In this study, we used a two-dimensional (2D) VR platform called Gather.town [16], which is a web-based and game-like 2D virtual conferencing tool in which users (e.g., educators and students) can access virtual rooms, as well as move around and interact with others in this environment. We also used a platform called Spatial.io [17], which is a three-dimensional (3D) based VR environment in which users (e.g., educators and students) can access virtual classrooms and engage in learning activities (e.g., presentation and discussion), as well as interact with others in such an environment. Lastly, we used the Zoom application to compare with the other two VR platforms in terms of usability and user experiences. The objectives of the study are outlined as follows:

- To investigate the usability of commercial VR platforms: Spatial.io and Gather.town for learning,
- To investigate Thai undergraduate students' engagement, enjoyment, and sociability in the above-mentioned VR platforms for learning,
- To understand differences in students' user experiences and usability among three different learning platforms: Spatial.io, Gather.town, and Zoom, and

- To propose a feasible solution for higher education in Thailand.

2   Method

2.1   Usability Test Setup

In this study, we aimed to investigate the usability of commercially available VR platforms: Spatial.io and Gather.town and Zoom application for Thai undergraduate students in learning. Also, we aimed to investigate Thai undergraduate students' engagement, enjoyment, and sociability in learning on such platforms. More importantly, in this usability testing, we aimed to understand the differences between these three platforms in terms of *Engagement, Usability, Sociability,* and *Enjoyment* to find an alternative solution for online learning in higher education in Thailand. We used usability testing in this study to achieve our objectives [8]. The preparation included *Participants Recruitment, Software and Hardware Set-up, Installation, and Preparation, Planned Tasks for Participants During the Test,* and *Data Collection Methods and Tools.* First, we recruited undergraduate students in Chulalongkorn University as well as other universities in Thailand who can voluntarily participate in the entire usability testing. We invited them through social media and instant messaging platforms such as Line and Discord. Participants in this study should age between 18 and 22 years, as well as they must belong to an undergraduate program in a university in Thailand. In addition, they should have sufficient experience in using e-learning tools, and be familiar with conferencing tools (e.g., Zoom or MS Team).

Regarding the setup of the usability testing, we aimed at collecting both quantitative and qualitative data from all three platforms. As this test would be conducted online due to the current pandemic restrictions, there would be a requirement regarding the hardware and software involved in this experimental setup. For instance, all participants were required to have a functioning computer/laptop with a stable internet connection since Gather.town and Spatial.io would be hosted and would run on their web browsers. Moreover, the participant was required to install the Zoom application on their computer/laptop to enter the Zoom session of this study. In this study, there were three members (UX researchers) for each session; one researcher was the host of the session and oversaw the overall session, and the other two researchers would be responsible for observing the participant groups during the brainstorming session as well as conducting the interviews and questionnaires to the participants.

In this study, each participant was required to attend three learning sessions: Spatial.io, Gather.town, and Zoom. In a particular platform (e.g., Gather.town), the participant was required to attend a lecture session while observers observed, listened, and took notes. As in each platform, there would have a few participants, they would be split into two groups where they could cooperate with others during the brainstorming session. After that, they would get to present their ideas. Finally, interview sessions and a questionnaire were carried out by a researcher at the end of the usability test. The experiments were conducted by having two groups of participants attending a mock-up educational session in which they would both watch the session's pre-recorded specific lecture video, followed by learning activities (e.g., brainstorming and discussion) followed by a questionnaire and interview session [9]. In this study, we used the *User*

Engagement Scale (UES) originally introduced by O'Brien [10]. The focus of this questionnaire is on the participants' engagement in learning during each session. We also used other questionnaires such as the *Usability Metric for User Experience* (UM-UX Lite), which was simplified from its original version by Lewis et al. [11]. The metric provides simplified measurements of the system usability [11]. In addition, we also used Usability Heuristics, created by Nielsen [12], which allows the evaluation which implies the full usability scores of each platform for the educational sessions and purposes. We also conducted an observational study to understand the participant's user experiences in using three different learning platforms.

2.2 Usability Test Method

The usability test was conducted on 6 consecutive days (a total of six sessions); taking approximately 1.5 h per session. In this study, we recruited 14 participants, and participants were randomly selected and divided into two groups (7 people in each group). As shown in Table 1, the first group filled in the first three study days (participated in the following sessions: Gather, Zoom, and Spatial Sessions respectively), while the second group occupied the final three study days (participated in the following sessions: Zoom, Gather and Spatial Sessions respectively). In this study, one session consisted of one moderator (the one who introduced the topic of the session) and two UX researchers (for interview and evaluation). In addition, the participants and arranging platform order were randomized into two groups to avoid the learning effects and order of the system. Table 1 shows the participants' assignments and details of the study design.

Table 1. Schedule of the study.

Day	Group no	Participants	Platform	The topic of the study
Day 1	1	P8, P9, P10, P11, P12, P13, P14	Gather Session 1	"Life Inside Metaverse"
Day 2	1	P8, P9, P10, P11, P12, P13, P14	Zoom Session 1	"Work Environment and Its Impact"
Day 3	1	P8, P9, P10, P11, P12, P13, P14	Spatial Session 1	"Game Design and Its Applications"
Day 4	2	P1, P2, P3, P4, P5, P6, P7	Zoom Session 2	"Work Environment and Its Impact"
Day 5	2	P1, P2, P3, P4, P5, P6, P7	Gather Session 2	"Life Inside Metaverse"
Day 6	2	P1, P2, P3, P4, P5, P6, P7	Spatial Session 2	"NFT and Its Applications"

As shown in Table 2, in this study, the learning activities (e.g., a lecture video) were to allow participants to learn a new topic of interest that was introduced, simulating a typical lecture period such as attending a lecture, group discussion, brainstorming, ideation, communication, and social interaction. All test days under the study followed a standardized procedure outlined below.

Table 2. Study Design and procedures.

Duration	Procedure steps	Participants	UX researchers' roles and responsibilities
5 min	Introduction	The participants provided their consent forms to participate.	A UX researcher requested consent from each participant of the session.
20 min	Video watching	The participants watched the video as a group, interacting (through the chat feature if applicable for that platform)	A UX Researcher observed the participant's interaction through the chat and answered any questions if needed.
30 min	Video discussion	After receiving topic questions from the moderator, participants discussed points based on the video; use of tools (e.g., Whiteboard sticky notes, if applicable for that platform)	A UX Researcher observed participants' interaction through the group discussion and answered any questions if needed.
10 min	Group presentation	Participants presented their ideas that were discussed during the group discussion.	A UX Researcher observed participants' interaction through the group presentation and answered any questions if needed.
2 min	Closing remarks	–	–
25 min	Interview and questionnaires	Each participant will privately join an interview session hosted by UX Researchers. Ones that are waiting in the queue will be doing questionnaires for the study.	A UX Researcher interviews the participant according to the questions that were prepared beforehand (see appendix B).

Usability Testing Procedures in Spatial.io. In this session, the participants were asked to create their accounts to access the platform; they would have an option to create their avatars (customized based on the uploaded pictures). At the beginning of the test, the participants were guided to the main virtual room in Spatial.io for the session introduction in which the purpose of our study was explained, followed by the lecture topic that was the main idea of the session. Then, the participants watched a lecture video related to that topic (e.g., *'Game Design and Its Applications* for the first Spatial session; *'NFT and Its Applications* for the second Spatial session). The topics were selected based on incoming trends today that could be applicable and suitable for all participants. Videos in Spatial.io were played through the screen sharing feature. After watching the lecture video, the participants were asked to enter pre-built separate virtual rooms. For instance, team one, which was randomly selected, went to the virtual world no.1; team two undertook it in a similar fashion created for the group discussion about that topic. The group discussion in Spatial.io was planned to replicate and simulate a brainstorming session held in a physical setting (e.g., gesture reaction to ideas, moving characters closer to the screen). After the discussion session, the participants came back to the main room; a group presentation was held to highlight the insights made during the discussion. The group presentation in Spatial.io was planned to simulate a presentation held in a physical setting (e.g., Avatar's clapping before and after the presentation, thumbs up, thumbs down, or any appropriate gesture) to show emotion. Finally, the session hosts (UX researchers) announced the closing remarks to conclude the session. After the session, interviews (through private virtual rooms in Spatial.io) were conducted for each participant; questionnaires, in which we used the *Google Forms* to measure users' engagement, enjoyment, and usability in the learning activities) were given out to the participants to complete during the idle period. During the session, the UX researchers interviewed the participants. Figure 1 shows the Spatial.io sessions during the test.

Fig. 1. An introduction session (left) and a presentation (right) in Spatial.io

Usability Testing Procedures in Gather.town. Before entering the virtual environment of Gather.town, the participants created their avatar-like figures. Then, one UX researcher guided the participants toward the main area in Gather.town. The introduction of the session was conducted; explaining the purpose of the study, as well as giving a brief instruction on controls and how bubbles (virtual whisperer) work (i.e., participants will only hear each other if they are in the same area). Next, a lecture video was conducted the same way as stated in Spatial.io; however, the topic would be different (e.g., '*I Spent 100 Days in the MetaVerse*' in the topic '*Life Inside Metaverse*' for all sessions of Gather.town). The participants were encouraged to interact while watching the video through the chat feature available in Gather.town. After watching the video, the participants were asked to enter two separate areas in Gather.town for group discussion (see Fig. 2). The participants used the digital objects in the area to increase interaction and enjoyment (e.g., chairs and tables for sitting in a group, whiteboards to brainstorm the session). Then, the participants were randomly selected for group discussion, and they were encouraged to do social interactions and communication as much as possible during the session. At the end of the group discussion, similar to the real world, the participants wandered around to other areas to interact with other participants as well. Following the discussion, participants used the microphone feature to present across groups for group presentation. Following the closing remark, Interviews were conducted one by one in a separate private room. Questionnaires were given out the same way as all sections during the idle period.

Fig. 2. A group presentation and discussion in Gather.town

Usability Testing Procedures in Zoom. As shown in Fig. 3, the usability testing procedures of the Zoom session would simulate a typical zoom online lecture conducted in the real world that includes a lecture session in the main meeting space, a discussion session in each breakout room, and a presentation in the main area again. Every part of the procedure was the same as on other platforms. The topic that was discussed was *"Work Environment and Its Impact"*, with the video *"Day in the Life of a Typical Japanese Office Worker in Tokyo"*.

Fig. 3. A group discussion in Zoom

3   Analysis and Results

In this study, for the quantitative data, we analyzed the questionnaire data by using descriptive analysis [14]. Using thematic analysis [15], in which qualitative data is analyzed in a group of codes that represent the meanings and patterns of such data, themes were created for proper analysis.

3.1 Demographic Data Analysis

First, we analyzed the demographic data of the participants. There was a total of 14 participants voluntarily engaged in the usability testing. Of these 14 participants, 10 were male participants (71.40%), and 4 were female participants (28.60%). The average mean age was 20.93 years old (SD = 0.27). Since this study was intended for Thailand's higher education, all the participant's nationalities are Thai. Their educational backgrounds are varied, but the majority of participants came from the *International School of Engineering* (ISE), Chulalongkorn University majoring in *Information and Communication Engineering* (ICE) having a percentage of 71.43% (n = 10). While some participants did not come from engineering-related fields such as Bachelor's in Economics, Thammasat University, and Singapore Institute of Management (SIM) majoring in Accounting Management with a total of 3 participants (21.43%). Concerning their experiences in using online learning platforms, all participants have used Zoom for their online education, while some of them have used Gather.town before (n = 6; 42.86%). However, although the participants have heard of VR platforms for learning or social gathering (e.g., Second Life), none of the participants have used Spatial.io before the study.

3.2 User Engagement Scale (UES)

For the quantitative data analysis, as shown in Table 3, we started with the participants' engagement in learning on these 3 platforms. For '*Focused Attention*' of the participants in three platforms, we found that both Spatial.io and Gather.town had a similar mean score, while Zoom had a slightly lesser mean score compared with the other two platforms (Spatial.io M = 3.23, SD = 1.01; Gather.town M = 3.23, SD = 1.0; Zoom M = 3.04, SD = 1.19). In '*Perceived Usability*', which was reversely calculated due to the question being negatively formulated, Spatial.io had the lowest score (M = 2.86, SD = 1.12), meaning that the system had some usability challenges. In contrast, Zoom had the highest usability score (M = 4.17, SD = 0.68), while Gather.town had a mean score of (M = 3.60, SD = 1.06). The results indicated that Zoom appeared to be the easiest among the platforms in this study. Concerning the '*Aesthetics*' aspect of all systems, Gather.town was the most appealing (M = 4.14, SD = 0.66), while Spatial.io had an above-average mean score (M = 3.12, SD = 0.99). Of these three platforms, Zoom was the least appealing (M = 2.79, SD = 0.83), as expected. Lastly, for '*Rewards*', the results indicated that Gather.town had the highest mean score, followed by Zoom; however, Spatial.io had the least mean score (Spatial.io M = 3.26, SD = 0.99; Gather.town M = 3.74, SD = 0.98; Zoom M = 3.38, SD = 0.90).

From the qualitative data, based on the interview results, the participants' insights of their engagement in Spatial.io were favored negative connotations. For instance, some

Table 3. User Engagement Scale.

		Spatial.io		Gather.town		Zoom	
		M	SD	M	SD	M	SD
Focused Attention (FA)							
FA-S1	I lost myself in this experience (totally immersed in Spatial.io).	3.21	1.12	3.07	1.00	3.07	1.33
FA-S.2	The time I spent using Spatial.io just slipped away	3.15	1.07	3.29	0.99	3.00	0.96
FA-S.3	I was absorbed in this experience in Spatial.io.	3.31	0.85	3.36	1.01	3.07	1.27
		3.23	**1.01**	**3.24**	**1.00**	**3.05**	**1.19**
Perceived Usability (PU)							
PU-S.1	I felt frustrated while using Spatial.io (reverse)	2.57	1.02	3.71	0.99	3.86	0.86
PU-S.2	I found Spatial.io to be confusing to use (reverse)	2.86	1.23	3.71	1.27	4.64	0.50
PU-S.3	Using Spatial.io was taxing (reverse)	3.14	1.10	3.36	0.93	4.00	0.68
		2.86	**1.12**	**3.60**	**1.06**	**4.17**	**0.68**
Aesthetics (AE)							
AE-S.1	Spatial.io was attractive	3.29	0.99	4.29	0.73	2.71	1.07
AE-S.2	Spatial.io was aesthetically appealing	3.57	1.09	4.43	0.65	2.50	0.76
AE-S.3	Spatial.io was worthwhile	2.79	0.89	3.71	0.61	3.14	0.66
		3.21	**0.99**	**4.14**	**0.66**	**2.79**	**0.83**
Rewards (RW)							

(*continued*)

Table 3. (*continued*)

		Spatial.io		*Gather.town*		*Zoom*	
		M	SD	M	SD	M	SD
RW-S.1	Spatial.io appealed to my senses	3.00	1.04	3.57	1.02	3.21	0.89
RW-S.2	My experience was rewarding	2.79	1.05	3.86	0.86	3.50	0.85
RW-S.3	I felt interested in this experience	4.00	0.88	3.79	1.05	3.43	0.94
		3.26	**0.99**	**3.74**	**0.98**	**3.38**	**0.90**

participants reported that they did not understand how to use the controls of Spatial.io, and thus, they encountered difficulties in moving their characters (avatars) in Spatital.io. The participants also explained that characters can be moved the same way in Gather.town but found it to be easier, much simpler. and less burdensome. Also, although interactive components (e.g., controls) in Spatial.io were richer and more attractive than in Gather.io and Zoom, to the best of researchers' knowledge, the chat feature was not provided, causing reluctance among the participants to interact as they would normally do in Zoom-based learning. The participants described that the elements and features available in Gather.town were useful in terms of collaboration, communication, and social interaction among peers. The virtual world in the Gather.town platform was also easily customizable, which allowed each session to be different and unique, resulting in reducing boredom for users. From the observational studies among all platforms, many participants were not familiar with Spatial.io, they felt taxed and needed help sometimes during the study. One technical challenge found in Spatial.io was that battery drainage was noticeably high, which caused frustration among the participants, and impacted their focus on the main topic of the session. Gather.town, on the other hand, exemplifies the interaction among the participants due to its game-like environment and features. Most participants were excited about using Gather. town in their learning compared with the other two platforms: Zoom and Spatial.io. As observed in Zoom, fewer participants opened their cameras compared to Gather town and Spatial.io; and the chat feature was only used by the participants, indicating that social interaction and communication were limited in learning.

3.3 Usability

As shown in Table 4, the usability of platforms was measured using two metrics: *Usability Metric for User Experience—Lite Version* (UMUX-Lite), and *Usability Heuristics*. For the UMUX-Lite, which only has two simple questions, we can see that the highest mean score belonged to Zoom (M = 4.18, SD = 0.54), followed by Gather.town with a score of (M = 3.82, SD = 1.04). In contrast, Spatial.io was found to have the lowest mean score far apart from the other two platforms with only a mean score (M = 2.89, SD = 1.08).

Table 4. UMUX-Lite (Usability) results.

	Spatial.io		Gather.town		Zoom	
UMUX-Lite	M	SD	M	SD	M	SD
1.Spatial.io's system capabilities meet my requirements	2.64	0.93	3.86	1.10	4.07	0.62
2.Spatial.io is easy to use	3.14	1.23	3.79	0.97	4.29	0.47
	2.89	**1.08**	**3.82**	**1.04**	**4.18**	**0.54**

In the aspect of *Usability Heuristics*, where the questions widely cover the usability aspect of a particular system (see Table 5), it is still clear that Gather.town and Zoom were ranked the highest among others, while Gather.town had a slightly higher mean score (M = 3.71, SD = 1.02) than Zoom, which had the score of (M = 3.6, SD = 0.92). It is still consistent UMUX-Lite in that Spatial.io still had the least mean score (M = 3.16, SD = 0.99). The findings from both UMUX-Lite and Usability Heuristics are consistent with the findings from the '*Perceived Usability*' of UES.

Table 5. Usability evaluation (Heuristics) results.

	Spatial.io		Gather.town		Zoom	
Heuristics	M	SD	M	SD	M	SD
Visibility of system status	3.14	0.95	3.71	0.91	3.93	0.83
Match between system and the real world	3.64	0.74	3.57	1.22	3.29	0.73
User control and freedom	3.29	1.27	4.14	0.86	3.29	0.91
Consistency	3.36	1.01	4.00	0.96	4.00	0.88
Prevent errors	2.43	0.94	3.71	0.83	3.79	0.97
Recognition rather than recall	3.00	0.88	3.57	1.09	3.64	1.01
Flexibility and efficiency of use	2.93	1.07	3.64	0.84	3.93	0.92
Aesthetics and minimalist design	3.57	0.94	3.64	1.22	3.79	0.80
Help users recognize, diagnose, and recover from errors	2.93	1.00	3.71	0.91	3.07	1.21
Help and documentation	3.29	1.07	3.43	1.40	3.29	0.99
	3.16	**0.99**	**3.71**	**1.02**	**3.60**	**0.92**

Regarding the qualitative data from the user interviews, the majority of the participants mentioned during the interview sessions that every session and platform tools for online education need to be simple and easy to use. Though they all agreed that all platforms were easy to use, especially Zoom, however, they reported that Spatial.io was found to be the most challenging tool to use. According to the interviews, the majority of the participants agreed that Spatial.io was an interesting and attractive virtual environment that resembles most of the real world. However, although it had low complexity in its system, it was a bit more challenging to use due to the platform's performance, compared with the other two platforms. As all participants were new to Spatial.io, learnability was important; however, they did not achieve this aspect during the testing. They also said that it was hard to move around and interact with other objects or people, thus, the usability and their user experiences were negatively impacted. In contrast, the other two platforms provided sufficient functionalities for learning, especially Gather.town. Most of the participants mentioned that compared with the other two platforms, Gather.town was the most useful for them due to its easy-to-understand user interface along with simple movement functions. Furthermore, they pointed out that the available features in Gather.town are suitable and usable for learning purposes (e.g., discussion, chat, and presentation). From the observation, the difficulty of usage for Spatial.io has been confirmed since many of the participants were disconnected due to some technical problems during the sessions and many of them carried frustrated facial expressions due to some technical and usability issues (e.g., character movements). However, the majority of the participants held no frustrated or confused expressions during the sessions of Gather. town and Zoom.

3.4 Enjoyment

With regards to the enjoyment of the participants, as shown in Table 6, all three platforms had differences in the mean scores: while the Gather.town platform had the highest score among these three platforms with a mean of (M = 4.00, SD = 0.78), followed by Zoom with a mean score of (M = 3.57, SD = 0.76), and Spatial.io with a mean score of (M = 3.21, SD = 0.80; See table 4.5), indicating that most participants enjoyed using Gather.town in learning.

Table 6. Enjoyment scores.

	Spatial.io		Gather.town		Zoom	
Enjoyment scale	M	SD	M	SD	M	SD
Overall, learning about this system is enjoyable.	3.21	0.80	4.00	0.78	3.57	0.76

According to the qualitative interview data, it can be said that Gather.town was the only platform where participants mentioned that it was enjoyable to be used for learning. Many users mentioned during the interview on Gather.town that they had a lot of fun using Gather.town. During the interview session on Zoom, the majority of participants mentioned that they enjoyed interacting with others using Zoom as well, especially during the brainstorming session conducted in the breakout room. However, for Spatial.io, the participants said during the interview that there were more interactive components than in Zoom, but less than Gather.town can offer. They also mentioned that they could not enjoy it since it was challenging to use such as they got disconnected from the system frequently. This led to their low enjoyment of using this system. Through the observations, many users enjoyed themselves during Gather.town sessions the most, especially whenever they were controlling their avatars. Many participants had joyful facial expressions or smiles during the activities conducted in Gather.town the most. While on Zoom, many participants seemed to have neutral facial expressions toward the sessions but seemed to be more joyful in the breakout rooms. On the other hand, for Spatial.io, many participants seemed exciting at first when they were learning something new, but their enjoyment slowly faded away as they encountered more issues within Spatial.io, thus, their enjoyment level dropped during the session.

3.5 Sociability

Regarding the sociability of the participants (see Table 7), it is clear that Gather.town had the highest mean score for the measure of (M = 4.1, SD = 0.79), followed by Zoom with the mean score of (M = 3.52, SD = 0.97) and Spatial.io had the lowest mean score (M = 3.36, SD = 0.88;), indicating that Gather.town, compared with other two platforms, could offer the best social elements and interactive experiences for users (e.g., chat feature). The following Table 7 shows the mean scores for the participants' sociability.

From the user interviews conducted, the majority of participants mentioned that they felt more of their social presence during the sessions of Gather.town due to the reason that Gather.town allowed them to move around easily and had a lot of cooperative learning tools that are easy to use and learn (e.g., video and chat). Most of the participants agreed that Gather.town provided the right environment for them to work with their teammates in the context of learning. For Zoom, some participants recognized it and praised Zoom for being efficient when there was a smaller number of people in the room since the communication does not get interrupted. However, many participants mentioned that Zoom could not provide the right environment for them to work as a team, such as the lack of cooperative tools on the platform, as well as limited social interactivity features. For Spatial.io, most of the participants agreed that Spatial.io had the potential to be improved in terms of sociability in the educational context since there are some cooperative tools provided by the system. Furthermore, Spatial.io is the most promising tool to simulate the real-world classroom-like environment in a virtual space. However, the current functions could not be properly used; thus, it did not improve the social presence of many of the participants.

Furthermore, with the observation data gained during each session, the statement from the interviews was supported. Since many of the participants seemed to talk and work together with their teammates the most during the sessions conducted in Gather.town. For Zoom, the social interaction seemed to be low during the main session, only a few participants talked or chatted. However, when they entered the breakout room,

Table 7. Sociability results.

		Spatial.io		Gather.town		Zoom	
	Sociability	M	SD	M	SD	M	SD
Q1	This Spatial.io environment enables me to easily contact my teammates	3.21	0.70	3.93	1.00	3.71	1.07
Q2	I do not feel lonely in this Spatial.io environment	3.57	0.94	4.29	0.61	3.71	0.99
Q3	The platform enables me to get a good impression of my teammates	3.64	0.63	3.93	0.73	3.71	0.91
Q4	The platform environment allows spontaneous informal conversation	3.14	1.10	4.29	0.91	3.71	1.07
Q5	The platform environment enables us to develop into a well performing team	3.00	1.04	4.00	0.68	3.36	0.84
Q6	The platform environment enables me to develop good work relationships with my teammates	3.43	0.76	4.07	0.73	3.21	0.80
Q7	The platform environment enables me to identify myself with the team	3.43	0.85	3.86	1.03	3.21	0.89
Q8	I feel comfortable with Spatial.io environment	3.14	0.95	3.93	0.83	3.93	0.73
Q9	The platform environment allows for non-task-related conversations	3.71	1.14	4.71	0.47	3.57	1.16
Q10	The platform environment enables me to make close friendships with my teammates	3.29	0.73	4.00	0.88	3.07	1.21
		3.36	**0.88**	**4.10**	**0.79**	**3.52**	**0.97**

they seemed to talk a lot more than they used to. On Spatial.io, they did not seem to walk around a lot despite the platform allowing the avatar's movements. However, they still performed some social interaction with each other during the brainstorming sessions, such as using post-it to put down some ideas while referring to them in the discussion with their friends.

4 Discussion

Based on the findings from the data analysis and results, in this section, we discussed the usability differences of the three platforms, as well as differences in the participants' user experiences in using these three platforms. Concerning the participants' engagement in learning on three different platforms, Spatial.io had some usability challenges and limitations including technical issues. This resulted in limited interaction among the participants. For instance, to our knowledge, there was no chat feature provided in the version of Spatial.io we used in the study. Consequently, it greatly impacted the participants' engagement during the learning session because they were used to utilizing primary chat features while using Zoom or other similar tools. Gather.town, on the other hand, offers an alternative for students to enhance their interaction experiences through a game-like environment and feature, which induce them to open the video and verbally discuss with each other. As a result, this resulted in higher user engagement in the learning session. Furthermore, features such as character movements and controls in Gather.town were simpler than in Spatial.io; especially when they provided a similar level of benefits, whereas the user experience was found to be taxing in Spatial.io.

In addition, a simple and game-like user interface in Gather.town seems beneficial for the participants where they can easily move around and be playful during learning, whereas such experience was limited in Zoom and challenging in Spatial.io. In general, it was found that the participants' engagement was higher in Gather.town compared to the other two platforms. Thus, Gather.town has an advantage over the other two platforms as it provides the best balance in terms of interaction, ease of use, and game-like experience that can provide an alternative for improving students' engagement in learning. It is assumed that engagement could signify the importance of how undergraduate students interact within their online classes; thus, those platforms that provide more of an interactive component such as communication features, or cooperative working elements will have the potential to be of great use for the online educational context. This finding is consistent with the existing literature [18]. In addition, students prefer a playful game-like environment that can encourage them to be engaged in the learning process.

In terms of system usability, all platforms allowed the participants to complete the intended tasks. However, there were some usability issues of Spatial.io discovered in this study, as discussed previously. For instance, its features (e.g., movements control) were not easy to use compared with the other two platforms. Technically, it seemed to require high computation power from hardware devices. In addition, internet connectivity seems to be a barrier to using Spatial.io which causes being lagged while using it. It should be noted that the participants in this study did not have prior experience in using Spatial.io; hence, it may have contributed to further opportunities to research with experienced users in this context. For Gather.town and Zoom, it was found to be usable and user-friendly for the participants, and they all could easily use them without any barriers or challenges. Based on the findings, it is highly important, especially in the educational context, for the platform used as a medium for online education during the COVID-19 pandemic to be usable and accessible by students. As usability plays a significant role when it comes to online education, the more usable the platform is, the more effective the classes will become. Also, students are likely to engage and feel motivated in such a learning platform. This finding is in-line with the existing literature [18].

Regarding the participants' enjoyment, Gather.town seemed to be the best platform referring to both quantitative and qualitative results. This platform offers a similar experience to a game-like environment, which made the participants excited and helped them enjoy the learning session. The features available on Gather.io are user-friendly and they are engaging as well. Thus, it results in increasing the participants' enjoyment compared with the other two platforms. The participants also mentioned that although Zoom is useful and user-friendly in learning, the social interaction is limited and the environment on this platform is less interesting and playful compared with Gather.io. For Spatial.io, the participants' enjoyment was the lowest among others due to its limitations and usability challenges as discussed previously. During online classes in the education world, enjoyment plays an important role in keeping the students attracted to the class session. Regardless of their age, students still seek enjoyment and fun in their every activity including learning; therefore, those platforms that provide engaging content, playful activity, and social interactivity can increase users' enjoyment of learning. However, it should be noteworthy that having too many enjoyment components in such an educational classroom could serve as a distraction for the students, thus, leading to more students losing focus on the intended educational content. This finding is in-line with the existing literature [19].

For the sociability aspect of the systems, the focus is to understand what and how a system can offer sufficient functionalities and an engaging environment for students to cooperate and socialize with each other. It is clear from the study that Gather.town offers the most sociable platform for students compared to the other two platforms. This could be due to various factors. For instance, the participants favored socializing in Gather.town because of its game-like environment and easy and user-friendly features. Since Gather.town allows users to create their own avatars and move them around as freely as they would like, along with many cooperative objects and tools that allow users to do a variety of tasks together with other users, such as a shared whiteboard, or a built-in board game. This may improve the effectiveness of social presence within the online world for the participants, thus increasing sociability for them as the result. Whereas Zoom, could not provide any means to help them cooperate as a team together. The participants will need to rely on the third-party tools most of the time while working together in Zoom during the brainstorming sessions. For Spatial.io, it does provide more tools than Zoom has to offer but the platform is challenging to access and unstable, causing the participants to give up on working together and thus, decrease their social presence. Sociability is what allows social interaction among users, especially in an online educational context where students could not gather physically. The platforms that provide a sufficient environment for students to cooperate and meet with each other similarly to the physical world the most could be one of the most promising alternatives that the online educational world is looking for. For instance, providing a specific area where only those within the indicted parameter could talk and hear each other as well as providing cooperative tools such as a shared whiteboard in Gather.town has proved to have more sociability impacts on the students where they are more likely to interact, communicate, and work with other students in the same session. It is noteworthy that although most participants mentioned that Spatial.io is the most realistic virtual platform in terms of social interaction compared with the other two platforms; however, as mentioned, due to its usability issues, it did not win over the other two platforms in the social aspect. All participants suggested that 3D-based VR platforms can be a substitute in the future because of their rapid development and a great attraction to people in many areas including education. These findings are consistent with the existing literature on usability and sociability in online communities [20].

Based on the findings from the study, we summarize as follows. First, the findings suggest that the current conferencing tools (e.g., Zoom) offer limited social interaction and fun elements for students, particularly in learning, that can lead to a decrease in students' engagement, enjoyment, and sociability. Two-dimensional virtual reality platforms (e.g., Gather.town) are found to be promising for students wherein they can not only engage in learning activities but also interact with each other through interactive tools and in a playful way. Furthermore, a game-like learning platform (e.g., Gather.town) can make students enjoy their learning, as well as it can enhance their overall engagement in learning through a game-like platform. Although 3D-based VR platforms (e.g., Spatial.io) are interesting, the current version may not be suitable to be integrated into learning yet. The study shows that improvements need to be made in usability and user experiences. Technical requirements (e.g., graphics and battery usage) are still a challenge for students to adopt such a system in learning. However, it does not mean that these 3D VR tools cannot be used in learning. Simply, they still need to be improved to fit with the existing educational landscape, particularly in Thailand. Although 3DVR-based learning platforms are not ready to be adopted at this moment, particularly in the Thailand educational section, it cannot be denied that they are promising for future adoption if they are designed based on users' needs. Based on the findings from this study, we suggest the following key takeaways for the higher education sector in Thailand:

1. The authorities and educators should consider adopting existing 2D VR platforms (e.g., Gather.town) in today's education system; by creating environments that could be customized freely by each organization (e.g., Gather Chula, Gather Thammasat) so that educators (professors) and students could be encouraged to engage and interact more freely in environments that have (high usability, and high UX/UI that leads to high engagement and enjoyment). Alternatively, they can consider developing their VR platforms for possibly all students in the university.

2. Possibility of a hybrid approach in which both a conferencing tool (e.g., Zoom) and a VR-based learning platform (e.g., Gather.town) will be adopted to improve students' interaction experience in university and close gaps in relationships that were built through online.

3. We also suggest the authorities of the Ministry of Education adopt a 2D VR-based educational model not only for higher education but also for primary and secondary education, etc.

4. Suggestion for a VR-based social gathering (extra-curricular) for undergraduate students.

References

1. William, R.S., Craig, A.B.: Understanding virtual reality: interface, application, and design. In: A volume in The Morgan Kaufmann Series in Computer Graphics. 2nd edn. Morgan Kaufmann (2018)
2. Frost, P., Warren, P.: Virtual reality used in a collaborative architectural design process. In: Proceedings of the 2000 IEEE Conference on Information Visualization. An International Conference on Computer Visualization and Graphics, pp. 586–573 (2000)
3. Kim, Y., Kim, H., Kim, Y.: Virtual reality and augmented reality in plastic surgery: a review. Arch. Plast. Surg. **44**(3), 179–187 (2017)
4. Sam, K., Luxton-Reilly, A., Wuensche, B., Beryl, P.: A systematic review of virtual reality in education. Themes Sci. Technol. Educ. **10**(2), 85–119 (2017)
5. Marr, B.: 10 Best Examples Of VR And AR In Education. https://www.forbes.com/sites/bernardmarr/2021/07/23/10-best-examples-of-vr-and-ar-in-education/?sh=581dd7cc1f48. Accessed 30 May 2022
6. Savage, E.N.: A conceptual framework for technology education: a historical perspective. J. Technol. Stud. **28**, 98–100 (2002)
7. Perkins, A., Kelly, S., Dumbleton, H., Whitfield, S.: Pandemic pupils: COVID-19 and the impact on student paramedics. Australas. J. Paramedicine (2020). https://doi.org/10.33151/ajp.17.811
8. Usability testing: https://www.usability.gov/how-to-and-tools/methods/usability-testing.html. Accessed 15 April 2022
9. Jeff, S., James, R.L.: Quantifying the User Experience. Practical Statistics for User Research. 2nd edn. Morgan Kaufmann, San Francisco, US (2012)
10. O'Brien, H.L., Cairns, P., Hall, M.: A practical approach to measuring user engagement with the refined user engagement scale (UES) and new UES short form. Int. J. Hum. Comput. Stud. **112**, 28–39 (2018)
11. Jeff, S.: Measuring usability: From the SUS to the UMUX-Lite. https://measuringu.com/umux-lite/. Accessed 30 May 2022
12. Jakob, N.: 10 Usability Heuristics for User Interface Design. https://www.nngroup.com/articles/ten-usability-heuristics/#poster. Accessed 30 May 2022
13. Office of the Research Ethics Review Committee for Research Involving Human Subjects: https://www.research.chula.ac.th/office-of-the-research-ethics-review-committee-for-research-involving-human-subjects/. Accessed 15 April 2022
14. Descriptive Analysis: How-to, types, examples. https://pestleanalysis.com/descriptive-analysis/. Accessed 15 April 2022
15. Braun, V., Clarke, V.: Using thematic analysis in psychology. Qual. Res. Psychol. **3**(2), 77–101 (2006)
16. Gather.town: https://www.gather.town/about. Accessed 05 May 2022
17. Spatial.io: https://spatial.io/about. Accessed 05 May 2022
18. Martin, F., Bolliger, D.U.: Engagement matters: student perceptions on the importance of engagement strategies in the online learning environment. Online Learn. **22**(1), 205–222 (2018)
19. Pangestu, H., Karsen, M.: Evaluation of usability in online learning. In: 2016 International Conference on Information Management and Technology (ICIMTech), pp. 267–271 (2016)
20. Phang, C.W., Kankanhalli, A., Sabherwal, R.: Usability and sociability in online communities: a comparative study of knowledge seeking and contribution. J. Assoc. Inf. Syst. **10**(10), 721–747 (2009)

Driving Well-being in the Information Society

A Review of Health Beliefs and Their Influence on Asylum Seekers and Refugees' Health-Seeking Behavior

Hamed Ahmadinia^(✉)

Information Studies, Åbo Akademi University, Turku, Finland
hamed.ahmadinia@abo.fi

Abstract. This article reviews health beliefs, and attitudes of asylum seekers and refugees, using an adapted framework of the Health Belief Model. The systematic review included 15 peer-reviewed records retrieved from CINAHL, Medline, PubMed, PsycINFO, and PsycArticles. Findings of this review show culture, tradition, fate or destiny, psychological factors, family, friends, and community were crucial influential factors in shaping asylum seekers, and refugees' perceived barriers, fear, severity, and susceptibility in their health-seeking activities. In addition, knowledge and awareness related to the benefits of using modern healthcare services were motivators for different ethnic groups to take care of their personal health. Healthcare providers, educational programs, and support from family, friends, and community had noteworthy influence on triggering the health-related decision-making process among asylum seekers and refugees. This study offers practical implications for healthcare providers and public health community to devise culturally relevant strategies that will effectively target asylum seekers and refugees with diverse cultural, traditional and attitudinal beliefs about healthcare and health seeking activities. This is one of the descriptive review studies on asylum seekers and refugees' health beliefs and their health-seeking behavior based on ethnicity grounds.

Keywords: Asylum seekers · Health beliefs · Health-seeking behavior · Refugees · Review

1 Introduction

In the recent decades, healthcare providers have investigated the health needs of refugees[1] and asylum seekers[2]. Still, since healthcare providers deal with vulnerable people, it is important to consider providing health services that are culturally adopted for minorities

---

[1] A refugee is an individual who have fled war, violence, conflict, or persecution and have crossed an international border to find safety in another country [1].

[2] An asylum-seeker is an individual who has left their country and is seeking protection from persecution and serious human rights violations in another country; However, an asylum-seeker hasn't yet been legally recognized as a refugee and is waiting to receive a decision on their asylum claim [2].

H. Li et al. (Eds.): WIS 2022, CCIS 1626, pp. 161–178, 2022.
https://doi.org/10.1007/978-3-031-14832-3_11

with diverse ethnic backgrounds [3]. Studies on resettled asylum seekers and refugees in a new country indicated different issues related to the healthcare, such as insufficient healthcare attention because of organizational barriers, cultural differences, language barrier, and access to social or healthcare services [3–6].

Moreover, refugees and asylum seekers may find it difficult to adapt to new environments and lifestyle, resulting in emotional and psychological issues [7–9]. Even though, it is expected migration influences value changes during adaptation, asylum seekers and refugees might continue with their own cultural practices to maintain their health and well-being, as health beliefs[3] typically do not change after migration [11–16].

Health beliefs are shaping people's perception of their health, cause of their health issues, and the ways through which they can overcome an illness [10]. There are many studies related to immigrants 'health beliefs and the influence of their beliefs on their health-seeking behavior[4]; however, there are only a few that cover the impact of health beliefs on asylum seekers and refugees' health-seeking behavior [18–22].

This review is designed based on the Health Belief Model (HBM) which has guided studies on health-seeking behavior; especially, health seeking behavior among minorities from different ethnic backgrounds [7, 23, 24]. Since early 1950s, HBM has been widely used as a conceptual framework in health behavior studies. The model was developed according to a well-established body of psychological and behavioral theory, focusing mainly on two variables, including the value placed by an individual on a particular goal, and an individual's estimated possibility of achieving that goal by a given action [25, 26]. When these variables were conceptualized in the context of health seeking behavior, the correspondences were: (1) wishing to avoid illness or recover from illness; and (2) the belief that a specific health information or action will prevent illness [26].

This paper aims to perform a descriptive review to provide a holistic picture of studies related to health beliefs, and attitudes of asylum seekers and refugees and their health-seeking behavior. The research objectives guiding this study are:

1. To explore asylum seekers and refugees' health beliefs and their health-seeking behavior.
2. To investigate influential factors on asylum seekers and refugees' health-seeking behavior according to their health beliefs and cultures.

2   Research Methods

This review started with a literature search conducted in January 2022, using the preferred reporting items for systematic reviews and meta-analyses (PRISMA) guidelines [27]. To be included in the review, studies had to (a) be published in English or English, along with another language, (b) focus on human health beliefs issues, (c) focus on asylum seekers, and/or refugees, and (d) be original studies, not a brief review of an original study published in a conference paper or editorial note. All kinds of quantitative and

---

[3] Health beliefs are what individuals believe about their health, what they think constitutes their health, what they consider the cause of their illness, and ways to overcome an illness it [10].

[4] Health seeking behavior is any activity undertaken by people who perceived themselves to have a health issue or to be sick aiming at finding an appropriate treatment [17].

qualitative study designs were considered, including focus group discussions, structured or semi structured interviews, observations, secondary data analyses, and surveys.

The main focus of the included studies was on investigating health belief of asylum seekers and refugees rather than describing healthcare providers' interpretations of their beliefs. The studies were excluded if their main focus was on indigenous ethnic minorities, subcultures, immigrants, or seasonal workers. Moreover, the studies were excluded when they did not provide original research findings, such as systematic reviews, literature reviews, editorial notes, or conference posters. Furthermore, all studies which investigate the research topic from different angles rather than health belief were excluded (i.e., human rights, health law, ambulatory care, safety science, mediators, health information systems, and health policy).

2.1   Research Adapted Framework

This review uses an adapted framework based on HBM to provide a comprehensive overview of literature findings related to asylum seekers and refugees' health seeking behavior and their health beliefs and cultures. The HBM has several primary concepts that predict why individuals will take a particular action to prevent, to screen for, or to control health conditions [28].

According to HBM, the three components influencing health-seeking behavior of asylum seekers and refugees include modifying factors, individual beliefs, and individual action (see Fig. 1).

- Modifying factors are described in the original model as demographic attributes of individuals, such as age, gender, ethnicity, socioeconomics, and knowledge [23]. The model proposed in this research includes modifying factors, such as gender, country of origin, county of residence, and residency ground.

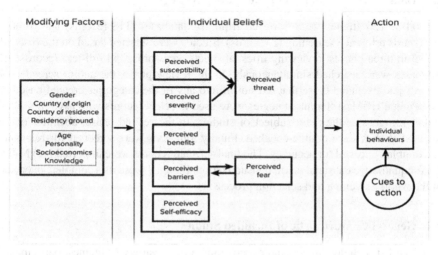

Fig. 1. Adapted framework based on health belief model components and linkages [25]

- Individual beliefs are described in the original model as perception about an illness, perceived benefits, perceived barriers, and perceived self-efficacy [23]. The proposed model for this review found perceived fear that may influence or be under influence from perceived barrier.
- Individual actions are described in the original model as individual behaviors and strategies to activate outcomes of the health seeking behavior [7, 25].

The concept in this study applied to providing a better understanding of individual beliefs and attitudes of this target group regarding their health and their health seeking behavior.

2.2 Information Sources and Search Strategy

Reviewer searched scientific databases through Web of Science (WoS), Scopus, and EBSCO for peer-reviewed journal articles, conference papers, books, and book chapters. Six databases (CINAHL (29 records), Medline (28 records), PubMed (35 records), PsycINFO (23 records), and PsycArticles (3 records)) were searched for the records on the association between asylum seekers, refugees and their beliefs and attitudes to health and illness.

This review started by searching for relevant studies through a medical subject heading (MeSH), truncation (*), and subject keywords adopted from Shahin et al. [28]. In addition, the terms "asylum seeker", and "refugee" along with all their synonyms and related terms were combined with proximity operators with a distance space of 10 (adj 10) to retrieve more results. The formulated search statement of this study was as follows: "health belief* OR attitude to health OR attitude to illness OR self-care OR self-management AND refuge* OR asylum seek*".

2.3 Data Extraction and Complete Search Strategy

A total of 120 studies were retrieved from six databases (118 records) and through backwards reference searching (2 records). Studies were selected based on the research model in three phases: reviewing titles, abstracts, keywords, and full-text records. All databases were searched simultaneously. In the review phase, the author screened all records and excluded those that did not fit into any of the categories created based on the original HBM; different strategies were used to select records with asylum seekers and/or refugees as the main subject of studies. In the second phase, abstracts of the selected studies were double-checked. Finally, full texts were screened for relevance and doubled checked for accuracy. The final selected records were imported into NVivo 1.6 for qualitative data analysis and visualization. Figure 2 presents a complete overview of the whole screening and selection process.

2.4 General Characteristic of Included Studies

The final list includes fifteen studies, covering a wide variety of themes, participants' genders, different sample size, various methods, and varied means of data gathering.

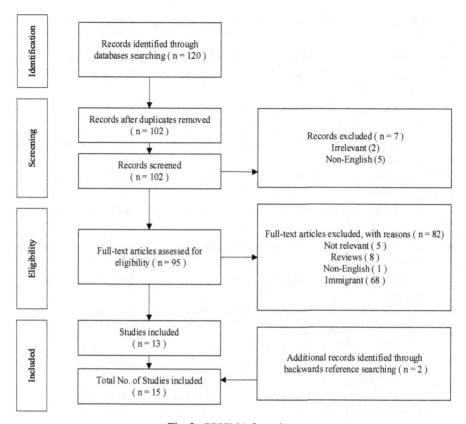

Fig. 2. PRISMA flow chart.

Majority of the included studies (8/15) were conducted in North America covering issues, including changing health beliefs and behaviors, cardiovascular disease, health beliefs and lifestyle, health beliefs and practices, health beliefs and women's health, and sexual health attitudes and beliefs (See Table 1).

This review includes studied with sample size ranging from eleven to approximately three hundred individuals, adopted both qualitative and quantitative methods, and utilized different means of data gathering, such as focus group, interviews, and observations. Table 2 and Appendix 1 provide additional information, such as vulnerable group categories, ethnic groups, current residency, and country of origin of the participants.

Table 1. Theme and methodological information of included studies in this review

ID	Theme	Gender	Size	Methodology	Data gathering
1	Health beliefs & women's health	Women	57	Qualitative	Semi-structured interview
2	Health beliefs & practices	Mixed	15	Qualitative	Focus group
3	Changing health beliefs & behaviors	Mixed	20	Qualitative	Semi-structured interview
4	Mental health beliefs & processes	Mixed	25	Qualitative	Semi-structured interview
5	Sexual health attitudes & beliefs	Mixed	11	Qualitative	Semi-structured interview
6	Sexual health attitudes & beliefs	Women	14	Qualitative	Semi-structured interview
7	Health beliefs & practices	Mixed	106	Qualitative	Semi-structured interview
8	Cardiovascular disease–related health beliefs & lifestyle	Mixed	195	Quantitative	Survey
9	Health beliefs & women's health	Mixed	45	Qualitative	Focus group
10	HIV & self-management skills	Mixed	19	Qualitative	Interviews & observations
11	Health beliefs & women's health	Men	38	Qualitative	Focus group & in-depth interviews
12	Diabetes & self-management skills	Mixed	292	Qualitative	Structured interviews
13	Health beliefs & practices	N/A	N/A	N A	N A
14	Health beliefs & practices	N/A	N/A	N A	N A
15	Health beliefs & practices	Mixed	119	Qualitative	Semi-structured interview

3 Results

An adapted framework based the HBM was used to examine attitudes and cultural beliefs concerning health-seeking behavior of asylum seekers and refugees in the world. We have identified three main categories, including modifying factors, individual beliefs, and individual action (See Fig. 1). The following subsections provide findings.

Table 2. General information related to included studies in this review

ID	Source	Target group	Residency	Origin
1	Saadi et al. 2015	Refugee	USA	Bosnian, Iraqi, and Somalin
2	Simmelink et al. 2013	Refugee	USA	Somalian, Ethiopian, and Eritrean
3	Brainard and Zaharlick 1989	Refugee	USA	Laotian
4	Savic et al. 2015	Refugee	Australia	Sudanese
5	Dean et al. 2016	Refugee	Australia	Sudanese
6	Dhar et al. 2017	Refugee	USA	Bhutanese
7	Papadopoulos et al. 2003	Refugee	UK	Ethiopian
8	Kamimura et al. 2017	Refugee	USA	Myanmarese
9	Ruzibiza 2021	Refugee	Rwanda	Burundian
10	Kennedy and Rogers 2009	Asylum seeker	UK	Sub-Saharan African
11	Piran 2004	Refugee	Iran	Afghan
12	Elliott et al. 2018	Refugee	Lebanon	Syrian
13	Kemp 1985	Refugee	USA	Cambodian
14	Rocereto 1981	Refugee	USA	Vietnamese
15	Gilman et al. 1992	Refugee	USA	Laotian

3.1 Perceived Susceptibility[5]

Table 3 provides common beliefs held across different ethnic groups within seven domains of the adapted HBM. First, common beliefs related to perceived susceptibility across all studied ethnic groups included lack of knowledge about health issues and its risk factors [13, 14, 16, 29–32], and Illnesses is caused by supernatural causes (God, Satan, or Evil spirits, magic, the evil eye) [15, 16, 29, 33–37]. These studies were in context of women's health, changing health beliefs and behaviors, mental health beliefs and processes, sexual health attitudes and beliefs, HIV and Diabetes and self-management skills. Second, perceived susceptibility and unique beliefs distinct to each ethnic group were: Sudanese key informants emphasized depression is white man's sickness [33], and Karen refugees resettled in the United States from the Thai-Myanmar (Burma) border [12] underscored lack of knowledge of the association between tobacco smoking and Cardiovascular disease.

---

[5] Perceived susceptibility "refers to beliefs about the likelihood of getting a disease or condition" [25].

Table 3. Common beliefs held across different ethnic groups

Adopted health belief model	Common beliefs	Ethnic groups
Barriers	Adhered to traditional normative beliefs	African, Asian, Middle-eastern
	Embarrassment	African, Asian, Balkan, Middle Eastern
	Fatalism	African, Asian, Balkan, Middle Eastern
	Inattentiveness to personal health	African, Asian, Balkan, Middle Eastern
	Poor patient provider communication skills	African, Asian, Balkan, Middle Eastern
	Presence of male providers	African, Asian, Balkan, Middle Eastern
	Psychosocial barriers	African, Asian, Balkan, Middle Eastern
Fear	Fear one's partner or family judgment	African, Middle Eastern
	Fear awareness of their community about preventive health issues	African, Balkan, Middle Eastern
	Fear of pain or diagnoses with breast cancer	African, Balkan, Middle Eastern
Benefits	Perceive the action as potentially beneficial by reducing the threat	African, Asian, Balkan, Middle Eastern
Severity	Belief about how serious a condition and its sequelae are	African, Asian
	Perceived susceptibility to and severity of illness or its sequelae	African, Asian, Balkan, Middle Eastern
Susceptibility	A lack of knowledge about health issues and its risk factors	African, Asian, Balkan, Middle Eastern
	Illnesses is caused by supernatural causes (God, Satan, or Evil spirits, magic, the evil eye)	African, Asian, Balkan, Middle Eastern
Self-efficacy	Confidence in one's ability to complete steps needed face with health issue	African, Balkan, Middle Eastern

(continued)

Table 3. (*continued*)

Adopted health belief model	Common beliefs	Ethnic groups
	Intentions to keep doctor's appointments	African, Balkan, Middle Eastern
Cues to action	A physician's recommendation	African, Asian, Balkan, Middle Eastern
	Flexibility in scheduling	African, Balkan, Middle Eastern
	Group educational program	African, Middle Eastern
	Help from physicians and other healthcare providers	African, Balkan, Middle Eastern
	Support from family friends	African, Asian, Middle Eastern

3.2 Perceived Severity[6]

Perceived susceptibility and perceived severity were two factors shaping perceived threat to health issues [25]. On the one hand, common health beliefs related to perceived severity included perceived susceptibility to and severity of illness or its sequelae with Bosnian, Somalian, Iraqi, Laotian, and Karen refugees in contexts of preventive health and breast cancer screening, changing health beliefs, traditional and modern health services, and cardiovascular disease respectively [12, 15, 29, 37]. On the other hand, belief about how serious a condition and its sequelae were common health beliefs among Ethiopian and Laotian in studies related to health beliefs and practices, and changing health beliefs and behaviors [15, 34]. Finally, unique beliefs distinct to African ethnic group related to perceived severity included beliefs that having HIV status would make life difficult and had considerable social problems, this was highlighted in a study with sub-Saharan asylum seekers with HIV [35].

3.3 Perceived Benefits[7]

Perceive the action as potentially beneficial by reducing the threat was noted among perceived benefits by African, Asian, Balkan, and Middle Eastern groups [12, 15, 29]. For instance, Iraqi and Bosnian woman mentioned, "*As long as the pain is for my own good in the end, I endure it,*" and "*Is not this for my own good? It is not for anyone else but me.*" [29]. Furthermore, several women from resettled Laotian refugees reported that "*they would have opted for a hospital birth because a hospital birth is safer if anything goes wrong, even had a traditional midwife been available.*" [15]. One particular perceived

---

[6] Perceived severity is "individual's beliefs related to the effects of a given health issue and the difficulties related to the health condition, such as pain, loss of work time, financial issues, and issues related to personal and family relationships" [38].

[7] Perceived benefits refers to "beliefs about the positive outcomes associated with a behavior in response to a real or perceived threat" [39].

Table 4. Unique beliefs distinct to each ethnic group

Adopted health belief model	Unique Beliefs	Ethnic groups
Barriers	Lack of family or community support	African
	Perceptions of racism	
	Silence (taboo)	
	Abrupt or hostile behavior of health care personnel	Asian
	Administrative barriers to care	
	Difficulty in finding interpreters	
	Distrust of the health care system	
	Preference for a physician from the same cultural background	
Fear	Fear awareness of their community about their mental health issues	African
	Fear of being considered sexually immoral	
	Fear of consequences associated with an unplanned pregnancy influenced condom use rather than fear of STIs or HIV	
	Fear of cultural shame	
	Fear of deportation	
	Fear that such conversations would encourage young people to do 'bad' things	
	Fear of western medicine	
	Fear of having blood drawn during medical examination	Asian
	Fear that IUDs will destroy the uterus	
Self-efficacy	Ability to recognize the threat to their health	African
	Adopting health-promoting behaviors through exercise or relaxation techniques to reduce stress	
	Confidence in one's knowledge & ability to explain the health results to others	
	Intentions to follow diet for health benefit	Asian
Cues to action	Support from community	African

(continued)

Table 4. (*continued*)

Adopted health belief model	Unique Beliefs	Ethnic groups
	Consulting with traditional healing specialists	Asian
	Consulting with local pharmacists	
	Access to gynaecological information	Middle Eastern
	Community health worker	

benefits form Laotian refugees study was perceiving "*western biomedicine stronger and more effective than traditional Laotian herbal remedies*" [15].

3.4 Perceived Barriers[8]

Perceived barriers were identified within four categories, including cultural and traditional factors, healthcare related barriers, health communication issues, and personal barriers.

3.4.1 Cultural and Traditional Factors

Embarrassment, fatalism, and presence of male providers were common perceived barriers in studies related to women's health, changing health beliefs, mental health, sexual health, and cardiovascular disease by African, Asian, Balkan, and Middle Eastern groups [12, 15, 29, 31, 33, 34, 40]. Different forms of expressions related to adhered to traditional normative beliefs was common perceived barriers by African, Asian, and Middle Eastern groups [13, 14, 16, 32, 35–37]. For example, both Cambodian and Vietnamese refugees in studies related to their health beliefs and practices mentioned "they do not like their head or shoulder touched" and "touching from shoulder up can be anxiety and soul may leave the body and cause health problems" [16, 37].

Lack of family or community support and silence (taboo) were specified as perceived barriers in studies on health beliefs and practices among Burundian, Eritrean, Ethiopian, and Somalian refugees [30, 34, 40]. As an example, silence was highlighted as a major barrier to effective implementation of adolescent sexual and reproductive health and rights program by Rwandan government [40]. A preference for a physician from the same cultural background was a perceived barrier mentioned in a study on cardiovascular disease–related health beliefs and lifestyle issues among Karen refugees [12].

---

[8] Perceived barriers are "the potential negative aspects of a particular health action and may act as impediments to undertaking recommended behaviors" [25].

3.4.2 Healthcare Related Barriers

Abrupt or hostile behavior of health care personnel, administrative barriers to care, and distrust of the healthcare system were mentioned as perceived barriers among Cambodian and Laotian refugees [16, 37]. Cambodian refugees mentioned issues related to language and cultural barriers, crowded waiting rooms, multiple interviews, and mysterious procedures as their perceived barriers to healthcare [16].

3.4.3 Health Communication Issues

Poor patient and healthcare provider communication skills were common perceived barriers in studies related to women health, changing health beliefs and practices by African, Asian, Balkan, and Middle Eastern groups [15, 29, 34, 36, 37]. Difficulty in finding interpreters was described as "limited availability of language interpreters and scheduled basis" as another perceived barrier related to health communication among Laotian refugees [37].

3.4.4 Personal Barriers

Inattentiveness to personal health and psychological barriers were commonly mentioned personal perceived barriers by African, Asian, Balkan, and Middle Eastern groups [12, 16, 29, 33]. For example, approximately two-thirds of women in a comparative qualitative study of refugee health beliefs on preventive health and breast cancer screening across Bosnian, Iraqi, and Somalian populations identified psychosocial barriers as barriers to uptake of preventive breast cancer screening [29]. Perceptions of racism was highlighted as Ethiopian refugees' individual perceived barriers [34].

3.5 Perceived Fear[9]

Fear awareness of their community about preventive health issues, and fear of pain or diagnosis with breast cancer were two common perceived fears in a study with Bosnian, Iraqi and Middle Eastern female women on preventive health and breast cancer screening [29]. Fear one's partner or family judgment was a common predictor of behavioral changes among sub-Saharan African and Afghan refugees in studies on asylum seekers with HIV, Afghan refugees and reproductive health attitudes [14, 35].

In terms of unique fear across African groups, different aspect of cultural, religious, community issues were mentioned by Burundian, Eastern African, Sundaneses, sub-Saharan African refugees in studies on mental health, sexual health, HIV and health beliefs, pregnancy and perinatal care, and health beliefs and practices (See Table 4) [13, 30, 33, 35, 40]. Cambodians' female refugees mentioned two perceiving or recognizing barriers to care as fear of having blood drawn during medical examination, and fear that IUDs will destroy the uterus [16].

---

[9] Perceived fear refers to an important predictor of behavioral changes and health-securing behaviors in response to perceiving or recognizing barriers to care [41].

3.6 Perceived Self-efficacy[10]

Confidence in one's ability to complete steps needed to face health issue, and intentions to keep doctor's appointments were the common expectations of self-efficacy among Bosnian, Iraqi, and Somali women in a study on refugee preventive health and Breast Cancer Screening [29].

Furthermore, positive elements of self-efficacy were identified among studies with African individuals, including ability to recognize the threat to their health, confidence in one's knowledge and ability to explain the health results to others, and adopting health-promoting behaviors through exercise or relaxation techniques to reduce stress in contexts of health practice and health beliefs, mental health, and HIV and self-management skills [30, 33–35]. Laotian refugees showed capabilities to organize and execute the courses of action required to manage their health through intentions to follow diet for their health benefit [37].

3.7 Cues to Action[11]

Commonly cited cues to action across African, Asian, Balkan, Middle Eastern populations included physician's recommendation [29, 37], flexibility in scheduling [29], group educational program [32, 35], help from physicians and other healthcare providers [29], and support from family and friends [30, 32, 34, 37] (see Table 4). There were also particular cues to action among different ethnic groups represented in this review. Consulting with traditional healing specialists, and consulting with local pharmacists were unique cues to action among Cambodian, Laotian, and Vietnamese refugees in different studies [15, 16, 36, 37]. Afghan and Syrian refugees mentioned access to gynecological information, and community health worker in studies on women's health and diabetes as their cues to action [14, 32]. Finally, support from community was an important motivator to seeking care by Somalian, Ethiopian, Eritrean, and Sudanese [30, 33].

4   Discussion and Conclusion

This review shed light on cultural beliefs and attitudes shaping asylum seekers and refugees' health beliefs, and their health-seeking behavior. The culture, tradition, fate or destiny, psychological factors, family, friends, and community were mentioned as the crucial influential factors in shaping how asylum seekers, and refugees perceived barriers, fear, severity, and susceptibility in their health seeking activities by African, Asian, Balkan, and Middle Eastern groups [13–16, 29, 32, 33, 36, 37].

More specifically, different forms of supernatural causes, fatalism, traditions and issues related to communications with healthcare providers were the common influential factors in health seeking activities by Asian and Middle Eastern asylum seekers and refugees [12, 14–16, 29, 32, 36, 37]. However, cultural shame, racism, and community

---

[10] Perceived self-efficacy refers to "beliefs in individual's capabilities to organize and execute the courses of action required to manage prospective situations" [42].

[11] Cues to action refers to "stimulus needed to trigger the decision-making process to accept a recommended health action" [43].

were mentioned as most influential factors in African refugees and asylum seekers health seeking behavior [30, 34, 40]. The increasing number of refugees and asylum seekers in the world leads to call upon healthcare providers and public health community to devise culturally relevant strategies that will effectively target different asylum seekers and refugees' groups with diverse cultural, traditional beliefs and attitudes about healthcare and health seeking activities.

Knowledge and awareness related to benefits of using modern healthcare services was highlighted as motivator for different ethnic groups to take care of their personal health [12, 15, 29]. More specifically, when the asylum seekers or refugees had enough information related to individual health, expectations of self-efficacy were found through different forms, including increasing confidence, intention, recognition, and adopting healthy lifestyle among refugees and asylum seekers [29, 30, 33, 34].

Adopting strategies, including providing health educational programs aiming at increasing asylum seekers and refugees' health literacy, knowledge, and awareness about health benefits of using modern healthcare services were highly recommended to the medical and public health community who are dealing with individuals with diverse ethnic backgrounds.

Physicians and healthcare providers, educational programs, and support from family, friends, and community had noteworthy influence on triggering the health-related decision-making process among asylum seekers and refugees [14, 16, 29, 30, 32–34, 36, 37]. This review shows the importance of engaging family and community support networks in health educational programs to eliminate or reduce the social stigma and cultural shame in using healthcare services as well as to bridge an understanding of cultural notions of health and disease among different ethnic groups of asylum seekers and refugees within the framework of modern healthcare structure.

This study proposed an adapted framework based on HBM and explored extensively health-seeking behavior of asylum seekers and refugees from cultural, psychological, religious, and traditional perspectives. However, there are limitations in applying adapted frameworks in terms of influential contextual factors in health seeking activities of the vulnerable groups, such as healthcare system and structure of different countries, which may have key role in shaping health beliefs and practices of these people but are not reflected in the model. Moreover, different studies related to the investigation of health beliefs of the vulnerable population have applied different methods (qualitative, quantitative, and mixed methods) in different contexts (i.e., women's health, mental health, cardiovascular disease, or diabetes) to examining health-seeking behavior that imposes significant limitations in the generalization of the findings.

The model proposed in this paper has different components influencing health-seeking behavior of asylum seekers and refugees in relation to modifying factors, individual beliefs, and individual action. However, included studies in the review did not consistently reflect information related to their studied groups in terms of age, gender, knowledge, and socioeconomic factors. Nonetheless, exploring health beliefs of vulnerable groups through adapted HBM provides significant information and understanding on cultural beliefs and attitudes that shape asylum seekers and refugees' health-seeking behavior. The outcome of applying such model is expected to provide practical guidelines for developing culturally appropriate health interventional programs to enhance compliance.

There were a few limitations in conducting this descriptive review. One of the primary limitations was the number of studies investigating health beliefs and behavior of asylum seekers and refugees. There was also inconsistency in providing information about studies of vulnerable group and their attitudes and behavior from the components of HBM perspectives. In addition, we also acknowledge that this review may not represent all relevant fields, as the scientific databases used in this review did not necessarily contain references to all the key publications. However, we are confident that the studies examined and evaluated in the review provide an overall overview of the body of academic publications within this multidisciplinary area of research.

5 Future Research Recommendation

The first recommendation for future studies calls upon healthcare providers, immigration authorities, policy makers, researchers, and surveyors to gather more comprehensive details on demographic, socio-cultural and migration-related information of refugees and asylum seekers. This information will facilitate recognizing asylum seekers and refugees' health beliefs, and their impact on their health-seeking behavior. Another recommendation is to conduct more studies related to asylum seekers and refugees' health beliefs to gain a better understanding of their needs for health services and health-related information and to develop health educational programs for their caregivers so that they are better able to meet these needs. The last recommendation is to shift away from solely investigating health service provision to adopting a cross-cultural and religious approach to provision of health services and health-related information for these people to meet the highest rate of satisfaction among these healthcare consumers.

Acknowledgement. This paper and the research behind it would not have been possible without the exceptional support of my supervisors, Dr Kristina Eriksson-Backa & Dr Shahrokh Nikou; and this research was supported by the grant from Finnish Cultural Foundation.

Appendix 1

Ethnic group and sub-ethnic groups of included studies in the review.

Ethnic group	Sub-ethnic group
African	Burundian, Ethiopian, Eritrean, Somalin, sub-Saharan African, Sudanese
Asian	Bhutanese, Cambodian, Laotian, Myanmarese, Vietnamese
Balkan	Bosnian
Middle Eastern	Afghan, Iraqi, Syrian

References

1. U.N.H.C.: What is a refugee. https://www.unhcr.org/what-is-a-refugee.html. Accessed 06 Mar 2022
2. Amnesty International Refugees: Asylum-seekers and Migrants. https://www.amnesty.org/en/what-we-do/refugees-asylum-seekers-and-migrants/. Accessed 06 Mar 2022
3. Alaoui, A., Patel, N., Subbiah, N., Choi, I., Scott, J., Tohme, W., Mun, S. K.: Health Information Sharing System for Refugees and Immigrants in Five States, In: 1st Transdisciplinary Conference on Distributed Diagnosis and Home Healthcare, D2H2., pp. 116–119. IEEE, Arlington, VA, USA (2006)
4. Benisovich, S.V., King, A.C.: Meaning and knowledge of health among older adult immigrants from Russia: a phenomenological study. Health Educ. Res. **18**(2), 135–144 (2003)
5. Katila, S., Wahlbeck, Ö.: The role of (transnational) social capital in the start-up processes of immigrant businesses: the case of Chinese and Turkish restaurant businesses in Finland. Int. Small Bus. J. **30**(3), 294–309 (2012)
6. Degni, F., Suominen, S., Essén, B., Ansari, W.E., Vehviläinen-Julkunen, K.: Communication and cultural issues in providing reproductive health care to immigrant women: health care providers' experiences in meeting the needs of [corrected] Somali women living in Finland. J. Immigr. Minor. Health **14**(2), 330–343 (2012)
7. Joseph, R., Fernandes, S., Derstine, S., McSpadden, M.: Complementary medicine & spirituality: health-seeking behaviors of Indian immigrants in the United States. J. Christ. Nurs. **36**(3), 190–195 (2019)
8. Pangas, J., et al.: Refugee women's experiences negotiating motherhood and maternity care in a new country: a meta-ethnographic review. Int. J. Nurs. Stud. **90**, 31–45 (2019)
9. Mangrio, E., Carlson, E., Zdravkovic, S.: Newly arrived refugee parents in Sweden and their experience of the resettlement process: a qualitative study. Scand. J. Public Health **48**(7), 699–706 (2020)
10. Misra, R., Kaster, E.C.: Health beliefs. In: Loue, S., Sajatovic, M. (eds.) Encyclopedia of Immigrant Health, pp. 766–768. Springer, New York (2012). https://doi.org/10.1007/978-1-4419-5659-0_332
11. Williams, N.E., Thornton, A., Young-DeMarco, L.C.: Migrant values and beliefs: how are they different and how do they change. J. Ethnic Migr. Stud. **40**(5), 796–813 (2014)
12. Kamimura, A., Sin, K., Pye, M., Meng, H.W.: Cardiovascular disease-related health beliefs and lifestyle issues among Karen refugees resettled in the United States from the Thai-Myanmar (Burma) border. J. Prev. Med. Public Health **50**(6), 386–392 (2017)
13. Dean, J., Mitchell, M., Stewart, D., Debattista, J.: Intergenerational variation in sexual health attitudes and beliefs among Sudanese refugee communities in Australia. Cult. Health Sex. **19**(1), 17–31 (2017)
14. Piran, P.: Effects of social interaction between Afghan refugees and Iranians on reproductive health attitudes. Disasters **28**(3), 283–293 (2004)
15. Brainard, J., Zaharlick, A.: Changing health beliefs and behaviors of resettled Laotian refugees: ethnic variation in adaptation. Soc. Sci. Med. **29**(7), 845–852 (1989)
16. Kemp, C.: Cambodian refugee health care beliefs and practices. J. Commun. Health Nurs. **2**(1), 41–52 (1985)
17. Ward, H., Mertens, T.E., Thomas, C.: Health seeking behaviour and the control of sexually transmitted disease. Health Policy Plan. **12**(1), 19–28 (1997)
18. Alvarez-Nieto, C., Pastor-Moreno, G., Grande-Gascón, M.L., Linares-Abad, M.: Sexual and reproductive health beliefs and practices of female immigrants in Spain: a qualitative study. Reprod. Health **12**(1), 1–10 (2015)

19. Jenkins, C.N.H., Le, T., McPhee, S.J., Stewart, S., Ha, N.T.: Health care access and preventive care among Vietnamese immigrants: do traditional beliefs and practices pose barriers. Soc. Sci. Med. **43**(7), 1049–1056 (1996)

20. Cooper Brathwaite, A., Lemonde, M.: Health beliefs and practices of African immigrants in Canada. Clin. Nurs. Res. **25**(6), 626–645 (2016)

21. Smith, A., et al.: The influence of culture on the oral health-related beliefs and behaviours of elderly Chinese immigrants: a meta-synthesis of the literature. J. Cross-Cult. Gerontol. **28**(1), 27–47 (2013)

22. Shah, S.M., Ayash, C., Pharaon, N.A., Gany, F.M.: Arab American immigrants in New York: health care and cancer knowledge, attitudes, and beliefs. J. Immigr. Minor. Health **10**(5), 429–436 (2008)

23. Becker, M.H.: The health belief model and sick role behavior. Health Educ. Monogr. **2**(4), 409–419 (1974)

24. Aalto, A.M., Uutela, A.: Glycemic control, self-care behaviors, and psychosocial factors among insulin treated diabetics: a test of an extended health belief model. Int. J. Behav. Med. **4**(3), 191–214 (1997)

25. Glanz, K., Rimer, B.K., Viswanath, K. (eds.): Health Behavior and Health Education: Theory, Research, and Practice, 4th edn. Jossey-Bass, San Francisco (2008)

26. Janz, N.K., Becker, M.H.: The health belief model: a decade later. Health Educ. Q. **11**(1), 1–47 (1984)

27. Shamseer, L., et al.: Preferred reporting items for systematic review and meta-analysis protocols (PRISMA-P) 2015: elaboration and explanation. BMJ **350**, 1–25 (2015)

28. Mckellar, K., Sillence, E.: Current research on sexual health and teenagers, Chap. 2. In: Mckellar, K., Sillence, E. (eds.) Teenagers, Sexual Health Information and the Digital Age, pp. 5–23. Academic Press (2020)

29. Saadi, A., Bond, B.E., Percac-Lima, S.: Bosnian, Iraqi, and Somali refugee women speak: a comparative qualitative study of refugee health beliefs on preventive health and breast cancer screening. Womens Health Issues **25**(5), 501–508 (2015)

30. Simmelink, J., Lightfoot, E., Dube, A., Blevins, J., Lum, T.: Understanding the health beliefs and practices of East African refugees. Am. J. Health Behav. **37**(2), 155–161 (2013)

31. Dhar, C.P., et al.: Attitudes and beliefs pertaining to sexual and reproductive health among unmarried, female Bhutanese refugee youth in Philadelphia. J. Adolesc. Health **61**(6), 791–794 (2017)

32. Elliott, J.A., et al.: A cross-sectional assessment of diabetes self-management, education and support needs of Syrian refugee patients living with diabetes in Bekaa Valley Lebanon. Confl. Health **12**(1), 40–50 (2018)

33. Savic, M., Chur-Hansen, A., Mahmood, M.A., Moore, V.M.: "We don't have to go and see a special person to solve this problem": trauma, mental health beliefs and processes for addressing "mental health issues" among Sudanese refugees in Australia. Int. J. Soc. Psychiatry **62**(1), 76–83 (2016)

34. Papadopoulos, R., Lay, M., Lees, S., Gebrehiwot, A.: The impact of migration on health beliefs and behaviours: the case of Ethiopian refugees in the UK. Contemp. Nurse **15**(3), 210–221 (2003)

35. Kennedy, A.P., Rogers, A.E.: The needs of others: the norms of self-management skills training and the differing priorities of asylum seekers with HIV. Health Sociol. Rev. **18**(2), 145–158 (2009)

36. Rocereto, L.: Selected health beliefs of Vietnamese refugees. J. School Health **51**(1), 63–64 (1981)

37. Gilman, S.C., Justice, J., Saepharn, K., Charles, G.: Use of traditional and modern health services by Laotian refugees. West. J. Med. **157**(3), 310–315 (1992)

38. Johnson, C.E., Mues, K.E., Mayne, S.L., Kiblawi, A.N.: Cervical cancer screening among immigrants and ethnic minorities: a systematic review using the health belief model. J. Lower Genital Tract Dis. **12**(3), 232–241 (2008)
39. NCI Perceived Benefits—Division of Cancer Control and Population Sciences (DCCPS). https://cancercontrol.cancer.gov/brp/research/constructs/perceived-benefits. Accessed 07 Mar 2022
40. Ruzibiza, Y.: Silence as self-care: pregnant adolescents and adolescent mothers concealing paternity in Mahama refugee camp. Rwanda. Sex. Cult. **26**, 994–1011 (2021)
41. Eder, S.J., et al.: Predicting fear and perceived health during the COVID-19 pandemic using machine learning: a cross-national longitudinal study. PLoS ONE **16**(3), e0247997 (2021)
42. Watts, R.E.: Self-efficacy in changing societies. J. Cogn. Psychother. **10**(4), 313–315 (1996)
43. LaMorte, W.: The Health Belief Model. https://sphweb.bumc.bu.edu/otlt/mph-modules/sb/behavioralchangetheories/behavioralchangetheories2.html. Accessed 07 Mar 2022

Measuring the Maturity of Healthcare Testbeds

Eva Collanus[1]([✉]) [ID], Emilia Kielo-Viljamaa[2] [ID], Janne Lahtiranta[1] [ID],
and Antti Tuomisto[1] [ID]

[1] University of Turku, Turku, Finland
evsico@utu.fi
[2] Novia University of Applied Sciences, Turku, Finland

Abstract. Co-creation is a commonly used method in health technology development. At the core of the approach is the development of solutions in collaboration with potential end-users or other experts that represent end-users' views. In Finland, co-creation is commonly carried through in testbeds: real-world environments or environments that closely simulate real-world conditions. Most testbed services are provided by hospitals, universities, or cities – public sector organizations that have mandated core operations (such as research or patient care) outside the testbed services. It follows from this that the quality of the services may vary. In our ongoing research, we will focus on understanding the quality of testbed services through maturity, the state of repeatability and readiness to serve the customers.

Keywords: Healthcare field · Co-creation · Testbeds · Maturity

1 Introduction

In Finland, testbeds have become the de facto way of conducting co-creative product development in the field of healthcare. Many of the domain testbeds focus on technology (e.g., HealthTech Lab operated by Turku University of Applied Sciences, and OYS Testlab operated by Oulu University Hospital). While there are no legal or otherwise binding limitations on who can offer testbed services in the domain, almost all testbed services are offered by public sector organizations, such as universities, hospital districts, or cities.

The few exceptions in the field are services offered by organizations that offer formal accreditation services, such as obtaining a CE marking. In addition, in the case of these private sector testbed service providers, the "loose" definition of testbed becomes problematic; are the offered services actually testbed services, or more akin to laboratory testing services, where the presence of the end-user may not be relevant at all. The fundamental question is, what counts as a testbed? On this matter, there are various, even contradictory, definitions in the literature. In this study, a testbed is defined as a platform for co-creation with customers, professionals, and other stakeholders; it can provide testing laboratories, simulation spaces or real-life environments [1]. There are many ways of naming the co-creation platforms in question. However, because the core

© The Author(s), under exclusive license to Springer Nature Switzerland AG 2022
H. Li et al. (Eds.): WIS 2022, CCIS 1626, pp. 179–191, 2022.
https://doi.org/10.1007/978-3-031-14832-3_12

idea is the same (i.e., providing co-creation services in a co-creation platform), we perceive testbeds, living labs, test labs, innovation labs and other co-creation platforms as corresponding concepts [c.f., 1]. In this article, we use the term testbed for consistency and link the discussion to the currently preferred terminology in Finland.

In the domain of healthcare, testbeds that offer co-creation opportunities have received significant attention in Finland over the last three years. Companies (and other stakeholders) have understood the benefits of developing solutions together with the actual end-users in real-world environments – or environments that simulate one. However, as the testbed services are complementary to the providers, the quality of testbed services varies. A patient care, research, and education are the primary services of these public sector organizations, and testbed services are commonly regarded as an added value to them.

Even though there have been testbeds in the field of healthcare for some time, there is little research on what makes a healthcare testbed "mature"; better in terms of quality of service and prepared to serve customers (esp. private sector companies). Better maturity leads to better testing, which can further develop products and services and thus positively affect care, for example, in social work. Some studies are made about the technical aspects of a testbed [c.f., 2], but the studies a) do not focus on the healthcare domain or b) regard the testbeds as co-creation facilities.

However, we argue that there is a definitive need for understanding the maturity of healthcare testbeds, and the first indications of this have already become exposed. For example, NHS England has reported their own testbed evaluation handbook [3], which presents different healthcare testbeds, and discusses how to evaluate their function. Another good indication of recent interest is the work by Jukić et al. [4], who discuss what makes co-creation mature in public and private organizations. However, outside these two publications, there is little discussion on what makes a healthcare testbed mature.

To fill this research gap, we have initiated a study in the field. In the first stages, we have investigated what kind of healthcare (co-creation) testbed services are provided in the Nordics and what kinds of factors are regarded by the potential customers (esp. companies) of the testbed services as an indication of a "good" testbed service. Having understood these factors, we have started a two-tiered work on 1) understanding the general framework that could be used for understanding the maturity of the domain testbeds and 2) what individual factors contribute to the analysis. This paper aims to understand how business process maturity models and factors can be applied to the context of healthcare testbeds in practice.

2   Why Maturity Models?

Maturity models – or maturity frameworks – are not just about a "good" way of conducting operations or providing services. They typically describe "the evolution of a specific entity over time" – usually, the evolution of a specific organizational area or function [5]. Maturity models commonly define different stages that represent the maturity or "business age" of the viewed entity. The models also describe what needs to be done to get to a higher or more "mature" level [6].

Maturity models tend to have three to six stages. Each stage typically has different dimensions and activities, which help apply the model to different settings [c.f., 7]. The business process maturity models that are our primary focus in the following are abundant in the literature. These are closely followed by software (IT) development models with a broad business audience. However, in some cases, the distinction between these two is not so evident.

Maturity models have gotten their part of criticism. For example, some models are blamed for oversimplifying reality and neglecting "the potential existence of multiple equally advantageous paths" [6, 8]. However, in counterarguments, the models are applauded for their comparativeness and prescriptiveness [6]. In our work, we see maturity models as diagnostic tools that can be used for a) understanding the current situation of a testbed, b) planning the road, and c) comparing testbed services against those of their peers.

3   Research Methods

The objective of this study is to understand how business process maturity models and factors can be applied to the context of healthcare testbeds. Our previous study [1] identified relevant factors by interviewing health technology companies and healthcare testbeds. In this study, we research them from a literature standpoint. For this, we have reviewed studies of business process maturity models and testbed papers. The traditional narrative review provides a coherent understanding of the topic when we aim to summarize previous theories and literature on the subject. On the other hand, we recognize there is room for different interpretations, which we should consider whilst collecting and analyzing studies.

The data collection was done in 2021 and 2022. As mentioned above, the maturity of healthcare testbeds is lacking; thus, we could not restrict our search only to the healthcare field. We emphasized healthcare and service business contexts. The selection prioritized recent publication years, but we soon recognized that the most relevant studies were not done in the last three years. The bases of business process maturity models required more broad inclusion. The strict restriction would have limited our knowledge. Only Finnish and English written papers were included. Our keywords include the healthcare field, testbeds, and maturity models. Considering research terms, we started with search terms "maturity model business process AND health" and "business process maturity model levels". We modified the keywords and research terms to address subjects we saw lacking. To understand the relevant maturity factors, we also researched studies on testbeds, living labs and other co-creation platforms that offer services for health technology companies or to other similar fields, such as the public sector. We used databases such as Web of Science and Business Source Complete, but soon we included Google Scholar, which enabled wider access to relevant and current research. Relevant data was found with the "snowball effect": this enabled us to find relevant, more referred studies that came up in the studies. When pondering suitable business process maturity models, current literature reviews helped explore best practices.

We know from previous studies [c.f., 1] that the research on healthcare testbed maturity is limited; hence, we decided to focus on business process maturity models. In addition to the richness of literature and experiences, we base our investigation on business models because of the kindship (not similarity) of healthcare testbed operations to generic business processes. These models commonly address business process performance and globalization [c.f., 9] and help organizations orient their services better to customer needs [10]. Of these two aspects, especially the latter, is of the essence when looking into how healthcare testbed services are currently offered and marketed in Finland. Furthermore, they helped validate the choice processes since there are a vast number of maturity models, most of which are not empirically tested in real-life situations.

4   Background: An Overview of Business Process Maturity Models

Business process maturity models (BPMMs) include process modelling, deployment, optimization and process management, and organizational culture and structure [9]. They give maturity stages and step-by-step guides to reach the higher maturity stage for business process management [11]. Tarhan et al. [12] list a total of 20 BPMMs, of which nine are counted as the most relevant ones. Furthermore, Felch and Asdecker [10] add three more relevant models to the list. Most of them are not empirically validated: whilst many different business process maturity models have been developed and sketched, only a few of them are actually tested in real-life situations. Manifold does not have any evidence of whether they really can improve the business processes or not [12]. The most studied and evaluated BPMMs are capability maturity model integration (CMMI), business process orientation maturity model (BPO-MM), business process management capability framework (BPM-CF), and process and enterprise maturity model (PEMM) [8, 10, 12] (see Table 1).

Table 1. Summary of business process maturity models.

Business process maturity model	Key element	Primary sources
CMMI	Most suitable for large organizations	[8–10, 13]
CMMI-SVC	Focuses on the organization's service practices	[8, 14, 15]
BPO-MM	Concentrates especially on cultural and structural aspects	[10–12, 16, 17]
BPM-CF	Emphasizes the role of organizational context	[10, 12, 18]
PEMM	Designed for self-assessment	[12, 17, 19]

Capability Maturity Model Integration. One of the most known and used process maturity model is capability maturity model integration (CMMI), which is also a base for many other models [9]. It is a framework used to measure the process development of the organization [8] so that the processes would be more suitable for the business needs

[13, p. 44]. CMMI is the most used of the maturity models and, according to the academic studies, is also the best one, especially for "large organizations rich in bureaucracy" [8]. The framework includes five maturity levels [13, p. 46], each indicating what can be expected from the processes and their results [13, p. 49]. The organization's current maturity level implicates which improvements are needed for the next maturity level: "– the higher maturity level of the organization, the more capable it is and the more predictable its results" [13].

Capability maturity model integration has variants for different situations. One of them is CMMI for services (CMMI-SVC) which aims to improve the organization's services practices [8]. The model is developed to help organizations that engage in service delivery. For example, the CMMI Product team [14] lists information technology, transportation and healthcare as suitable sectors that benefit from using the CMMI-SVC model. CMMI-SVC has 24 process areas in total, for example, capacity and availability management, service continuity, work monitoring and control, work planning, organizational process performance, and process and product quality assurance [15].

Even though – and perhaps precisely because of it – the CMMI models are the most popular maturity model frameworks, they have also received much criticism. Capability maturity model integration has been criticized for focusing only on the processes while ignoring the whole organization, its culture and people, even though these factors are vital for success [8]. It is also stated that the maturity models only give specific steps that improve the organization's maturity level and processes instead of giving broader instructions. In addition, CMMI requires "a specific type of training and experience", which has made many practitioners criticize it [8].

Business Process Orientation Maturity Model. The business process orientation maturity model (BPO-MMs) focuses on several cultural and structural aspects: customer orientation, organizational integration, process performance characteristics, culture, values and beliefs, people management characteristics, process supportive IT, and supplier orientation [11, 16]. The better business process orientation maturity the organization has, the more defined structural characteristics it has [11]. Business process orientation can be defined as the level where the organization considers its relevant processes [16]. Willaert et al. [16] have described detailed overviews of the different components. MMO has four described maturity stages; however, there is no assessment guide for determining maturity scores [17].

BPO-MM is one of the only BPMMs that refers to empirical studies about its development, application, and validation. Some studies even claim to link the BPO-MM usage with better business performance. BPO-MM has the largest amount of research on business environment testing, making it the most popular business process maturity model [12].

Business Process Management Capability Framework. Another popular business process maturity model is the business process management capability framework (BPM-CF), which has also been empirically tested to improve the organization's processes [12]. It was developed by Rosemann and de Bruin [18], who emphasized that the maturity level is always based on the context. It includes six factors impacting process success: strategic alignment, culture, people, governance, methods, and information technology. The framework has five maturity levels. However, even though the 5th level is the highest, it does not mean it might not be the best way for the organization's business process management. Instead, level 5 is the most sophisticated level, which might be suitable for certain business process management contexts [18].

BPM-CF is one of the most referred maturity models. Some studies actually involve empirical evidence on its development, application and validation, which is uncommon among maturity models [12].

Process and Enterprise Maturity Model. The process and enterprise maturity model (PEMM) is designed by Hammer [19]. It consists of two parts: process enablers and enterprise capabilities. Interdependent process enablers (design, performers, owner, infrastructure, and metrics) and supportive environments offering enterprise capabilities (leadership, culture, expertise, and governance) suit organizations of any industry and all their processes [19]. Thus, PEMM gives basic descriptive properties [12]. According to Tarhan et al. [12], using models such as PEMM is primarily diagnostic because they do not contribute to a process improvement guide.

The PEMM evaluation is designed so that organizations can assess their process enablers and enterprise capabilities themselves. Hammer [19] says even new personnel could use and interpret the framework. It is designed to be so simple that organizations do not need to "rely on experts or consultants – employees are more likely to believe in and act on such assessments" [19]. In addition, involving employees in the evaluation processes can engage them, and they might not resist the changes made to improve maturity.

PEMM is one of the few process maturity models that give examples of real-life applications and not just theoretical implementations [17].

5   Maturity Factors for Testbeds

Even though the four introduced maturity models have their own aspects of business processes, they have a few things in common: they concentrate on strategic alignment, culture (how a company reacts to changes), and people.

Testbeds and healthcare have their own characteristics and thus need to consider different things when discussing general business processes. For example, we need to take certain contextual ethical issues into consideration. There are some similarities, especially with the CMMI-SVC model, which considers work planning, quality assurance and service continuity, for instance. However, the model observes such a substantial number of factors that using CMMI-SVC purely would require specific training, and it could be too time-consuming to measure testbeds' maturity with it. BPO-MM, BPM-CF, and PEMM are applicable but do not include all the factors we have noted relevant for testbeds' maturity. What we can learn from the existing process maturity models, however, is the necessity of testing and validation in a real-life environment.

As mentioned above, some lessons can be learned outside BPMMs per se. Because the possibilities of co-creation and participatory development are becoming de facto standard, all parties are interested in testbed readiness too. NHS England has a Test Bed Programme that aims to improve healthcare through potential technologies [20]. The goal of the programme is, for example, to prevent unnecessary hospital admissions and support "frontline workers to deliver care more effectively and efficiently" [3, p. 1]. It also aims for better collaboration between relevant stakeholders, such as academia, industry, patient groups, and the NHS. It emphasizes how testbed evaluation is essential since it tells what has worked and what areas could be improved [3, p. 1]. It discloses several important aspects, such as resources, evaluation governance, ethical approval, and data collection and sharing [3, p. 11], as well as the importance of logic model development [3, p. 25], evaluation protocols [3, p. 27], and communication challenges [3, p. 30]. The NHS Test Beds Programme evaluation learning handbook addresses several key factors of testbed maturity, indicating we are on the right track with our maturity factors.

In this paper, we use Rosemann and de Bruin's [18] definition of the maturity factor. That is a specific and independent entity that reflects a "fundamental and distinct characteristic" that helps to describe the strengths and weaknesses of the subject. Thus, it is vital to identify suitable maturity factors that fit the context, in this case, healthcare and health technology development.

In 2021, we interviewed 13 healthcare testbeds in Nordic countries, focusing on Finnish testbeds [1]. These helped us to gather preliminary maturity factors. These were: resources, facilities, marketing and communications, repeatability, contract models, certification and standards compliance, and time in the market area. Then, after an expert panel, we operationalized the factors. Now, the factor categories are: 1) management, 2) staff, 3) quality, 4) operational processes, 5) funding, 6) facilities, 7) marketing and communications, and 8) ecosystems (see Table 2).

Staff. Staff includes not only the personnel of the testbed but also the recruitment of patients and customers participating in co-creation; and other staff that can be recruited if necessary, such as students and researchers. At a minimum, a testbed engages single coordinators or project leaders; at a maximum, it also employs researchers and healthcare professionals.

Testbeds give the opportunity to co-create with different stakeholders, such as researchers, patients, and clinicians [21]. For example, suppose the testbed has access to certain stakeholders and can designate suitable healthcare personnel to test certain products. In that case, it may indicate that the testbed has established its activities in the healthcare field. Successful patient and customer recruitment can also imply higher maturity: according to NHS [3, p. 17], testbeds are often too ambitious in the amounts of patients they try to recruit to participate.

On the issue of the business process maturity models, they do not address recruitment per se. However, all four of them focus more on personnel and other stakeholders' skills, knowledge, training, and motivation [14, 16, 18, 19].

Quality. A testbed's quality is difficult to measure per se. However, there are some things we can consider. For example, testbeds can ensure their quality by using quality manuals, defining different processes, and utilizing certifications or standards such as ISO 9001. Low-level maturity in this factor means the testbed does not have process descriptions or contract models, but high-level maturity implies tailorable process descriptions and contract models.

In terms of quality, studies emphasize management and evaluations; for example, NHS England [3] emphasizes the vitality of evaluation. According to [3], suitable data ownership processes and ethical approvals are important when assessing readiness.

On the other hand, it is possible to stress process and product management and assurance [22]. The introduced maturity models emphasize the process quality and evaluations. In CMMI-SVC, process and product quality assurance aim to "provide staff and management with objective insight into processes and associated work products" [23], while PBO-MM finds process documentation and process performance measurement vital [16]. Likewise, BPM-CF [24] and PEMM [19] underline the importance of measuring processes according to their priorities.

In addition, a testbed can assure their quality with (external) evaluations and with a steering group. This is also noticed in NHS England [3], which recommends that testbeds use evaluation advisory groups and/or local evaluation teams to ensure the testbed's process quality.

Operational Processes. Operational processes cover the base objects: for example, to whom the services are directed, who is the main customer (e.g., public sector or organizations), how long the testbed has provided its services, and how many times. Low-level maturity in operational processes stands for single testing activities, while high-level maturity in this factor means continuous co-creation.

Even though the time of existence or the quantities of service provided do not disclose the maturity per se, they give time to polish processes. By repetition, the testbed can notice issues that arise from certain situations that are not foreseeable. Likewise, if the testbed is planned to be a permanent part of the organization, they may have more time to understand operations and processes than in a fixed-term situation. If the testbed is based on a project, it may no longer be used after the project is finished [21]. However, it is more convenient to count service quantities rather than finances: after all, financial performance does not give much information on success or maturity [16]. For example, clinical testing in real-life situations can be more expensive than simple usability testing in a laboratory setting; however, it does not tell if the processes are more mature.

As mentioned above, customers are also part of operational processes: who can buy the services and who is the main customer. Therefore, as specified by both PEMM [19] and BPM-CF [24], it is important for organizations to know their customers, understand their needs and develop the processes accordingly.

Funding. Funding covers whether the testbed can fund product innovations and how the pricing of the services is designed (e.g., are the services free, or is the pricing market-based) is part of the factor. For instance, if the funding is coming only through a project, it implies it has a lower maturity level in this factor. However, if the funding is part of the organization's business activities, the testbed has higher maturity.

Financial models vary greatly between testbeds. They can be business-driven when the funding comes independently or from both public and private funding, or they can be research-driven, which is mainly government-subsidized [21]. Often the universities have the latter type of financial model, thus "heavily depending on public funding" [25].

Introduced business process maturity models do not focus on funding as their process areas or factors. However, it does not mean it is not vital to consider it in the healthcare testbed context. Testbeds often arise from projects that aim to develop them suitable for their purposes. Unfortunately, testbeds based on a project are sometimes no longer in use [21]. If it is tied to the organization's business activities, it can have a better chance of continuity and hence more time to become more mature in general, not only in the funding perspective.

Facilities. The testbed's facilities can be testing or laboratory environments [21], simulation laboratories [26] and/or real-life environments [26]. Sometimes the testbed aims to offer testing settings that enable co-creation and development before going to the real environment; however, the testbed is considered more mature if it offers the possibility to develop products or services in real-life settings (e.g., in hospitals). While classic laboratory settings provide important opportunities to develop, they fail to give real-life context and the possibility to see how the developed product/service would be used in its authentic setting by its ultimate end-users [21].

CMMI-SVC, BPO-MM, BPM-CF or PEMM does not address facilities in the same meaning; however, they all highlight IT and infrastructures that support business processes and make the work possible [16, 19, 23, 24].

Marketing and Communications. In our framework, the marketing and communications factor includes used communications channels (e.g., social media, webpages, or newspapers), communication plans, brand, and personnel responsible for marketing and communications. Testbeds that only use social media and a single webpage, but are not active on these platforms, do not have plans, or do not have the corresponding employee for marketing and communications, have lower maturity. Likewise, higher maturity means that the testbed also organizes meaningful events, has a marketing and communications plan, executes it actively, and has someone in charge of the related activities.

Maturity can be seen in testbeds when they "desire for positive public image" [4]. Functional marketing and communication can also reflect good customer relationships and the goal of approaching customers in a way the testbed is seen and noticed publicly. It prevents a situation where only a few selected organizations or individuals know its existence and recognize the situations and products that could benefit from the services of the testbed. In addition, the broader the audience uses the testbed, the more different applications and application scenarios can be recognized.

According to BPO-MM [16], it decreases confusion if certain people are responsible for certain things, e.g., marketing. Likewise, if people are responsible for many different things, or many are responsible for the same things, it can create tensions in the organization. On the other hand, BPM-CF [18, 24] highlights the importance of communication between stakeholders: not only in the marketing setting but also in the development processes.

Ecosystems. Ecosystems mean the networks and ecosystems the testbed is part of and their other partners. Different values are given to the testbed that is part of local, national, or international networks and ecosystems – the best situation being that they are involved in each kind.

Networks, such as the European Network of Living Labs (ENoLL), can help individuals and testbeds. Firstly, it helps individuals and organizations find the testbed, not only nationally but also internationally. Contrastingly, it can give testbeds an idea of what other testbeds are doing so that there would not be as much overlap in their services [21]. As reported by Santonen et al. [25], many testbeds are an essential part of local and regional innovation networks and ecosystems.

BPO-MM [16] emphasizes the supplier perspective of business. Nowadays, the roles between supplier and manufacturer are fading, making suppliers more partners: and partnerships can arise even globally, enhancing possibilities for success in a broader area. Thus, one cannot forget the importance of partners, networks, and ecosystems.

Table 2. Summary of maturity factors.

Maturity factor	Explanation	Primary sources
Staff	Testbed personnel, external workforce (e.g., students), customer and patient recruitment	[14, 16–19, 21]
Quality	The quality manuals, steering groups, evaluation processes, and documents ensuring uniform testbed services	[3, 16, 19, 22–24]
Operational processes	Customers, the number of services provided, age of the testbed	[16, 19, 21, 24]
Funding	Service pricing and funding possibilities	[21, 25]
Facilities	The facilities and settings the testbed provide to the customers (laboratory, simulation, real-life settings)	[21, 26]
Marketing and communications	Communication channels, marketing personnel, communication plans	[4, 16, 18, 24]
Ecosystems	Networks and ecosystems the testbed is part of and its partners	[16, 21, 25]

6   Discussion and Future Steps

We have already learnt from the existing maturity models and current literature about the need for continuous development of maturity models. Used models must live with time – they must be tested, evaluated, and validated in real-world environments. In the case of BPMMs, they are typically evaluated through "demonstration with a prototype, experiment with prototype or system, benchmarking, survey, expert interview, focus group" [10]. From this perspective, our next step in which the status of our work is validated using local healthcare testbeds as a benchmark and then refined for further use with wider audiences is in line with the MOs used in the field.

We have published a paper addressing the seven initial maturity factors and how they are visible in the interviewed Nordic testbeds. Now we have also addressed how literature sees the factors. The fact that testbeds are usually facilitated by universities, hospitals and cities lead to the fact the testbed business is not the core operations of these actors. This impacts how the facilitation is executed, managed, and developed. Thus, this study concentrates on practical contributions.

To develop a maturity framework, we need to break up the initial maturity factors into more detailed ones, which are used for a more detailed analysis of the testbeds. We also need to consider if some factors and components are more critical than others. Furthermore, we need to define maturity stages to build a measurement instrument. The studies of BPMMs and other maturity models help us understand these. The structure and the content of the framework and the instrument have been assessed by an expert panel, which gave us valuable feedback for revisions. Now, the maturity framework is under piloting and testing. This gives us more data used to polish the framework even further.

It is vital to note that piloting and testing help us understand the aspects of companies and testbeds and the perspective of clinical workers and other product end-users. Because our environment is healthcare and co-creation and testbeds are all about including different stakeholders, we cannot focus only on the developers and facilitators. The testing will give us more understanding of perspectives on testbed participation.

The goal of the project is not just to make an assessment instrument. The developed and tested framework that helps improve the maturity of testbed activities can really enhance the health technology co-creation and development activities – and that way, help companies make better products that are beneficial for product end-users, clinical workers, and patients. For instance, a quality testbed can help develop social services and provide more ways to improve the work of social workers and the treatment of patients in different situations. Furthermore, the quality of the testbed ensures that this is done in a resource-wise manner, with high-quality results and fruitful collaboration with the participants. All this enhances the RDI ecosystem of the area, which is crucial for the sustainable development of society.

Limitations. This study has potential limitations. Whilst narrative literature review suited our aim, it has flaws: our biases could have affected the selection of studies. Because there is little prior knowledge of testbeds' maturity, we did not limit our data collection only to the most recent publications. Furthermore, we selected only Finnish or English written research, which may have dropped off relevant studies written in other languages.

Acknowledgements. This paper was conducted by the project Health Campus Turku 2.0 (337640), funded by the Academy of Finland.

References

1. Kielo-Viljamaa, E., Collanus, E., Lahtiranta, J., Tuomisto, A.: Maturity of health care testbeds – a qualitative mapping at the Nordic context. FinJeHeW **14**, 92–103 (2022). https://doi.org/10.23996/fjhw.111734

2. Hermenier, F., Ricci, R.: How to build a better testbed: lessons from a decade of network experiments on emulab. In: Korakis, T., Zink, M., Ott, M. (eds.) TridentCom 2012. LNICSSITE, vol. 44, pp. 287–304. Springer, Heidelberg (2012). https://doi.org/10.1007/978-3-642-35576-9_24

3. NHS England: NHS England Test Bed Programme: Evaluation learning from Wave 1 (2018)

4. Jukić, T., Pluchinotta, I., Hržica, R., Vrbek, S.: Organizational maturity for co-creation: towards a multi-attribute decision support model for public organizations. Gov. Inf. Q. **39**, 101623 (2022). https://doi.org/10.1016/j.giq.2021.101623

5. Tapia, R.S., Daneva, M., van Eck, P., Wieringa, R.: Towards a business-IT aligned maturity model for collaborative networked organizations. In: 2008 12th Enterprise Distributed Object Computing Conference Workshops, pp. 276–287. IEEE, Munich (2008)

6. Pöppelbuß, J., Röglinger, M.: What makes a useful maturity model? A framework of general design principles for maturity models and its demonstration in business process management. In: ECIS (2011)

7. Mettler, T., Blondiau, A.: HCMM - a maturity model for measuring and assessing the quality of cooperation between and within hospitals. In: 2012 25th IEEE International Symposium on Computer-Based Medical Systems (CBMS), pp. 1–6. IEEE, Rome, Italy (2012)

8. Albliwi, S.A., Antony, J., Arshed, N.: Critical literature review on maturity models for business process excellence. In: 2014 IEEE International Conference on Industrial Engineering and Engineering Management, pp. 79–83. IEEE, Selangor Darul Ehsan, Malaysia (2014)

9. Van Looy, A., Poels, G., Snoeck, M.: Evaluating business process maturity models. JAIS **18**, 461–486 (2017). https://doi.org/10.17705/1jais.00460. Ghent University, Faculty of Business and Economics, K.U. Leuven

10. Felch, V., Asdecker, B.: Quo vadis, business process maturity model? Learning from the past to envision the future. In: Fahland, D., Ghidini, C., Becker, J., Dumas, M. (eds.) BPM 2020. LNCS, vol. 12168, pp. 368–383. Springer, Cham (2020). https://doi.org/10.1007/978-3-030-58666-9_21

11. Van Looy, A., Backer, M.D., Poels, G., Snoeck, M.: Choosing the right business process maturity model. Inf. Manag. **50**, 466–488 (2013). https://doi.org/10.1016/j.im.2013.06.002

12. Tarhan, A., Turetken, O., Reijers, H.A.: Business process maturity models: a systematic literature review. Inf. Softw. Technol. **75**, 122–134 (2016). https://doi.org/10.1016/j.infsof.2016.01.010

13. O'Regan, G.: Capability maturity model integration. In: Introduction to Software Process Improvement, pp. 43–65. Springer, London (2011). https://doi.org/10.1007/978-0-85729-172-1_3

14. CMMI Product Team: CMMI for Services, Version 1.3. 4315959 Bytes (2010). https://doi.org/10.1184/R1/6572375.V1

15. Kusakabe, S.: Analyzing key process areas in process improvement model for service provider organization, CMMI-SVC. In: 2015 IIAI 4th International Congress on Advanced Applied Informatics, pp. 103–108. IEEE, Okayama, Japan (2015)

16. Willaert, P., Van den Bergh, J., Willems, J., Deschoolmeester, D.: The process-oriented organisation: a holistic view developing a framework for business process orientation maturity. In: Alonso, G., Dadam, P., Rosemann, M. (eds.) BPM 2007. LNCS, vol. 4714, pp. 1–15. Springer, Heidelberg (2007). https://doi.org/10.1007/978-3-540-75183-0_1

17. Röglinger, M., Pöppelbuß, J., Becker, J.: Maturity models in business process management. Bus. Process Manag. J. **18**, 328–346 (2012). https://doi.org/10.1108/14637151211225225

18. Rosemann, M., de Bruin, T.: Towards a business process management maturity model. In: Proceedings of the 13th European Conference on Information Systems, pp. 521–532 (2005)

19. Hammer, M.: The process audit. Harvard Bus. Rev. **2007**, 20 (2007)

20. NHS England: Test beds. https://www.england.nhs.uk/aac/what-we-do/how-can-the-aac-help-me/test-beds/

21. Grotenhuis, F.D.J.: Living labs as service providers: from proliferation to coordination. Glob. Bus. Organ. Excellence **36**, 52–57 (2017). https://doi.org/10.1002/joe.21790
22. Alonso, J., Martínez, I., de Soria, L., Orue-Echevarria, M.V.: Enterprise collaboration maturity model (ECMM): preliminary definition and future challenges. In: Popplewell, K., Harding, J., Poler, R., Chalmeta, R. (eds.) Enterprise Interoperability IV, pp. 429–438. Springer, London (2010). https://doi.org/10.1007/978-1-84996-257-5_40
23. Wibas: CMMI for Services (CMMI-SVC) v1.3 (n.d.)
24. Rosemann, M., vom Brocke, J.: The six core elements of business process management. In: vom Brocke, J., Rosemann, M. (eds.) Handbook on Business Process Management 1. IHIS, pp. 105–122. Springer, Heidelberg (2010). https://doi.org/10.1007/978-3-642-45100-3_5
25. Santonen, T., Kjellson, F., Andersson, K., Hirvikoski, T.: Developing maturity model for transnational living lab collaboration. In: Bitran, I., Conn, S., Gernreich, C., Heber, M., Huizingh, K.R.E., Kokshagina, O., Torkkeli, M. (eds.) Proceedings of the 2020 ISPIM Innovation Conference (Virtual) Event "Innovating in Times of Crisis" held on 7 to 10 June 2020. International Society for Professional Innovation Management (2020)
26. Haukipuro, L., Väinämö, S., Hyrkäs, P.: Innovation instruments to co-create needs-based solutions in a living lab. Technol. Innov. Manag. Rev. **8**, 22–35 (2018). https://doi.org/10.22215/timreview/1156

Study Structures in the Interplay of Stress and Coping in Higher Education

Eija-Liisa Heikka[1]([✉]) [iD], Pia Hurmelinna-Laukkanen[1] [iD], Outi Keränen[1] [iD], and Pia Partanen[2]

[1] University of Oulu Business School, Oulu, Finland
{eija-liisa.heikka,pia.hurmelinna-laukkanen,
outi.keranen}@oulu.fi
[2] University of Oulu, Oulu, Finland
pia.partanen@oulu.fi

Abstract. Stress and coping have attracted examination from viewpoints of students and faculty, but often separately. We aim to combine these perspectives by considering the interplay of stress and coping, and how these emerge among students and teachers at a business school where study structures have changed. Our findings indicate a strong connection between the stress experienced by students and by faculty. We subsequently categorise the various stressors as (1) those for which effective coping mechanisms exist, (2) those that exhibit tensions and require active management, and (3) those that are difficult to overcome because the coping mechanism for one group increases the stress of the other. Our findings contribute to the existing knowledge on stress and coping in higher education by combining the viewpoints of students and teachers. The study also extends understanding of business education and the role of study structures in the well-being of business students and faculty.

Keywords: Stress · Coping · Study structures · Higher education

1 Introduction

In evaluating a situational threat, individuals assess whether they have enough resources to cope with it, influencing their perception [11]. Conversely, stress emerges when the individual's resources are taxed or exceeded [5]. While the stressor itself is neutral, an individual's response can be positive or negative [10, 18], but such interpretation influences an individual's well-being in both cases.

Well-being has been researched in many working environments [1], and recent studies have also examined the well-being in higher education [7]. University students have been found to stress over balancing work, family, and student life [15], and faculty members experience stress from the pressure to publish [14], acquire funding, participate in various administrative activities, and manage student feedback – all of which need to be balanced with other areas of their lives [3]. These issues can also affect how teachers approach their students, and greater recognition of the stressful nature of higher

© The Author(s), under exclusive license to Springer Nature Switzerland AG 2022
H. Li et al. (Eds.): WIS 2022, CCIS 1626, pp. 192–203, 2022.
https://doi.org/10.1007/978-3-031-14832-3_13

education is therefore needed [15]. In addition, research is needed to understand how some coping strategies work for teachers and others for students [17]. However, existing literature seems to focus either on students or faculty, and relatively little attention has been paid to the dynamics between the different stressors and coping mechanisms of the two groups. The interplay between these elements could be important in helping to resolve some of the emergent well-being challenges in higher education.

Thus, we examine *how experienced stress and coping mechanisms for students and teachers in higher education are connected in relation to study structures.* We contribute to existing knowledge on stress and coping mechanisms in higher education by combining the student and teacher viewpoints of stress and coping in a business education context. As a specific contribution, we identify effective formal and informal support frameworks, tensions that call for active management, and inbuilt contradictions that present as irreconcilable stress factors. Acknowledging these issues will allow measures to be taken to improve the well-being of both students and teachers.

2 Structures Related to Stress and Coping in Higher Education

In higher education, varying formal and informal structures guide the activities of students and faculty. Study structures show how studies are meant to progress, and support systems such as student administration (including counselling, personal study plans, etc.) are relevant functions that give practical support to their realisation and fluency [9]. In addition, different informal structures, such as peer communities, guide teachers' and students' conduct [19].

This study suggests that stress can be observed in people's reactions to these structures. In higher education, stress is typically associated with requirements stemming from study structures for students to pass courses, progress in a certain timeframe, and achieve high enough grades [14]. Sometimes, stress can be found to be positive, pushing both students and teachers to better results. However, Zimmerman et al. [21] also note that levels of student burnout can often be traced to changes in programme organisation and that study-related structures can also increase the workload for teachers, limiting the ways in which they can balance their teaching, research, and administrative duties [14]. For instance, while international accreditation is a means of pursuing legitimacy and global status, it seems to generate stress [14]. Similarly, informal structures may induce stress. For example, a competitive educational culture can result in students spending more time on their studies. This may improve their performance but may also lead to feeling that they cannot show any tiredness to peers or family [12].

The existing research tends to focus on the negative side of stress [21], covering the demands of academic work for students, such as workload, social issues, and worries over job prospects. These stressors may be intertwined with the pressure of time management and meeting deadlines [12], accelerated by the need to take part-time jobs [17]. Correspondingly, studies on higher education faculty have reported that work tends to occupy free time and holidays [14]. Subsequently, the relevance of preventive strategies for dealing with academic stress and mental health problems has increased their importance [16].

Coping mechanisms are an individual's cognitive and behavioural attempts to deal with internal and external demands and the conflicts between them [4]. In the literature, coping has been characterised as problem-focused (removing or circumventing the stressor, e.g., through self-leadership [8]; emotion-focused, e.g., through positive affect [8]; or avoidance focused, e.g., ignoring the situation [2].

Like stress, coping mechanisms may be approached by looking into structures. For students, there are many formal support services in universities [13]. It also has been found that satisfaction with social support networks can act as a buffer against stress for both students and teachers [2]. Peer mentoring tends to influence student well-being, and hence developing relevant prevention and intervention programmes can manage academic stressors [20].

However, coping mechanisms do not always have the intended effect [21]. Students might not be aware of the support provided for them [19] or even recognise when they are stressed [17]. In addition, the negative approach to stress may make individuals feel ashamed of seeking help [16]. Another challenge is that a structure that has been established to support one group may increase the stress of others. A student may, for example, benefit from the dedicated support of a teacher-tutor but the teacher may become stressed about finding enough time for the task. In addition, the teacher's inability to help the student due to certain rules or a lack of professional knowledge about mental health can be a stress-causing combination [9]. Similarly, faculty might benefit from clear rules around grading and retakes, although students can find them too rigid [21].

It can be concluded that the stress felt by students resonates with their teachers' stressors, influencing the quality of teaching and the performance of students. Tensions can emerge when the needs of students and teachers collide, and the efficiency of their coping mechanisms is limited; the same structure can sometimes have an opposite effect on the stress of the two groups. For example, increased use of information technology might increase flexibility while simultaneously increasing the stress of the other party. Different structures may also have similar influences on different groups. To better understand these issues, we turn to empirical examination.

3 Methodology

This study uses a qualitative case study to allow a view of stress and coping from the perspective of both students and teachers. The study context is a business school of a Nordic public university, where the organisation of the degree programmes and the application process were changed significantly a few years ago. Although the new study-related structures were designed to allow students to finalise their studies within a specific timeframe and with curriculum personalisation, they have been identified as stressors for students and teachers. Since the changes, students apply for specific majors in the later stages of their bachelor programme, not when entering the school. The final selection is based on the popularity of the desired majors and grade averages, which creates competition among the students and prompts exam retakes. Subsequently, the business school has developed several formal support structures, such as tutor-teacher activities and systems for developing pedagogical skills.

3.1 Data Collection

The data comprises organisational documentation, interviews, and multiple survey responses. Three surveys were conducted in 2019, 2020, and 2021 to collect student insights through around 60 Likert-scaled and qualitative open-ended questions on study-work-life balance, programme structure and difficulty level, and stress, well-being, and coping. In total, 232 responses were received in 2019, 267 in 2020, and 285 in 2021, representing a response rate of between 16 and 19%.

The teachers' views were gathered using an email questionnaire sent in 2019 and 2020 containing open questions regarding workload, perceptions of study structures, and student interaction. The questionnaire was sent to 156 individuals on the business school's email list, and 20 teachers responded. This limited response is at least partially because not everyone receiving the questionnaire was long-term faculty and, to be able to respond, an individual needed to have worked at the business school both before and after the changes. This adjustment brings the response rate in line with that of the students. To understand the teachers' insights more thoroughly, seven in-depth interviews were conducted in spring 2020 (Table 1). In addition to the survey and interview data, a report of staff well-being survey (2020), the school's webpages and annual reports, and accreditation-related and tutor-teacher training materials were examined.

Table 1. The interview data.

Interviewee	Date	Duration
Professor A	5 June 2020	45 min
Professor B	8 June 2020	1 h 20 min
Professor C	8 June 2020	52 min
Professor D	8 June 2020	20 min
University Lecturer	10 June 2020	31 min
University Lecturer	17 June 2020	30 min
Assistant Professor	23 June 2020	58 min

3.2 Analysis

First, each dataset was separately analysed to distinguish recurring patterns relating to stress and coping, and subcategories were then created to identify links between them [6]. This step showed how the identified stressors and coping mechanisms were related to study, formal, or informal support structures. Next, the datasets were combined and analysed from the viewpoints of students and teachers. In the final phase of analysis, the groups' views were combined using the structures as the point of connection to analyse the interactions between the stressors and the coping mechanisms for each group.

The qualitative analysis was conducted by two researchers, first separately and then discussing their findings to reach a consensus. The stressor and coping categorisations of the two researchers were nearly identical, and there were no significant disagreements. A third researcher ran statistical tests on the quantitative student survey data to check that the qualitative data was in line with the overall patterns. Very similar connections were detected, so we proceeded with the qualitative assessment, the findings of which are presented below.

4 Findings

The findings revealed extensive variety in how individuals experience stress and cope with it. The data collected from the students clearly showed that their most significant stressor was uncertainty related to applying for majors. This stemmed from the highly competitive atmosphere around selection and the related pressure of achieving good grades, which increased the perceived need for retakes and caused time management and workload issues since retakes are typically held simultaneously as other exams. Another central point is that the curriculum's general nature and the required modules created a lack of motivation as students must take subjects that they do not feel are particularly important. Stress emerged due to problems in passing mandatory courses and subsequently proceeding with studies, applying to a specific major, or graduating on time. The generality of the programme generated additional worry about being inadequately qualified on graduation. Table 2 summarises the findings related to stressors and their relation to structures.

Table 2. Structural factors and related stressors for students.

Structural factor	Stressor	Quotes
Major selection	Grade competition	"The average of your grades that influence applying to majors has caused stress."
Time frame	Workload	"Specifically, courses that influence majors are retaken multiple times, creating lots of extra work."
	Scheduling	"Scheduling, and if there are too many exams and courses simultaneously."
	Keeping up with the timeframe	"It stresses the most if I am able to complete enough courses to apply to the master's program."
	Expiring study rights or student allowance months	"Master's thesis and graduation on time and expiring study right."
Obligatory studies	Lack of motivation	"Challenging courses, for which you are not motivated."

(continued)

Table 2. (*continued*)

Structural factor	Stressor	Quotes
	Passing courses	"Graduating on time and passing certain courses."
Generality of curriculum	Lack of proficiency	"The general Bachelor's program does not teach anything properly."
	Job prospects	"Generalistic bachelor's programs do not provide qualification to any work task."

Among the students' coping mechanisms, formal support structures were important. The students indicated that knowing where to ask for help for various problems is vital. Official support systems, such as tutoring activities, were deemed beneficial in forming social relationships and becoming familiar with the new environment. Electronic examination emerged as a specific example of a structure that can ease student stress; 'e-exams' were less stressful than normal modes of assessment as they were perceived to support time management and write higher quality answers. The significance of tools that enable distance learning increased during the pandemic. While remote teaching and learning during COVID-19 caused stress for most students, there was also an appreciation of new learning methods that improved performance and lowered stress. Overall, students expected that opportunities to engage in distance learning would assist them in managing their time.

Student coping mechanisms are more complex when observed in terms of study structures. For example, although the uncertainty around major selection was stressful for most respondents, it eased stress for others; they felt that studying a range of subjects in the bachelor's programme developed familiarity with different majors, which eased

Table 3. Structural factors and related coping mechanisms for students.

Structural factor	Coping mechanism	Quotes
Remote learning/e-exam	Flexibility	"The e-exam helps you in coordinating work and study lives."
	Control	"With a computer, you can write more thoughtful and decent answers."
Generality of curriculum	Better decisions	"After having general knowledge from all majors, it is easier to decide about the major."
Social support	Friends and meaningfulness	"I have felt studying meaningful and made wonderful new friends."

decision-making. Informal support structures were also seen to have varying influences. While the comparison to friends and peers caused pressure around improving grades, having friends enhanced the meaningfulness of and progress in studies. Table 3 illustrates the findings related to students' coping mechanisms and their relation to structures.

Similarly, teachers reported mixed experiences regarding study structures. The increases in student intake resulting from changes to the bachelor's and master's programmes increased workload and challenged effective delivery of teaching and assessment, thereby increasing stress (see Table 4). The generality of the bachelor's degree was seen to pose demands regarding the course content, especially regarding the students' base level of knowledge. Over recent years, there has been a decrease in courses and learning activities that would develop basic academic skills. Therefore, a need has emerged to adjust first-year courses accordingly. This subsequently affects the skills with

Table 4. Structural factors and related stressors for teachers.

Structural factor	Stressor	Quotes
Increased student intake	Teaching and evaluation methods	"The increased number of students caused that the assessment needed to be changed."
	Workload	"Teaching takes double work [...] because the number of students per course has increased and demands of diverse teaching add even more work."
	Course content	"In the past, students had much broader (major-specific) knowledge."
Generality of curriculum	Insecurity	"We need to supervise all kinds of topics, and sometimes I feel not competent enough."
	Lack of motivation	"There might be students who have primarily applied to some other major. Motivating these students creates challenges."
Major selection	Retakes	"When we have a highly competitive bachelor's program, the grade is a disappointment for many, causing a lot of work."
	Aggressive attitudes	"The grade goals are high and [...] the result is aggressive complaints, looking for errors in the teacher [...] and atmosphere may even be hostile."

which students begin their majors. The most significant stressors of teachers are linked to student attitudes towards these compulsory basic courses and retakes. The grade goals of the students are high because of competition, which had been found sometimes to generate aggressive criticism and a hostile atmosphere. In the worst cases, students focused on looking for teaching errors. This type of grade-oriented, instead of learning-oriented behaviour, was mentally challenging for teachers.

On the other hand, clear rules help the teachers to communicate with the students, as does being able to refer to study structures when students make inquiries for special arrangements. Teaching is described as more coordinated now with effective programme management and a focus on the assurance of learning. As the structure is more controlled, it is easier to know what the students have already studied, and teachers can better position their courses. A sense of belonging provides an appropriate social pressure to develop teaching.

Most faculty respondents consider stress and workload levels reasonable even though the pandemic created a new type of pressure to utilise various platforms and tools. Teachers manage many stressors through pedagogical training and discussions with their peers. Especially informal support systems and support from superiors remain highly relevant. Table 5 illustrates the coping mechanisms of teachers and their relation to structures.

Table 5. Structural factors and related coping mechanisms for teachers.

Structural factor	Coping mechanism	Quotes
Student intake and major selection	Pedagogical training	"More interactive methods in both teaching and course evaluation."
	Peer discussions	"Discussion with colleagues assists in developing pedagogical issues."
Program-level coordination	Collaboration and sense of belonging	"It is easier to know what the students have already studied. This way, I can locate my course and teaching in the program and make use of the connections with other courses."
	Common guidelines	"We are pleased with the common policy for not allowing retakes of course assignments."

5   Discussion

The main findings of our study show the multitude of stressors and coping mechanisms for students and teachers in higher education. A closer examination highlights the dynamic role of structures in this relationship. As Lazarus and Opton [10] suggest, the meaning of the same stressor can vary, and we demonstrate this variance in the context of business education.

While some stressors are discrete, many of them are multifaceted in that the same factor can have a different role within and between the groups of actors, even to the level of a stressor becoming a coping mechanism. For example, study-related structures reduce rather than increase stress for some students and teachers. Students can feel either frustration or advantage at having more time to decide which major to apply to, and such structures can pose demands for teachers but also provide them with opportunities for collaboration that will ease their workload [10]. Teachers can feel stressed by the requirements for high-quality teaching and reporting for accreditation purposes [14], but these study structures can also increase the clarity of what is expected from them.

It seems that formal and informal support structures bear different meanings for students and teachers. Teachers appear to benefit from informal structures, especially peer support, which emphasises the importance of emotional coping [8]. On the other hand, formal structures, such as tutor-teacher arrangements, often generate additional demands. For students, the situation seems reversed. Formal structures such as the provision of e-exams mitigate their stress by providing a problem- or avoidance-based means of coping [2], while informal social connections are more complex. Although peer and family support are essential, they may also increase stress [12]. However, the vicious stress circle here seems rooted in the individual student's appraisal of the situation [5]. Applying for a particular major has been judged a competitive process, and this is mirrored in the students' speech and actions, creating and maintaining a culture of competition, even unnecessarily, as most students still end up in the desired major.

Our findings indicate that the students' and teachers' stressors are often intertwined, giving rise to different chain reactions, and accelerated or hindered by varying perceptions and the conditions under which they emerge. Hence, although the stressor itself is neutral, the response is labelled positive or negative according to the quality of an individual's relationship with it [18]. While teachers may have a more objective view of major selection, it is hard for them to respond to the students' concerns in a way that would genuinely remove stress [21]. As the competitive culture in the business school is strong, there is a risk that it will be embraced by incoming first years and continue to influence future cohorts. It is therefore essential to pay attention to how the programme structure is communicated to students, especially through formal support.

By observing the dynamic interplay between stress factors and coping strategies of students and teachers, we can identify three categories. The first category includes coping mechanisms that are mutually beneficial for the two groups, such as the utilisation of e-exams. The second category covers stressors and mechanisms involving tensions that demand more active management; coping mechanisms are not always readily available or may fail to remove distress [17]. The stressors are addressable with appropriate measures, but only if they are conducted in the right way. Finally, some contradictions emerged as irreconcilable; there are coping mechanisms that are effective for lowering stress for one party but become stressors for the other (e.g., tutor-teacher arrangements). Such contradictory settings may be impossible to remove completely, but their occurrence could be limited by carefully aligning study structures with formal and informal support systems.

6 Conclusions

While earlier studies have considered the reasons for stress and various means of relief [11], existing literature does not adequately acknowledge the dynamic interplay between stressors and coping mechanisms between different higher education groups [2, 14]. This study contributes to prior knowledge by responding to this issue by examining how stress and coping for students and teachers in higher education are connected. We show how study structures act as a platform for complex relationships of stressors and coping mechanisms and how structural examination brings forth the tensions inherent in coping with stress in the business school context.

Our study indicates, first, that stress and coping mechanisms can be categorised into three groups, in each of which the role of structures is somewhat different. In the first category, structures such as counselling services and associated coping mechanisms are generally beneficial in removing harmful stress if the culture of a higher education organisation allows their effective utilisation. In the second category, there are sources of stress and coping mechanisms that are more controversial in potentially generating tensions that necessitate removing the causes of ineffectiveness and/or identifying negative cycles in the interactions between teachers and students. For example, tensions may emerge due to individual circumstances, and reallocating tasks or moving a student to a different group may help restore the effectiveness of a coping mechanism. On the other hand, our findings also indicate that a third category is more challenging; some stressors cannot be removed for all parties and, even if addressed, will continue to cause stress in some other part of the higher education organisation. In these cases, certain structures can become the means of diminishing the contradictions. For example, if stressors in the study-related structures cannot be removed, formal or informal support structures may ease some challenges.

Second, our findings reveal that possibilities for addressing the limitations of coping mechanisms connect to deviations between the groups of higher education actors regarding the role of structures. For example, many support and counselling services are available for students, and they are actively encouraged to use those [9]. However, teachers might not be aware of their own stressors and might consider them a normal part of their work. Similarly, they might not be able to identify personal coping mechanisms that would enhance their well-being and stress management [3]. Considering that structures also may generate different stressors for students and teachers, such differences call for active attention in the academic community, such as recognising teachers' individual strengths and actively searching for emotion-based coping tools [2]. Balancing the effects of structures calls for managerial attention and is essential because they have both direct and indirect effects on the well-being of students [21] and teachers.

Our study has its limitations, such as only observing students and teachers in one business school. While this research setting was favourable in many ways, such as providing the chance to observe structural change, the relatively limited demographic knowledge about participants and access to primary data limit the generalisability of the study. As with any small-scale study, the findings are restricted to a relatively small group and a specific context, thus affecting generalisability. Also, not all the possible participants responded, and those who did might be somehow more interested in stressors/coping, which can affect the findings. Nevertheless, we believe that the findings reveal relevant aspects and represent a fruitful basis for future research on the limits of each coping mechanism and the role of technology in easing irreconcilable situations, for example.

References

1. Alatalo, S., et al.: Linking concepts of playfulness and well-being at work in retail sector. J. Retail. Consum. Serv. **43**, 226–233 (2018)
2. Amirkhan, J.H., Bowers, G.K., Logan, C.: Applying stress theory to higher education: lessons from a study of first-year students. Stud. High. Educ. **45**(11), 2231–2244 (2020)
3. Barry, K.M., Woods, M., Warnecke, E., Stirling, C., Martin, A.: Psychological health of doctoral candidates, study-related challenges and perceived performance. High. Educ. Res. Dev. **37**(3), 468–483 (2018)
4. Folkman, S., Lazarus, R.S.: An analysis of coping in a middle-aged community sample. J. Health Soc. Behav. **21**(3), 219–239 (1980)
5. Folkman, S., Lazarus, R.S.: If it changes it must be a process: study of emotion and coping during three stages of a college examination. J. Pers. Soc. Psychol. **48**(1), 150–170 (1985)
6. Guest, G., MacQueen, K.M., Namey, E.E.: Applied Thematic Analysis. Sage, Thousand Oaks (2011)
7. Guthrie, S., Lichten, C.A., Van Belle, J., Ball, S., Knack, A., Hofman, J.: Understanding mental health in the research environment: a rapid evidence assessment. Rand Health Q. **7**(3), 2 (2018)
8. Houghton, J.D., Wu, J., Godwin, J.L., Neck, C.P., Manz, C.C.: Effective stress management: a model of emotional intelligence, self-leadership, and student stress coping. J. Manag. Educ. **36**(2), 220–238 (2012)
9. Kotera, Y., Conway, E., Van Gordon, W.: Mental health of UK university business students: relationship with shame, motivation and self-compassion. J. Educ. Bus. **94**(1), 11–20 (2019)
10. Lazarus, R.S., Opton, E.M., Jr.: The study of psychological stress: a summary of theoretical formulations and experimental findings. In: Spielberger, C.D. (ed.) Anxiety and Behavior, pp. 225–262. Academic Press Inc., New York and London (1966)
11. Lazarus, R.S., Folkman, S.: Stress, Appraisal, and Coping. Springer, New York (1984)
12. Misra, R., McKean, M., West, S., Russo, T.: Academic stress of college students: comparison of student and faculty perceptions. Coll. Stud. J. **34**(2), 236–245 (2000)
13. Oswalt, S.B., Riddock, C.C.: What to do about being overwhelmed: graduate students, stress and university services. Coll. Stud. Aff. J. **27**(1), 24–44 (2007)
14. Prasad, A., Segarra, P., Villanueva, C.E.: Academic life under institutional pressures for AACSB accreditation: insights from faculty members in Mexican business schools. Stud. High. Educ. **44**(9), 1605–1618 (2019)
15. Razak, A.Z.A.A., Yunus, N.K.Y.Y., Samsudin, N., Ab Wahid, H., Wahid, Z.W.: Social support moderating effect between work-family conflict and health and stress of working students in UPSI. Int. Bus. Educ. J. **12**, 25–38 (2019)
16. Reavley, N., Jorm, A.F.: Prevention and early intervention to improve mental health in higher education students: a review. Early Interv. Psychiatry **4**(2), 132–142 (2010)
17. Robotham, D.: Stress among higher education students: towards a research agenda. High. Educ. **56**(6), 735–746 (2008)

18. Simmons, B.L., Nelson, D.L.: Eustress at work: extending the holistic stress model. In: Nelson, D.L., Cooper, C.L. (eds.) Positive Organisational Behavior – Accentuating the Positive at Work, pp. 40–53. Sage, London, Thousand Lakes and New Delhi (2007)
19. Stecker, T.: Well-being in an academic environment. Med. Educ. **38**, 465–478 (2004)
20. Stoliker, B.E., Lafreniere, K.D.: The influence of perceived stress, loneliness, and learning burnout on university students' educational experience. Coll. Stud. J. **49**(1), 146–160 (2015)
21. Zimmermann, F., Rösler, L., Möller, J., Köller, O.: How learning conditions and program structure predict burnout and satisfaction in teacher education. Eur. J. Teach. Educ. **41**(3), 318–342 (2018)

What Drives User Engagement of Theme Park Apps? Utilitarian, Hedonic, or Social Gratifications

Ting Long[1,2](✉) [ID]

[1] Turku School of Economics, University of Turku, Turku, Finland
ting.long@utu.fi
[2] National Research Center of Cultural Industries, Central China Normal University, Wuhan, China

Abstract. This study seeks to examine the determinants of user engagement in theme park apps from a uses and gratification perspective. Specifically, three different gratifications: utilitarian (i.e., utilitarian value, perceived ease of use, and convenience), hedonic (i.e., hedonic value and curiosity fulfillment), and social (i.e., social interaction and presence) gratifications are proposed to affect user engagement, which comprises three dimensions: cognitive, affective, and behavioral engagement. The research model was tested by collecting data via an online survey (N = 347). The results show that all utilitarian, hedonic, and social gratifications can facilitate users' cognitive and affective engagement, while behavioral engagement is only affected by utilitarian and hedonic gratification. This study enriches the understanding of what motivates user engagement in theme park apps and offers practical implications for park managers.

Keywords: Theme park · Mobile applications · User engagement · Uses and gratification

1 Introduction

The growth of mobile applications (apps) and the ubiquitous access to wireless Internet have dramatically changed the way people visit theme parks. An increasing number of theme parks have launched dedicated apps to improve visitors' experience [1]. Theme park apps are intentionally designed for theme park visitors and offer multi-functional services to satisfy visitors' various needs throughout the journey [2]. For instance, visitors can use such apps to obtain official event information, book digital tickets, arrange visit routes, reserve a digital fast-pass ticket for specific attractions, take photos, and interact with others. Particularly, under the COVID-19 pandemic situation, theme park apps are important for theme park visitors to obtain safety notifications and touchless services. However, user engagement is still crucial of successful implementation for theme park apps [3, 4]. Prior research has indicated that many users are willing to download mobile travel apps, but about 50% of users will delete the apps later [5]. Thus, it is important to investigate what sustains user engagement in theme park apps.

© The Author(s), under exclusive license to Springer Nature Switzerland AG 2022
H. Li et al. (Eds.): WIS 2022, CCIS 1626, pp. 204–219, 2022.
https://doi.org/10.1007/978-3-031-14832-3_14

Recent studies have examined the factors influencing user engagement of travel-related mobile apps from different perspectives. For instance, based on Stimulus-Organism-Response (S-O-R) model, Tian et al. [6] found that user engagement in travel apps is affected by perceived usefulness, price advantage, and user interface attractiveness. Similarly, Tak and Gupta [7] identified visual design, information design, and collaboration design are determinants of user engagement in travel apps. Although these studies have offered important insights into understanding what motivates user engagement in theme park apps, several issues require further investigation. First, prior studies have mainly focused on the technological perspectives; few studies have examined the impacts of hedonic and social impacts on user engagement in theme park apps. Indeed, the existing theme park apps have included some functions to fulfill users' hedonic (e.g., listening to music) and social needs (e.g., communicating with other users), which may influence user engagement. Second, while user engagement is a multidimensional concept, most prior studies only touch on one particular dimension, and few have examined multiple different dimensions of user engagement. Users may engage in theme park apps differently (e.g., cognitively, emotionally, or behaviorally); thereby, it is essential to understand what affects such differences.

To address the research gap, the current study seeks to examine the determinants of user engagement in theme park apps from a uses and gratification perspective. Specifically, three different gratifications, namely, utilitarian (i.e., utilitarian value, perceived ease of use, and convenience), hedonic (i.e., hedonic value and curiosity fulfillment), and social (i.e., social interaction and presence) gratifications are proposed to affect user engagement. Additionally, user engagement has three dimensions: cognitive, affective, and behavioral engagement. The research model was tested by collecting data via an online survey (N = 347). In so doing, the present study contributes to the literature by offering an in-depth understanding of the different roles of different gratification in triggering different dimensions of user engagement in theme park apps.

The remainder of the paper is structured as follows. Section 2 offers the theoretical background, and Sect. 3 proposes the research model and hypotheses. Section 4 introduces the research methods, and Sect. 5 shows the results. Finally, the paper is closed through conclusions, limitations, and future research directions.

2 Theoretical Background

2.1 Uses and Gratification Theory

Uses and gratification theory (U&G) originated in communication research, aiming to explain why and how people actively select a specific media to fulfill their specific needs [8]. It offers a theoretical framework to identify psychological needs of individuals when using a specific media [8, 9]. It has been widely used in IS field to examine user behaviors in different contexts, such as online games [10], mobile apps [11–13], and microblogs [14].

Prior research has applied this theory to classify different gratifications and examine their different roles in determining users' behavioral intentions toward a new IS. For instance, when studying WeChat, Gan and Li [11] categorized gratification into hedonic, utilitarian, social, and technical dimensions. They found that hedonic, utilitarian, and technical gratifications positively affect users' continuance intention of WeChat, while social gratification does not. Regarding the tourist attraction fan page, Ho and See-To [15] classified gratification as entertainment, informativeness, and socializing gratifications, and found that all gratifications have a positive influence on user attitude on the fan page. In the work of Gamage et al. [16], social, process, and content gratifications are found to affect users' decision-making of hotel choices through WeChat. Although prior studies examine how IS gratifies users' needs using similar factors, there are several inconsistent findings.

In summary, U&G theory has been applied to explain how individuals use an IS in different contexts, including travel-related IS. We selected it as the research framework for this study due to following reasons. First, this theory can help explain user engagement on the individual level. Second, it can identify the types of gratifications obtained from previous use of a theme park app and help understand whether different gratifications play different roles in predicting individuals' user engagement.

2.2 User Engagement

In prior literature, user engagement is defined differently, but most definitions agree that its core reflects users "investment in interactions with an object" [17]. The understanding of user engagement has evolved in past years. Initial user engagement was considered as unidimensional, focusing on users' behavioral responses to an object, such as continuance behaviors [17, 18]. Recent studies agree that user engagement is a complex and multidimensional concept that involves different types of psychological states and behaviors. One commonly used category of user engagement was developed by Dessart et al. [19]: cognitive, affective, and behavioral engagement. Cognitive engagement refers to how users pay attention to the interaction with the object; affective engagement refers to how users enjoy interacting with an object; and behavioral engagement refers to users' actual behaviors to interact with the object, such as sharing, learning, and endorsing [17, 19].

Many scholars have used this classification to examine user engagement in various IS. For instance, when studying online brand communities, Islam et al. [20] tested user engagement as a reflective second-order construct comprising affective, behavioral, and cognitive engagement, and found that user engagement is influenced by self-brand image congruity and value congruity. In the context of mobile travel apps, Tian et al. [18] found that perceived ease of use only affects behavioral engagement positively, while has no significant impact on cognitive and affective engagement. Both compatibility and UI attractiveness have significant influences on all affective, behavioral, and cognitive dimensions of engagement. These studies show that the multidimensions of user engagement may be helpful in explaining how users engage in theme park apps variously. Thus, the three dimensions of user engagement, including cognitive, affective, and behavioral dimensions, are applied in this study.

3 Research Model and Hypotheses

Based on U&G theory, this study operationalizes utilitarian value, perceived ease of use, and perceived convenience as utilitarian gratification; hedonic value and curiosity fulfillment as hedonic gratification; social presence and social interaction as social gratification. All gratifications have positive impacts on user engagement, which includes cognitive, affective, and behavioral engagement. Figure 1 illustrates the research model.

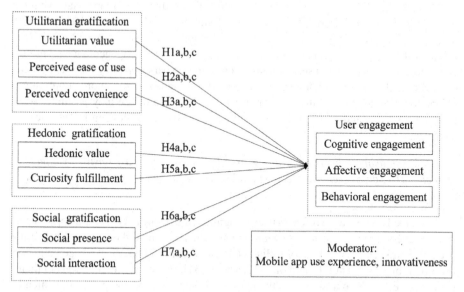

Fig. 1. Research model.

3.1 Relationship Between Utilitarian Gratification and User Engagement

Utilitarian value refers to users' cognitive evaluation of problem-solving in using a theme park app [21]. Previous research has found that users use various IS to help them accomplish tasks, such as online banking systems [22] and mobile social apps [23]. In this study's context, the theme park app often provides multiple functions to help tourists solve problems when visiting a theme park, such as assisting users in making a travel plan via offering official information on attractions and events and assisting visitors to quickly locate and find the path to a specific attraction via a GPS-based map. When users perceive that a theme park app is useful for enhancing their visiting experience, they are likely to pay more cognitive effort to know the app. Meanwhile, when problems have been solved, users may form positive emotions toward the app, which in turn improve their willingness to interact with the app emotionally. Furthermore, user perceptions of usefulness in solving problems may directly influence their use behavior. Prior studies have indicated that users' perceptions of usefulness can affect users' affective and cognitive engagement in online learning platforms [24]. And users' utilitarian motivation positively influences their behaviors regarding mobile phones [25]. Thus, it is reasonable to assume that utilitarian value can enhance users' cognitive, affective, and behavioral engagement. Therefore, the following hypotheses are developed:

H1: When using a theme park app, users' perceived utilitarian value positively affects their (a) cognitive engagement, (b) affective engagement, and (c) behavioral engagement.

Perceived ease of use refers to users' belief that a theme park app that using the app would be free of effort [26]. It has been found to be an important determinant of individuals' behaviors toward IS, such as adoption and continuance usage [26, 27]. Prior research also suggested that perceived ease of use can affect user engagement with mobile apps [28]. Similarly, when users can easily use a theme park app, they may feel greater control over the usage, which may improve their willingness to pay more attention and efforts to learn how to use it. Additionally, perceived ease of use may promote users' positive emotions and willingness to use the app. Thus, the following hypotheses are suggested:

H2: When using a theme park app, users' perceived ease of use positively affects their (a) cognitive engagement, (b) affective engagement, and (c) behavioral engagement.

Perceived convenience refers to users' cognition that using a theme park app can help them to accomplish tasks in a convenient way when visiting a theme park [29]. It has been identified as a critical factor influencing users' behaviors, such as usage behaviors toward mobile payment [30] and online learning [31]. Indeed, many functions in theme park apps seek to help users visit a theme park at the right time and place conveniently. When users perceived the app as convenient, they are likely to engage with the app. Thus, the following hypotheses are proposed:

H3: When using a theme park app, users' perceived convenience positively affects their (a) cognitive engagement, (b) affective engagement, and (c) behavioral engagement.

3.2 Relationship Between Hedonic Gratification and User Engagement

Hedonic value refers to users' pleasurable experience via using a theme park app [21, 32]. It has been found to be an important factor influencing use behaviors of mobile apps, such as the mobile fitness app [33] and mobile travel app [32]. Indeed, many hedonic elements have been included in theme park design, such as photos, music, video, and even mini-games. When users perceive a mobile app is fun to use, they are likely to interact with it. Therefore, it is reasonable to assume that the more hedonic value users perceived in using a theme park app, the more likely they are to engage with it. Thus, we hypothesize the following:

H4: When using a theme park app, users' perceived hedonic value positively affects their (a) cognitive engagement, (b) affective engagement, and (c) behavioral engagement.

Curiosity fulfillment refers to users' perceptions of cognitive exploration in seeking out new things and experience via using a theme park app [34]. Theme park apps provide users with many channels to fulfill such needs, for instance, official information on attractions and events, the discussion forum for users to share experiences, or photos and videos. All these channels can satisfy users' curiosity about the theme parks and other visitors' experiences, stimulating their interest in the park. Prior research has demonstrated that curiosity fulfillment is an important component of hedonic value of social media, which affects continued usage [34]. Therefore, this study assumes when users' curiosity is fulfilled by using a theme park app, they are more likely to engage with the app from cognitive, affective, and behavioral perspectives. Thus, the following hypotheses are developed:

H5: When using a theme park app, users' curiosity fulfillment positively affects their (a) cognitive engagement, (b) affective engagement, and (c) behavioral engagement.

3.3 Relationship Between Social Gratification and User Engagement

Social presence refers to users' psychological sense of establishing connections with others via using theme park apps [10]. People are motivated to use IS with high levels of social presence to meet their needs for psychological connection with others. Prior studies have found that social presence positively affects user behaviors, such as continuance intention toward social virtual world [35] or social network sites [36]. Many theme park apps included social elements to satisfy such social needs. When users feel more likely to connect with others through theme park apps, they have a stronger intention to engage with the app. Thus, the following hypotheses are recommended:

H6: When using a theme park app, users' perceived social presence positively affects their (a) cognitive engagement, (b) affective engagement, and (c) behavioral engagement.

Social interaction refers to users could obtain opportunities to get acquainted or become familiar with others via using a theme park app [37]. It has been found to be an essential factor affecting individuals' engagement with IS. For instance, Cheung et al. [38] found that social interaction significantly impacts users' sharing behavior in online communities. In the work of Li et al. [10], social interaction positively affects users' continuance intention of online games. Likewise, when users feel that a theme park app can satisfy their social needs through social functions (e.g., forming a friendship with others), they have a stronger willingness to engage with the app. Thus, the following hypotheses are suggested:

H7: When using a theme park app, users' perceived social interaction positively affects their (a) cognitive engagement, (b) affective engagement, and (c) behavioral engagement.

4 Research Method

4.1 Data Collection

This study conducted an online survey via wjx.cn in China to collect empirical data. The target population was theme park app users who had used the app when they were visiting a theme park. The snowball sampling method was employed to reach the target respondents. The questionnaire was first sent to different theme park fans' groups via QQ and Weibo (Chinese famous social media platforms), then the respondents were encouraged to spread the survey to other theme park fans' communities or their friends. Each respondent who completed the questionnaire got a virtual red packet with random money from RMB 0.1 to 2.

A total of 361 completed questionnaires were received. Among the received questionnaires, 14 invalid submissions (e.g., same answers for all questions) were removed. Thus, 347 valid responses were used for further analysis. Table 1 shows the demographics of the respondents, 47% were males, 54.8% aged between 26 and 35, 74.4% earned income over RMB 4500 per month, 60.8% held bachelor's degrees, 97.7% visited theme parks once per year, 55% used mobile phone 3–6 h per day.

4.2 Data Measures

The measurements of this research were adapted from previously validated instruments and further modified to fit the theme park app context. The seven-point Likert scale (from "1 = strongly disagree" to "7 = strongly agree") was used to measure all constructs. The measurement items for utilitarian value and hedonic value were adapted from Fang et al. [32] and Zhou et al. [21]. The items of perceived ease of use were modified from Davis [26]. The items of perceived convenience were taken from Souiden et al. [29]. The items of curiosity fulfillment were adopted from Hu et al. [34]. The items of social presence were modified from Li et al. [10]. The items of social interaction were adapted from Kim et al. [37]. The items of cognitive engagement, affective engagement, and behavioral engagement were taken from McLean and Wilson [39].

To collect data from theme park app users in China, the author of this study, who is fluent in both Chinese and English, translated the questionnaire from English to Chinese, and two IS experts checked both versions of the questionnaire. Additionally, a pilot study was conducted among 30 theme park app users from social media platforms. Based on the feedback from respondents, some of the questions were reworded, and the layout of the whole questionnaire was modified to improve the coherence.

4.3 Common Method Variance

The common method variance (CMV) was tested by two methods: (1) The Harman's single-factor test. The result showed that the highest total variance for any factor was 47.97%, lower than the recommended maximum of 50% [40]. (2) The full collinearity test was suggested by Kock and Lynn [41]. The result showed that the variance inflation factors (VIFs) range from 1.647 to 3.848, lower than the 5, thereby suggesting collinearity was also not a critical concern in this research [41].

Table 1. Demographic information of respondents (N = 347).

Measure	Item	Frequency	Percentage (%)
Gender	Male	163	47.0
	Female	182	52.4
	Unwilling to disclose	2	0.6
Age	18–25	86	24.8
	26–35	190	54.8
	36–45	67	19.3
	46–55	4	1.2
Monthly income	Under RMB 1500	16	4.6
	RMB 1501—3000	39	11.2
	RMB 3001—4500	34	9.8
	RMB 4501—6000	74	21.3
	RMB 6001—7500	64	18.4
	RMB 7501—9000	52	15.0
	RMB 9001—10500	31	8.9
	RMB 10500 or above	37	10.7
Education	Below college	35	10.1
	Junior college	50	14.4
	Bachelor or above	262	75.5
Yearly theme park visit experience	0	8	2.3
	1	132	38.0
	2	139	40.1
	3 or above	68	19.6
Daily mobile phone usage	>0 and ≤1 h	4	1.2
	>1 and ≤3 h	69	19.9
	>3 and ≤6 h	191	55.0
	>6 and ≤9 h	50	14.4
	>9 h	33	9.5

5 Data Analysis and Results

The partial least squares structural equation modeling (PLS-SEM) was used to evaluate the research model, including the test of measurement and structural models.

5.1 Measurement Model

The convergent validity and discriminant validity were applied to examine the measurement model. Convergent validity was evaluated by examining composite reliability (CR), average variance extracted (AVE), and Cronbach's alpha (CA) [42]. Discriminant validity was demonstrated by accessing item loadings and square root of each construct's AVE. Item loadings should be higher on the measured construct than the cross-loading on

Table 2. The results for test reliability and convergent validity.

Construct	Item	Factor loadings	Cronbach's alpha	Composite reliability	Average Variance Extracted (AVE)
Utilitarian value (UTIV)	UTIV1	0.873	0.837	0.902	0.755
	UTIV2	0.851			
	UTIV3	0.881			
Perceived ease of use (PEOU)	PEOU1	0.754	0.881	0.910	0.628
	PEOU2	0.797			
	PEOU3	0.859			
	PEOU4	0.771			
	PEOU5	0.804			
	PEOU6	0.764			
Perceived convenience (CONV)	CONV1	0.760	0.892	0.917	0.650
	CONV2	0.764			
	CONV3	0.845			
	CONV4	0.806			
	CONV5	0.820			
	CONV6	0.836			
Hedonic value (HEDV)	HEDV1	0.867	0.869	0.920	0.793
	HEDV2	0.893			
	HEDV3	0.910			
Curiosity fulfillment (CURI)	CURI1	0.890	0.893	0.934	0.824
	CURI2	0.905			
	CURI3	0.928			
Social presence (SOCP)	SOCP1	0.915	0.909	0.943	0.846
	SOCP2	0.916			

(continued)

Table 2. (*continued*)

Construct	Item	Factor loadings	Cronbach's alpha	Composite reliability	Average Variance Extracted (AVE)
	SOCP3	0.929			
Social interaction (SOCI)	SOCI1	0.899	0.907	0.942	0.843
	SOCI2	0.913			
	SOCI3	0.942			
Cognitive engagement (COGE)	COGE1	0.832	0.792	0.878	0.706
	COGE2	0.812			
	COGE3	0.876			
Affective engagement (AFFE)	AFFE1	0.867	0.874	0.922	0.799
	AFFE2	0.886			
	AFFE3	0.927			
Behavioral engagement (BEHE)	BEHE1	0.877	0.854	0.911	0.774
	BEHE2	0.874			
	BEHE3	0.889			

other constructs. In addition, the square root of each construct's AVE should be greater than the correlations with other constructs. Table 2 shows that the value of CR (CR > 0.7), AVE (AVE > 0.5), and CA (CA > 0.7) all exceed the thresholds [43]; thus, the convergent validity of the measurement model in this study was confirmed. The result in Table 3 indicates that the scales of this measurement model had sufficient discriminant validity [43].

5.2 Structural Model

The structural model was tested by using the bootstrapping technique in Smart PLS, including the test of the significance of path coefficients, the coefficient of determination (R^2), and the predictive relevance (Q^2). The results show the R^2 value for cognitive engagement was 68.9%, affective engagement was 71.6%, and behavioral engagement was 62.9%. The Q^2 values for cognitive engagement, affective engagement, and behavioral engagement were 0.451, 0.534, and 0.453, respectively. These indicate that the proposed research model has strong explanatory power and predictive power. There were 11 hypotheses supported at the 0.05 significance level (see Table 4). The results showed that utilitarian value exerted significant effects on cognitive engagement (β = 0.370, p < 0.001), affective engagement (β = 0.173, p < 0.05) and behavioral engagement (β = 0.233, p < 0.01). Perceived ease of use exerted significant effects on both cognitive engagement (β = 0.170, p < 0.05) and behavioral engagement (β = 0.183, p < 0.05). There is no significant association between perceived convenience and user

Table 3. Discriminant validity: Fornell-Larcker criterion.

	UTIV	PEOU	CONV	HEDV	CURI	SOCP	SOCI	COGE	AFFE	BEHE
UTIV	0.869									
PEOU	0.774	0.792								
CONV	0.757	0.780	0.806							
HEDV	0.807	0.749	0.755	0.890						
CURI	0.703	0.583	0.613	0.702	0.908					
SOCP	0.651	0.555	0.605	0.718	0.795	0.920				
SOCI	0.646	0.587	0.609	0.718	0.686	0.751	0.918			
COGE	0.782	0.722	0.696	0.756	0.609	0.636	0.616	0.840		
AFFE	0.750	0.692	0.691	0.787	0.680	0.724	0.705	0.791	0.894	
BEHE	0.728	0.675	0.656	0.725	0.662	0.638	0.619	0.749	0.750	0.880

(Note: UTIV: Utilitarian value; PEOU: Perceived ease of use; CONV: Perceived convenience; HEDV: Hedonic value; CURI: Curiosity fulfilment; SOCP: Social presence; SOCI: Social interaction; COGE: Cognitive engagement; AFFE: Affective engagement; BEHE: Behavioral engagement)

engagement. Thus, H1a, H1b, H1c, H2a, and H2c were supported, while H2b, H3a, H3b, and H3c were not. Additionally, hedonic value exerted significant effects on cognitive engagement ($\beta = 0.202$, $p < 0.05$), affective engagement ($\beta = 0.255$, $p < 0.001$) and behavioral engagement ($\beta = 0.163$, $p \leq 0.05$). There is no significant association between curiosity fulfillment and user engagement. Therefore, H4a, H4b, and H4c were supported, while H5a, H5b, and H5c were not. Furthermore, social presence exerted significant effects on both cognitive engagement ($\beta = 0.187$, $p < 0.05$), and affective engagement ($\beta = 0.227$, $p < 0.01$). Social interaction exerted significant effects on affective engagement ($\beta = 0.136$, $p < 0.05$). Thus, H6a, H6b, and H7b were supported, while H6c, H7a, and H7c were not.

Regarding the control variables, age showed significant effects on cognitive engagement within theme park app ($\beta = 0.062$, $p < 0.05$). There were no significant effects from other control variables.

Table 4. Hypotheses results

Hypotheses	Path coefficients	P value	t value	f^2 value	Result
H1a: UTIV → COGE	0.370	0.000	4.444	0.108	Support
H1b: UTIV → AFFE	0.173	0.020	2.323	0.026	Support
H1c: UTIV → BEHE	0.233	0.007	2.716	0.036	Support
H2a: PEOU → COGE	0.170	0.018	2.363	0.027	Support

(*continued*)

Table 4. (*continued*)

Hypotheses	Path coefficients	P value	t value	f^2 value	Result
H2b: PEOU → AFFE	0.119	0.055	1.920	0.014	Not support
H2c: PEOU → BEHE	0.183	0.015	2.438	0.026	Support
H3a: CONV → COGE	0.071	0.341	0.952	0.005	Not support
H3b: CONV → AFFE	0.060	0.364	0.909	0.004	Not support
H3c: CONV → BEHE	0.036	0.640	0.467	0.001	Not support
H4a: HEDV → COGE	0.202	0.018	2.369	0.030	Support
H4b: HEDV → AFFE	0.255	0.000	3.491	0.052	Support
H4c: HEDV → BEHE	0.163	0.050	1.964	0.016	Support
H5a: CURI → COGE	−0.089	0.230	1.201	0.007	Not support
H5b: CURI → AFFE	−0.006	0.930	1.459	0.000	Not support
H5c: CURI → BEHE	0.139	0.145	1.459	0.015	Not support
H6a: SOCP → COGE	0.187	0.017	2.379	0.029	Support
H6b: SOCP → AFFE	0.227	0.007	2.691	0.047	Support
H6c: SOCP → BEHE	0.064	0.474	0.715	0.003	Not support
H7a: SOCI → COGE	0.019	0.766	0.298	0.000	Not support
H7b: SOCI → AFFE	0.136	0.032	2.148	0.023	Support
H7c: SOCI → BEHE	0.056	0.447	0.761	0.003	Not support

(Note: UTIV: Utilitarian value; PEOU: Perceived ease of use; CONV: Perceived convenience; HEDV: Hedonic value; CURI: Curiosity fulfillment; SOCP: Social presence; SOCI: Social interaction; COGE: Cognitive engagement; AFFE: Affective engagement; BEHE: Behavioral engagement)

6 Discussion and Conclusion

This study investigates the antecedents of user engagement in theme park apps in China. The results indicate that utilitarian, hedonic, and social gratifications play different roles in determining different sub-dimensions of user engagement in theme park apps. Specifically, regarding the antecedents of cognitive engagement, utilitarian gratifications (i.e., utilitarian value and perceived ease of use), hedonic gratifications (i.e., hedonic value), and social gratifications (i.e., social presence) are found to affect cognitive engagement positively. These results are consistent with previous research. For instance, prior research has found that utilitarian value affects cognitive engagement in online learning [24], perceived ease of use influences IS continuance significantly [27], hedonic value is an antecedent of travel app engagement [32], and social presence exerts significant influence on user engagement with social network sites [36]. When users perceive a theme park app as useful, easy to use, enjoyable, and can fulfill their need to connect with others, they are likely to engage with the app cognitively, such as pay more attention and effort to know and learn the app.

Moreover, regarding the determinants of affective engagement, utilitarian gratification (i.e., utilitarian value), hedonic gratification (i.e., hedonic value), and social gratification (i.e., social interaction and presence) are found to be significant predictors. These findings are consistent with previous research. For instance, utilitarian and hedonic values have been reported to facilitate users to form positive emotions toward Airbnb, which in turn, affect user satisfaction and loyalty [44]. Social presence has been found to have a positive influence on affective engagement in the context of online collaborative learning [45]. Social interaction is reported as a determinant of user engagement in fitness apps [46]. Thereby, similar to cognitive engagement, when users' utilitarian, hedonic, and social needs are gratified, they are likely to engage with the theme park apps emotionally.

Furthermore, regarding the antecedents of behavioral engagement, utilitarian gratification (i.e., utilitarian value and perceived ease of use) and hedonic gratification (i.e., hedonic value) are significant, while social gratifications are not. The possible reason for the insignificant relationship between social gratification and behavioral engagement is that other widely used alternatives exist, such as social network sites. Even though theme park apps offer social functions, they are not enough to trigger users' behavioral engagement directly. This also indicates the different roles of each gratification in motivating different user engagement dimensions.

Other factors, including perceived convenience and curiosity fulfillment are not predictors of all dimensions of user engagement. A possible explanation for the insignificant impact of perceived convenience is that convenience offered by theme park apps is limited, and cannot facilitate user engagement adequately. Likewise, curiosity fulfillment also cannot motivate engagement, as users may use other information channels (such as word of mouth, popular social media, or advertising) to satisfy their curiosity.

6.1 Theoretical Implications

This study contributes to the literature in the following ways: first, unlike prior studies mainly focusing on technical dimension, this study extends the user engagement research by examining the roles of three types of gratifications in motivating user engagement based on U&G theory. The findings show that user engagement in theme park apps depends on how users' needs are gratified; when utilitarian, hedonic, and social needs are all satisfied, they tend to engage with the app. The findings also help explain the multipurpose and multi-functional nature of theme park apps.

Second, unlike prior studies mainly touch on one dimension of user engagement, this study enriches prior literature by unfolding three dimensions of user engagement, including cognitive, affective, and behavioral engagement. The findings show that different dimension of user engagement has different antecedents. This helps distinguish the differences in user engagement dimensions.

Third, the theoretical perspective of U&G yields new insights into the mechanisms underlying user engagement of theme park apps. The findings show that utilitarian, hedonic, and social gratifications motivate user engagement, indicating the U&G theory is a useful theoretical framework to explain user engagement with IS.

6.2 Managerial Implications

This study offers managerial implications: first, to improve user engagement, managers should focus on the strategies to improve utilitarian value, perceived ease of use, and hedonic value. For instance, managers should improve the usefulness for users to solve problems during the visit, such as offering detailed event information, GPS-based map, and virtual queue functions. Also, the app should be easy to use, such as a concise and clear interface, fast response speed, and a detailed help manual. Moreover, the app should be fun to use, such as including music, video, and mini-games related to the theme park.

Furthermore, this study found that social presence is also important to improving users' cognitive and affective engagement. Social interaction is a determinant of affective engagement. Thus, managers should highlight the strategies to improve the social gratification related functions. For instance, the app should include some social functions or integrate with other social network apps (e.g., Facebook or Twitter) to allow users to build relationships and share moments with others.

6.3 Limitations and Future Research

This study has several limitations. First, the empirical data was only collected in China. Thus, future research could gather data in other countries to generalize this study's findings or uncover the differences among users in different nations. Second, this study focuses on the users' cognition impacts on user engagement; thus, user emotions, such as surprise and joy, could be studied in future research. Third, the relationships between three different dimensions of user engagement could also be examined in future research.

Acknowledgements. This study is supported by the Finnish Foundation for Economic Education (Under grant 20-11123).

References

1. Omnico: Theme Park Mobile Barometer. https://content.omnicogroup.com/theme-park-mobile-barometer. Accessed 30 Nov 2021
2. Kamboj, S., Joshi, R.: Examining the factors influencing smartphone apps use at tourism destinations: a UTAUT model perspective. Int. J. Tour. Cities 7(1), 135–157 (2021)
3. Gupta, A., Dogra, N., George, B.: What determines tourist adoption of smartphone apps? J. Hosp. Tour. Technol. 9(1), 50–64 (2018)
4. Lu, J., Mao, Z., Wang, M., Hu, L.: Goodbye maps, hello apps? Exploring the influential determinants of travel app adoption. Curr. Issue Tour. 18(11), 1059–1079 (2015)
5. Linton, H., Kwortnik, R.J.: The mobile revolution is here: are you ready?. Center for Hospitality Research Publications, Cornell University, New York (2015)
6. Tian, Z., Lu, M., Cheng, Q.: The relationships among mobile travel application attributes, customer engagement, and brand equity. Soc. Behav. Pers. 49(7), 1–10 (2021)
7. Tak, P., Gupta, M.: Examining travel mobile app attributes and its impact on consumer engagement: an application of S-O-R framework. J. Internet Commer. 20(3), 293–318 (2021)
8. Katz, E., Blumer, J.G., Gurevitch, M.: Utilization of mass communication by the individual. In: The Uses of Mass Communications: Current Perspectives on Gratifications Research, pp. 19–32. SAGE, London, England (1974)

9. Xu, J., Fedorowicz, J., Williams, C.B.: Effects of symbol sets and needs gratifications on audience engagement: contextualizing police social media communication. J. Assoc. Inf. Syst. **20**(5), 536–569 (2019)
10. Li, H.X., Liu, Y., Xu, X.Y., Heikkila, J., van der Heijden, H.: Modeling hedonic is continuance through the uses and gratifications theory: an empirical study in online games. Comput. Hum. Behav. **48**, 261–272 (2015)
11. Gan, C.M., Li, H.X.: Understanding the effects of gratifications on the continuance intention to use WeChat in China: a perspective on uses and gratifications. Comput. Hum. Behav. **78**, 306–315 (2018)
12. Lee, H.E., Cho, J.: What motivates users to continue using diet and fitness apps? Application of the uses and gratifications approach. Health Commun. **32**(12), 1445–1453 (2017)
13. Kaur, P., Dhir, A., Chen, S., Malibari, A., Almotairi, M.: Why do people purchase virtual goods? A uses and gratification (U&G) theory perspective. Telematics Inform. **53**, 101376 (2020)
14. Liu, X.D., Min, Q.F., Han, S.N.: Understanding users' continuous content contribution behaviours on microblogs: an integrated perspective of uses and gratification theory and social influence theory. Behav. Inf. Technol. **39**(5), 525–543 (2020)
15. Ho, K.K.W., See-To, E.W.K.: The impact of the uses and gratifications of tourist attraction fan page. Internet Res. **28**(3), 587–603 (2018)
16. Gamage, T.C., Tajeddini, K., Tajeddini, O.: Why Chinese travelers use WeChat to make hotel choice decisions: a uses and gratifications theory perspective. J. Glob. Scholars Market. Sci. **32**(2), 285–312 (2022)
17. Dessart, L., Aldas-Manzano, J., Veloutsou, C.: Unveiling heterogeneous engagement-based loyalty in brand communities. Eur. J. Mark. **53**(9), 1854–1881 (2019)
18. Tian, Z., Shi, Z., Cheng, Q.: Examining the antecedents and consequences of mobile travel app engagement. PLoS One **16**(3), e0248460 (2021)
19. Dessart, L., Veloutsou, C., Morgan-Thomas, A.: Consumer engagement in online brand communities: a social media perspective. J. Prod. Brand Manag. **24**(1), 28–42 (2015)
20. Islam, J.U., Rahman, Z., Hollebeek, L.D.: Consumer engagement in online brand communities: a solicitation of congruity theory. Internet Res. **28**(1), 23–45 (2018)
21. Zhou, Z., Fang, Y., Vogel, D.R., Jin, X.-L., Zhang, X.: Attracted to or locked in? Predicting continuance intention in social virtual world services. J. Manag. Inf. Syst. **29**(1), 273–306 (2012)
22. Bhattacherjee, A.: Understanding information systems continuance: an expectation-confirmation model. MIS Q. **25**(3), 351–370 (2001)
23. Akdim, K., Casaló, L.V., Flavián, C.: The role of utilitarian and hedonic aspects in the continuance intention to use social mobile apps. J. Retail. Consum. Serv. **66**, 102888 (2022)
24. El-Sayad, G., Md Saad, N.H., Thurasamy, R.: How higher education students in Egypt perceived online learning engagement and satisfaction during the COVID-19 pandemic. J. Comput. Educ. **8**(4), 527–550 (2021)
25. Kim, Y.H., Kim, D.J., Wachter, K.: A study of mobile user engagement (MoEN): engagement motivations, perceived value, satisfaction, and continued engagement intention. Decis. Support Syst. **56**, 361–370 (2013)
26. Davis, F.D.: Perceived usefulness, perceived ease of use, and user acceptance of information technology. MIS Q. **13**(3), 319–340 (1989)
27. Venkatesh, V., Morris, M.G., Davis, G.B., Davis, F.D.: User acceptance of information technology: toward a unified view. MIS Q. **27**(3), 425–478 (2003)
28. McLean, G.: Examining the determinants and outcomes of mobile app engagement - a longitudinal perspective. Comput. Hum. Behav. **84**, 392–403 (2018)

29. Souiden, N., Chaouali, W., Baccouche, M.: Consumers' attitude and adoption of location-based coupons: the case of the retail fast food sector. J. Retail. Consum. Serv. **47**, 116–132 (2019)
30. Pal, A., Herath, T., De', R., Rao, H.R.: Is the convenience worth the risk? An investigation of mobile payment usage. Inf. Syst. Front. **23**(4), 941–961 (2021)
31. Hsu, J.-Y., Chen, C.-C., Ting, P.-F.: Understanding MOOC continuance: an empirical examination of social support theory. Interact. Learn. Environ. **26**(8), 1100–1118 (2018)
32. Fang, J., Zhao, Z., Wen, C., Wang, R.: Design and performance attributes driving mobile travel application engagement. Int. J. Inf. Manage. **37**(4), 269–283 (2017)
33. Huang, G., Ren, Y.: Linking technological functions of fitness mobile apps with continuance usage among Chinese users: moderating role of exercise self-efficacy. Comput. Hum. Behav. **103**, 151–160 (2020)
34. Hu, T., Kettinger, W.J., Poston, R.S.: The effect of online social value on satisfaction and continued use of social media. Eur. J. Inf. Syst. **24**(4), 391–410 (2015)
35. Mäntymäki, M., Riemer, K.: Digital natives in social virtual worlds: a multi-method study of gratifications and social influences in Habbo Hotel. Int. J. Inf. Manage. **34**(2), 210–220 (2014)
36. Lin, H., Fan, W., Chau, P.Y.K.: Determinants of users' continuance of social networking sites: a self-regulation perspective. Inf. Manag. **51**(5), 595–603 (2014)
37. Kim, M.J., Lee, C.-K., Contractor, N.S.: Seniors' usage of mobile social network sites: applying theories of innovation diffusion and uses and gratifications. Comput. Hum. Behav. **90**, 60–73 (2019)
38. Cheung, C.M.K., Liu, I.L.B., Lee, M.K.O.: How online social interactions influence customer information contribution behavior in online social shopping communities: a social learning theory perspective. J. Am. Soc. Inf. Sci. **66**(12), 2511–2521 (2015)
39. McLean, G., Wilson, A.: Shopping in the digital world: examining customer engagement through augmented reality mobile applications. Comput. Hum. Behav. **101**, 210–224 (2019)
40. Podsakoff, P.M., MacKenzie, S.B., Lee, J.Y., Podsakoff, N.P.: Common method biases in behavioral research: a critical review of the literature and recommended remedies. J. Appl. Psychol. **88**(5), 879–903 (2003)
41. Kock, N., Lynn, G.S.: Lateral collinearity and misleading results in variance-based SEM: an illustration and recommendations. J. Assoc. Inf. Syst. **13**(7), 546–580 (2012)
42. Hair, J.F., Jr., Hult, G.T.M., Ringle, C.M., Sarstedt, M.: A Primer on Partial Least Squares Structural Equation Modeling (PLS-SEM). Sage Publications, Thousand Oaks (2021)
43. Petter, S., Straub, D., Rai, A.: Specifying formative constructs in information systems research. MIS Q. **31**(4), 623–656 (2007)
44. Lee, S., Kim, D.-Y.: The effect of hedonic and utilitarian values on satisfaction and loyalty of Airbnb users. Int. J. Contemp. Hosp. Manag. **30**(3), 1332–1351 (2018)
45. Molinillo, S., Aguilar-Illescas, R., Anaya-Sánchez, R., Vallespín-Arán, M.: Exploring the impacts of interactions, social presence and emotional engagement on active collaborative learning in a social web-based environment. Comput. Educ. **123**, 41–52 (2018)
46. Eisingerich, A.B., Marchand, A., Fritze, M.P., Dong, L.: Hook vs. hope: how to enhance customer engagement through gamification. Int. J. Res. Market. **36**(2), 200–215 (2019)

Author Index

Printed in the United States
by Baker & Taylor Publisher Services